Third Edition

Keith Harding and Rachel Appleby

INTERNATIONAL EXPRESS

PRE-INTERMEDIATE

Student's Book

with Pocket Book

OXFORD

UNIVERSITY PRESS

OXFORD
UNIVERSITY PRESS

Great Clarendon Street, Oxford, OX2 6DP, United Kingdom

Oxford University Press is a department of the University of Oxford.
It furthers the University's objective of excellence in research, scholarship,
and education by publishing worldwide. Oxford is a registered trade
mark of Oxford University Press in the UK and in certain other countries

ISBN: 978 0 19 459759 3

Printed in China

This book is printed on paper from certified and well-managed sources

ACKNOWLEDGEMENTS

*The Publishers would like to thank the following for their kind permission to reproduce
photographs and other copyright material:* Alamy Images pp.8 (smartphone
with map/Yankee), 9 (car production line/vario images GmbH & Co.KG),
(computer assembly line/Imagebroker), 10 (Corte Inglés/Kevin Fox), (Ford car
show/Alexey Zarubin), (Lavazza coffee/Rachel Dayman), 18 (Palio di Siena/
Kim Petersen), (Sapporo Snow Festival/JTB Media Creation, Inc.), (Scarlet
Sails festival/Bogomyako), 21 (electrician/Bill Stephenson), (plumber/Mark
Chivers), 30 (Dan Seddiqui in coal plant/AlamyCelebrity), (Dan Seddiqui in
field/AlamyCelebrity), (Dan Seddiqui in recording studio/AlamyCelebrity),
37 (list passenger/Drive Images), (Japanese police station/Mark Bassett),
44 (Basking Robbins sign/Maurice Savage), (Amazon packaging/Maurice
Savage), (FedEx plane/Stan Rohrer), (NBC building/Kevin Foy), 52 (handbag/
AR Images), 57 (iron railing/Mira), (coal/Guy Edwardes Photography), (oil/Paul
Rapson), 66 (park/Ian Dagnall), (tram/Alex Segre), (shopping district/SFL Travel
), 80 (Sony Playstation/1exposure), (Philips tape player/Interfoto), 90 (meeting
audience/Stuart Foster India), (two people in office/Stuart Forster), 92 (food/
Kari Marttila), (group hug in office/Adrian Weinbrecht), (handing business
card/Vincent Hazat), 94 (classroom/Jeremy Sutton-Hibbert), 95 (man raising
hand in meeting/Yuri Arcus), 96 (bar in Rio/Mechika), 97 (Niterói Museum/
Thomas Cockrem), 104 (Jack Dorsey and team/Aurora Photos), 105 (fast food/
David Levenson), (cycling/Scottish Viewpoint), (man with juice maker/i love
images), 106 (sport balls/D. Hurst), (rugby ball/numb), (sport balls/PhotosIndia),
108 (distribution centre/Apex News and Pictures Agency), 109 (broken-down
van/Justin Kase zninez), (zipper/PRILL Mediendesign), 114 (Kindle/Jeff Morgan
08), (paying in cash/Jonathan Goldberg), (Selexyz bookshop/Jochen Tack),
117 (woman at computer/Morgan Lane Photography); Bridgeman Art Library
Ltd pp.43 (Major Walter Clopton Wingfield/Private Collection/Look and Learn/
Peter Jackson); Corbis pp.10 (LG presentation/Corbis Wire), 11 (woman in
office/Blink), 21 (hotel receptionist/John Smith), (photographer/Ivy), (woman
in fabric shop/Latitude), 32 (woman with suitcase/Comet), 34 (luggage/
Passage), (train station/Architecture), (ticket inspector/Corbis Wire), 42 (Da
Vinci Codex/Documentary), (Edvard Munch, The Scream/Corbis Wire),
44 (Sun Microsystems sign/Reuters), 45 (man with map/Jordan Siemens),
54 (Atacama desert/Encyclopedia), (Chile miners rescue/Corbis Wire), 56 (man
running/Comet), (burger/Bridge), (man running through airport/Blend),
57 (plastic bottles/moodboard), 59 (healthy food/Galeries), 62 (paper/Bridge),
63 (coffee/Food Passionates), 68 (Dubai/Latitude), 90 (hotel guest with porter/
Radius Images), 91 (desert/Matt MoyerNational Geographic), 92 (women
exchanging gifts/Image Source), 94 (man working at home/Blink), 102 (Mark
Zuckerberg/Corbis News), 105 (washing up/Comet), (people in cinema/
moodboard), 117 (businessman/Ariel Skelley/Blend Images), (architect/Ivy),
120 (Copacabana Palace Hotel/Richard T. NowitzEncyclopedia), 130 (Caterina
Fake and Stewart Butterfield/Patrick Fraser/Outline); Getty Images pp.9 (oil
rig/Ryan Lindsay/E+), (department store/Anna Bryukhanova/E+), (airplane/
Erik SimonsenPhotographer's Choice), (coffee/narvikk/E+), (taking cash out/
ML HarrisImage Bank), (mobile shopping/Gregor Schuster/Photographer's
Choice), 11 (woman in grocery store/Jon FeingershBlend Images), (man/John
FedeleBlend Images), 19 (woman/Hill Street StudiosBlend Images), 20 (man
in office/Nick DavidTaxi), 21 (taxi driver/altrendo images), (woman in office/
Matilde GattoniarabianEye), 34 (woman on airplane/Westend61), (check-in
desk/quavondo/E+), (airport lounge/Jon ShiremanPhotonica), 37 (man in taxi/
Stockbyte), (woman at airport/Kazuhiro Tanda/Digital Vision), 40 (beach/
Neil SetchfieldLonely Planet Images), (diver/Zac MacaulayPhotographer's
Choice), (Sagrada Familia/Visions Of Our LandPhtolibrary), (mountain biking/
MichaelSvoboda/E+), 43 (Pierre Omidyar/Bloomberg), 45 (businesswoman with
luggage/Rich Legg/E+), 47 (people in meeting/Joshua Hodge Photography),
57 (fruit/Dorling Kindersley), (timber/Panoramic Images), 59 (exercise class/
Clay McLachlanAurora), 63 (milk/Burke/Triolo Productions/FoodPix), (flour/
Paola ZucchiPhotolibrary), 66 (outdoor cafe/L WheatleyPhotolibrary),
68 (Zurich/Hans Georg Eiben/Look), (Shanghai/Wei Fang/Flickr), 69 (Kraków
old town/Thomas Stankiewicz/Look), (Sukiennice, Kraków/Jacek Kadaj/Flickr),
70 (man in street/Helen Cathcart/Taxi), 71 (doctor's desk/Ghislain & Marie
David de LossyCultura), 78 (gramophone/Russell Knight/Hulton Archive),
79 (couple in record store/Fuse), 80 (Akio Morita/Kurita Kaku/Gamma-Photo),
84 (business man/David Hanover/Photographer's Choice), 85 (man in office/
Jetta Productions/Iconica), 94 (business opening/Jupiterimages/Workbook
Stock), 96 (Portugese Library, Rio de Janeiro/Paul Bernhardt/Lonely Planet
Images), (Brazil village/Peter AdamsPhotolibrary), (Rio de Janeiro/Ian Trower/
Robert Harding World Imagery), 105 (students/John Fedele/Blend Images),
106 (pool ball/Maria Toutoudaki), 109 (delivery/Andersen Ross/Iconica),
114 (class at blackboard/blue jean images), (student at computer/Hill Street
Studios/Blend Images RM), (mobile phone payment/Philippe Huguen/AFP),
117 (people in office/Aura/Taxi), 118 (people applauding/lalfor/the Agency
Collection); iStock pp.8 (calendar with pin), (calendar), 48 (sports t-shirt), (pink
shirt), (blue shirt), (orange fleece), (checked shirt), 63 (cake); North Carolina
Museum of History pp.43 (Caleb Bradham, 1910-1915/North Carolina Museum
of History); Philips pp.80 (Gerard Philips/Philips), (Frederik Philips); Oxford
University Press pp.8 (cycle helmet/Finnbarr Webster), (clock/Photodisc),
9 (woman in TV studio), 21 (architect on site/EdBockStock/Stutterstock),
(chef/Plush Studios), 24 (Rio de Janeiro beach/Corbis/Digital Stock), 34 (plane
ticket/Photodisc), (passports/Stockbyte), (air hostess/image100), 52 (espresso
machine/Creative Crop), 57 (gas cooker/Photodisc), 62 (coffee/Piotr
Skubisz), 63 (water bottle/Martin Wiernik), (bread/D. Hurst), 105 (shopping/
Photographer's Choice), 106 (golf ball/Photodisc); PA Photos pp.54 ('Estamos
Bien'/Hector Retamal/AP), 116 (Bangladeshi Info Ladies/A.M. Ahad/AP),
(Bangladeshi Info Ladies/A.M. Ahad/AP); Rex Features pp.42 (Wittelsbach-
Graff Diamond/Keystone USA/Zuma), 102 (Cameron Winklevoss and Tyler
Winklevoss/David Hartley), 119 (Amazon Kindle/James Looker/Future
Publishing); Science Photo Library pp.21 (eye examination/Public Health
England).

Cover images by kind permission: Corbis (Ponte Vasco da Gama, Lisbon/Image
Source), (Conference table/Marnie Burkhart), (Woman with cell phone/
Westend61); Getty Images (Cafe table and chairs/Ron Chapple), (Confident
businessman/Martin Barraud/OJO Images).

Commissioned Photography by: Mark Bassett pp.3, 4, 5 (functions), 6, 7, 8 (ex8.1,
12), 13, 25, 36, 49, 60, 72, 120.

Illustrations by: Roarr Design pp.12, 81, 82, 88; Fred Van Deelan/The
Organisation pp.30, 69; Mark Duffin pp.46, 78, 83; Satoshi Hashimoto/Dutch
Uncle Agency pp.20, 22, 58, 73, 127; Nick Lowndes/Eastwing p.93.

Welcome to *International Express*

Your guide to the Student's Book Pack

The **Student's Book Pack** contains the Student's Book and the Pocket Book.

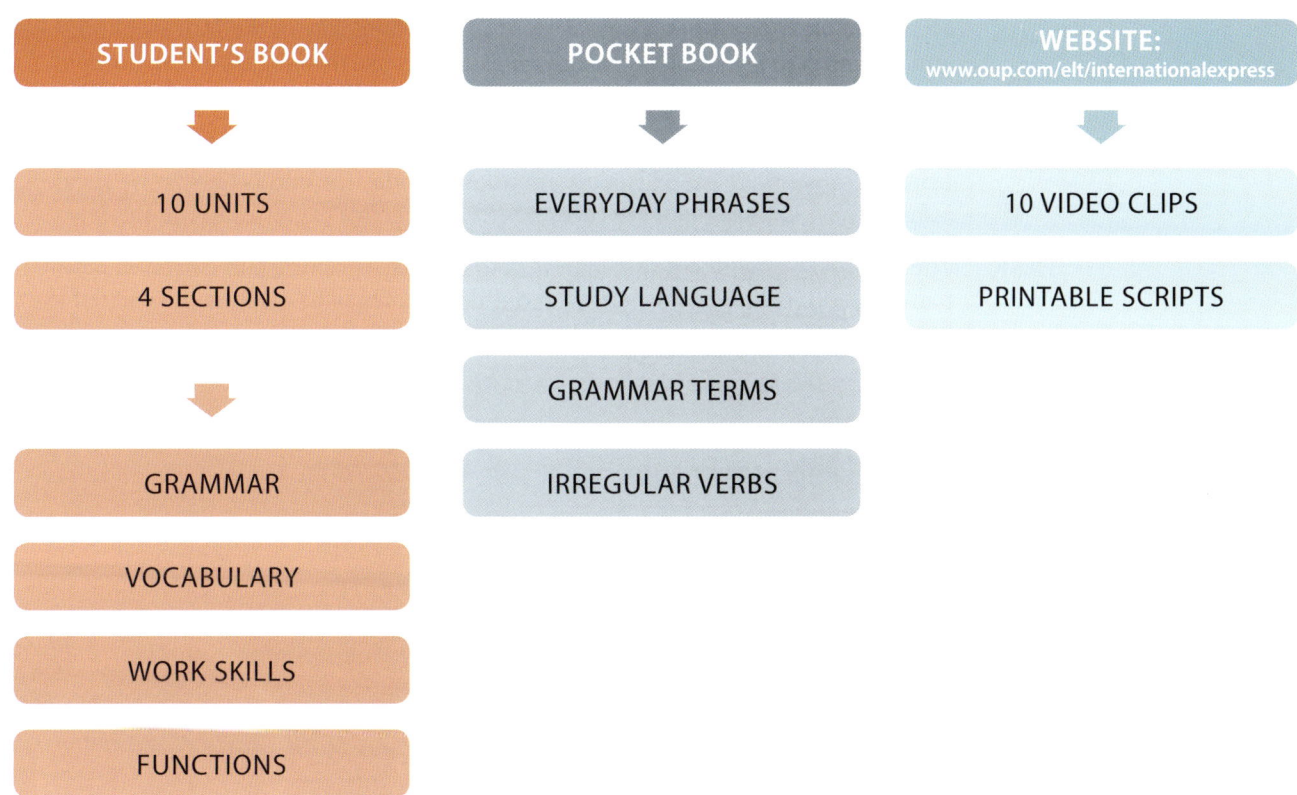

STUDENT'S BOOK	POCKET BOOK	WEBSITE: www.oup.com/elt/internationalexpress
10 UNITS	EVERYDAY PHRASES	10 VIDEO CLIPS
4 SECTIONS	STUDY LANGUAGE	PRINTABLE SCRIPTS
	GRAMMAR TERMS	
GRAMMAR	IRREGULAR VERBS	
VOCABULARY		
WORK SKILLS		
FUNCTIONS		

The **Student's Book** has 10 units and each unit has four sections: Grammar, Vocabulary, Work skills, and Functions. One unit is eight pages, and is followed by a Review section of four pages. The Review section can be done in class or for self-study.

The **Pocket Book** contains examples of everyday phrases taken from the Student's Book. This can be used at work or for travel to help remember and use key phrases. There is also a section that gives examples of useful phrases for the classroom. *Grammar terms* has details about key words and phrases we use to talk about grammar. This is followed by a list of irregular verbs.

There is one video clip for every unit on the website. The topic of the video is linked to the topic of the unit.

How a unit works

The **Grammar** and **Functions** sections have four stages: Introduction, Focus, Practice, and Task.

INTRODUCTION

The language is introduced in a recorded conversation or in a reading text. There are questions to check understanding of the conversation or the text.

FOCUS

The Focus stage highlights the main areas of the language in the Introduction stage and asks some questions about how we form and use the language. The notes in the **Review** section help answer these questions.

PRACTICE

The Practice stage has activities to practise the language from the Introduction, using the answers to the Focus questions as a guide. The aim is to practise speaking as much as possible. There are further written practice exercises in the **Review**.

TASK

The section ends with a more open task to practise speaking and communicating in pairs or groups. More information about the tasks may be given at the back of the book in the **Task and activity notes**.

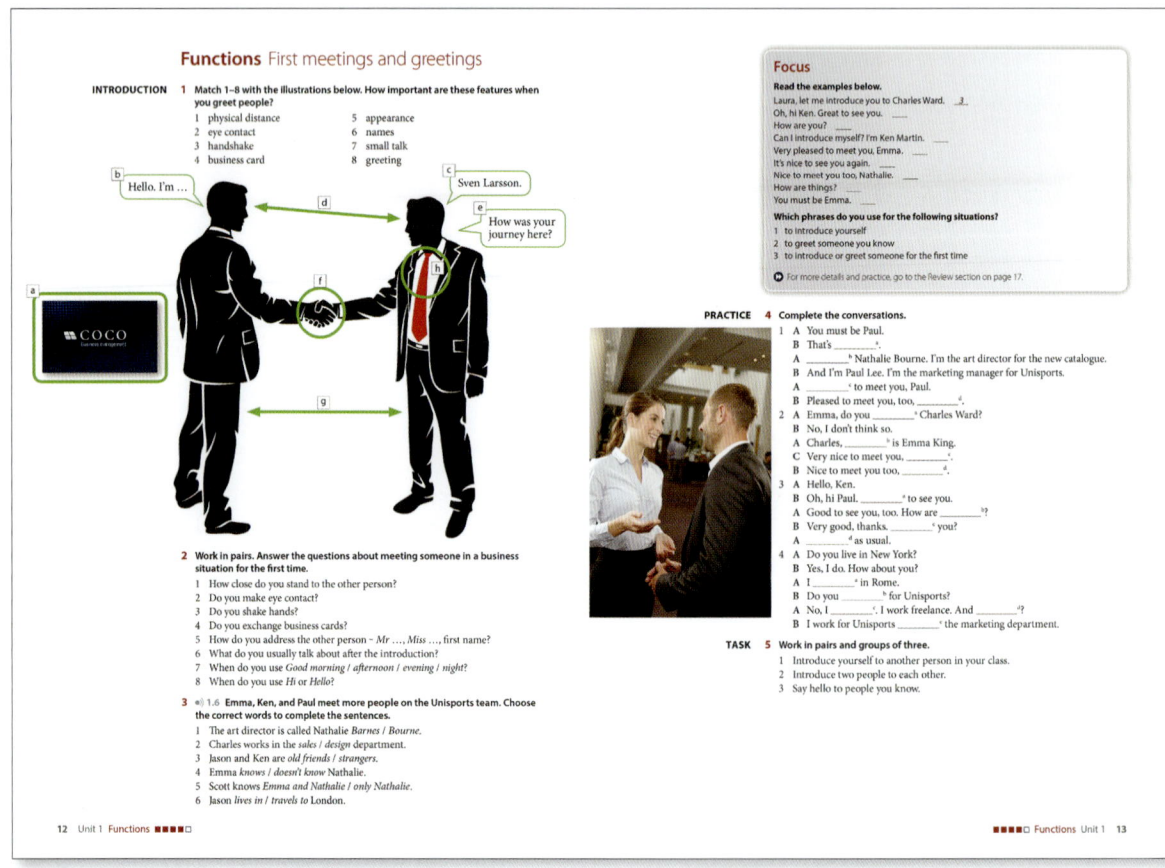

The **Vocabulary** and **Work skills** sections work in a similar way to the **Grammar** and **Functions** sections but have a more flexible format which allows for a variety of vocabulary and work skills to be studied and practised. There are further practice activities for both of these sections in the **Review**.

REVIEW

There is a **Review** at the end of each unit. It contains notes on the form and use of the language in the **Grammar** and **Functions** sections, and practice and review exercises for all four sections. There are listening, reading, and writing exercises which can be done as self-study or in class time.

TASK AND ACTIVITY NOTES

This section has notes for the tasks and activities in the unit. For some tasks, there are notes for Student A and Student B on different pages.

SCRIPTS

This section has all the scripts for the conversations and listening practice activities.

ANSWER KEY

The answers for activities and exercises in the units can be found here.

Contents

Getting started

Grammar Present Simple: *do, be,* and question words

1 **What do these people do? Match the photos with the business cards.**

2 **Read the details on the business cards and complete the sentences.**

1 Paul lives in _____ .
2 Emma is a _____ . She works in _____ .
3 Ken lives in _____ . He's a _____ .
4 Laura designs _____ .
5 Emma's family name is _____ .
6 Paul is a _____ . He works for _____ .

3 •)) **1.1** **Listen to Laura, Ken, and Paul meet at the Unisports headquarters. Are these statements true or false?**

1 Ken knows Laura.
2 Laura works in a studio.
3 Ken works for a company.
4 Paul knows Ken.
5 Paul suggests they have a drink.

4 •)) **1.2** **Laura, Ken, and Paul meet Emma. Listen and choose the correct word.**

1 Emma is in a *running* / *cycling* team.
2 She works for a *travel* / *model* agency.
3 She usually trains in the *morning* / *afternoon*.
4 Ken and Laura have both got *cars* / *bikes*.
5 Paul and Laura take the *bus* / *train* to work.

Focus

Read the examples.

Positive	Negative
I **live** in New York. She **works** for a model agency. I**'m** in a new studio.	I **don't** work for a sports magazine. It **doesn't** go very fast. Rome **isn't** a safe place to ride a bike.
Questions	**Answers**
Do you **do** a lot of training? Where **do** you **train**? How **are** you?	Yes, I **do**. I **live** near the river so I usually **train** there. I**'m** very well, thanks.

Frequency adverbs

0% ———————————————————————→ 100%
never   rarely   sometimes   often   usually   always

I *sometimes* go running.
I'm *always* too busy.

Wh- and How question words

What   Where   Who   When   Why   Which
How + much, many, far, often, long

What do you do?   I'm a photographer.
How often do you go training?   I usually go cycling before breakfast every day.

Complete the rules with these words.

before   beginning   be   not   facts   -s / -es

We add _____ to the verb for *he*, *she*, and *it*.
We use the verbs *do* and _____ to make questions.
We use _____ to make negative statements.
We use the Present Simple to talk about _____ and regular activities.
Wh- and *How* question words come at the _____ of a sentence.
We usually put frequency adverbs _____ all verbs except *be*.

⏩ For more details and practice, go to the Review section on page 14.

PRACTICE

5   Complete the sentences. Use the words in brackets.

Example   Laura *lives* in Rome. (live)

1   Ken _____ photographs. (take)
2   Laura _____ men's suits. (not design)
3   Ken and Laura _____ friends. (be)
4   Emma _____ in Scotland. (not live)
5   Paul _____ Cantonese, but he _____ Japanese. (speak) (not speak)
6   Ken _____ for a sports magazine. (not work)
7   Paul and Laura _____ to work. (not cycle)
8   Paul _____ a sales manager. (not be)

6   Work in pairs. Ask and answer questions for the sentences in 5.

Example   A   Does Laura live in Rome?
                 B   Yes, she does.

7   Talk to other people in the class. Find out the following information.

their name   what they do   where they work   where they live

8 Match the question words with the pictures.

what   what time   when   where   which   who

   A or B

1 _____   2 _____   3 _____   4 _____   5 _____   6 _____

how far   how long   how many   how much   how often

£1.70 + 50p = ?   Madrid ↓ Barcelona?         1 hour? 1½ hours? 2 hours?

7 _____   8 _____   9 _____   10 _____   11 _____

9 Write the questions for these answers. Use the words in brackets.

1 She's a sportswear designer. (what / Laura)
2 He knows Laura, but he doesn't know Emma. (who / Ken)
3 She lives in Rome. (where / Laura)
4 She trains every morning. (how often / Emma)
5 She cycles for about two hours. (how long / Emma)
6 He works for Unisports. (which company / Paul)
7 She gets up at 5.30. (what time / Emma)
8 She goes to the sports centre after cycling. (when / Emma)
9 He runs two or three kilometres. (how far / Ken)

10 Work in pairs. Take it in turns to ask and answer the questions in **9**.

11 Work in pairs. Go to page 126. Find out how hard your partner works.

TASK 12 Work in pairs. Read the details about Paul and Emma. Student A writes five questions about Paul. Student B writes five questions about Emma. Take it in turns to ask and answer your questions.

Paul Lee

Paul works in the Hong Kong branch of Unisports. Unisports is a sportswear producer and they make clothes for a variety of sports including running, cycling, and tennis. Paul speaks English, Mandarin Chinese, and Cantonese. He travels to the States and the UK on business a lot, but takes his holidays in Asia. He loves food, especially spicy food from Thailand or Sichuan in China. He enjoys playing tennis and plays every weekend when he is at home.

Emma King

Emma is from Scotland and lives in London. She sometimes travels abroad for cycling events and for her modelling. She models for sportswear companies and cosmetic products. Her father is Scottish and her mother is from Hungary so she speaks some Hungarian. She enjoys listening to music and watching films. She goes to the cinema about once a month.

Vocabulary Talking about companies

1 Match the type of company with the pictures. Think of examples of some companies.

airline   bank   car manufacturer   coffee producer   department store
electronic goods producer   oil company   e-commerce company   television company

2 Which type of company in **1** offers the following services and products? Add one more item to each group.

1 loans, mortgages
2 fridges, toasters
3 personal shoppers, home delivery
4 espresso roast, whole bean
5 petrol, kerosene
6 news programmes, dramas
7 saloon cars, sports cars
8 online check-in, upgrades
9 music downloads, online shopping

3 ◗)) 1.3 Listen to two people talking about a company. Complete the company profile.

1 Name _____
2 Nationality _____
3 Headquarters _____
4 Type of company _____
5 How old _____
6 Number of employees _____
7 Revenue _____
8 Main competitor _____

4 Complete the sentences using the information about the company in **3**.

1 The company's called _____ .
2 It's a _____ company.
3 The headquarters are in _____ .
4 It's an _____ company. It produces _____ .
5 It started in _____ .
6 It employs _____ people.
7 Its annual revenue is _____ .
8 Its main competitor is _____ .

5 ◀)) **1.4** Listen to four company descriptions. Number the pictures in the order you hear them.

1 _____ 2 _____ 3 _____ 4 _____

a

c

b

d

6 Write the questions.

1 What nationality / company?
2 How old?
3 Where / headquarters?
4 How many people / employ?

5 What type / company?
6 What / annual revenue?
7 What / produce?
8 Who / main competitor?

7 Work in pairs. Complete the chart by asking and answering questions about the companies. Use the questions in **6**.

Student A   Look at the chart below.
Student B   Go to page 126.

	Company name	Nationality	Headquarters	Type of company	Start	Revenue / Employees
1	Credit Suisse					
2	EMI	British	London	music	1931	£1.072 billion / 5,500
3	Amazon					
4	Louis Vuitton	French	Paris	fashion	1854	€2.5 billion / 18,000
5	Bayer					
6	K-Line	Japanese	Ichikawa	shipping company	1919	¥497 billion / 659

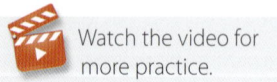
Watch the video for more practice.

8 Work in pairs. Play a company guessing game.

Student A   Think of a company you know well. Answer Student B's questions.
Student B   Ask Student A questions to help you guess the name of the company.

Example   B What type of company is it?
            A It's a car company.
            B What nationality is it?
            A It's French.

Work skills Talking about your job

1 1.5 **Listen to three people introducing themselves. Complete the table.**

	Junko	Linda	Karl
1 Job			
2 Company			
3 Department			
4 Responsibilities			
5 Full- / Part-time			
6 Hours per week			
7 Colleagues, other people			
8 Place of work			
9 Travel			

2 Complete the questions with the words below. Now work in pairs. Take turns to ask and answer questions about your jobs. Complete the answers.

Can Do (×2) How many What What type Where Which Who (×2)

1 ________ do you do?
I'm a / an ________________.

2 ________ do you work for?
I work for ________________. / I'm self-employed. / I work freelance.
/ I run my own company.

3 ________________ of company is it?
It's a / an ________________.

4 ________ department are you in?
I work in the ________________ department.

5 ________ you work full-time?
Yes, I do. / No, I don't. I work part-time.

6 ________________ hours do you work a week?
I work about ________________.

7 ________ do you work with?
I work with ________________.

8 ________ do you usually work – in an office?
I usually work ________________.

9 ________ you travel much for work?
Yes, I travel ________________. / No, I don't.

10 ________ you tell me what you do in your job?
I'm responsible for ________________. This involves ________________.

Functions First meetings and greetings

INTRODUCTION

1 Match 1–8 with the illustrations below. How important are these features when you greet people?

1 physical distance
2 eye contact
3 handshake
4 business card

5 appearance
6 names
7 small talk
8 greeting

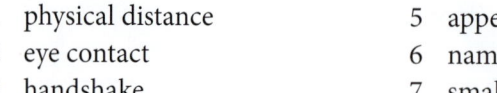

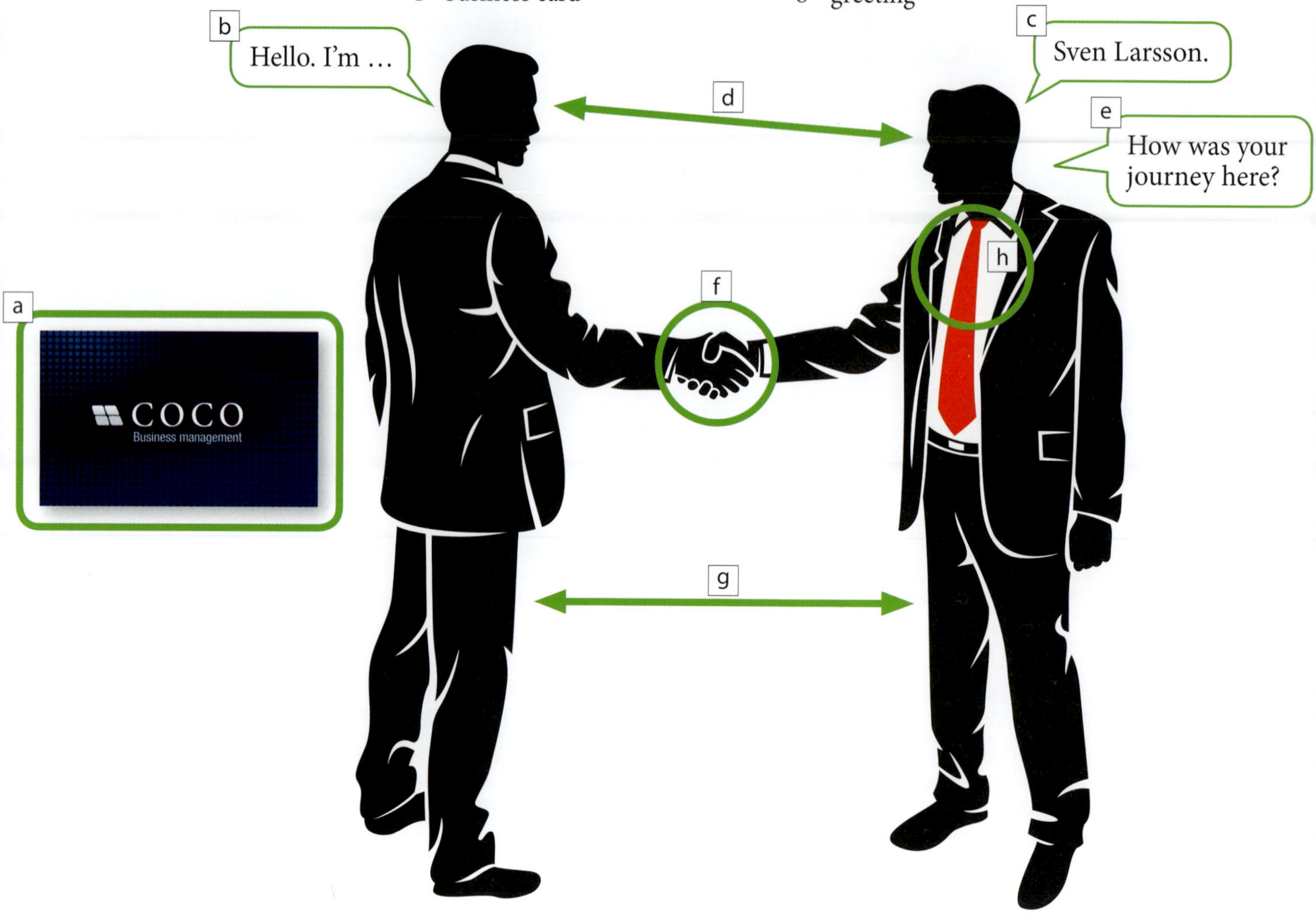

b Hello. I'm …

c Sven Larsson.

e How was your journey here?

d

h

f

a

COCO
Business management

g

2 Work in pairs. Answer the questions about meeting someone in a business situation for the first time.

1 How close do you stand to the other person?
2 Do you make eye contact?
3 Do you shake hands?
4 Do you exchange business cards?
5 How do you address the other person – *Mr …*, *Miss …*, first name?
6 What do you usually talk about after the introduction?
7 When do you use *Good morning / afternoon / evening / night*?
8 When do you use *Hi* or *Hello*?

3 ●)) **1.6** Emma, Ken, and Paul meet more people on the Unisports team. Choose the correct words to complete the sentences.

1 The art director is called Nathalie *Barnes / Bourne*.
2 Charles works in the *sales / design* department.
3 Jason and Ken are *old friends / strangers*.
4 Emma *knows / doesn't know* Nathalie.
5 Scott knows *Emma and Nathalie / only Nathalie*.
6 Jason *lives in / travels to* London.

Focus

Read the examples below.

Laura, let me introduce you to Charles Ward.   _3_
Oh, hi Ken. Great to see you.   ___
How are you?   ___
Can I introduce myself? I'm Ken Martin.   ___
Very pleased to meet you, Emma.   ___
It's nice to see you again.   ___
Nice to meet you too, Nathalie.   ___
How are things?   ___
You must be Emma.   ___

Which phrases do you use for the following situations?

1 to introduce yourself
2 to greet someone you know
3 to introduce or greet someone for the first time

For more details and practice, go to the Review section on page 17.

PRACTICE   **4** **Complete the conversations.**

1 A You must be Paul.
   B That's _____ ª.
   A _____ ᵇ Nathalie Bourne. I'm the art director for the new catalogue.
   B And I'm Paul Lee. I'm the marketing manager for Unisports.
   A _____ ᶜ to meet you, Paul.
   B Pleased to meet you, too, _____ ᵈ.

2 A Emma, do you _____ ª Charles Ward?
   B No, I don't think so.
   A Charles, _____ ᵇ is Emma King.
   C Very nice to meet you, _____ ᶜ.
   B Nice to meet you too, _____ ᵈ.

3 A Hello, Ken.
   B Oh, hi Paul. _____ ª to see you.
   A Good to see you, too. How are _____ ᵇ?
   B Very good, thanks. _____ ᶜ you?
   A _____ ᵈ as usual.

4 A Do you live in New York?
   B Yes, I do. How about you?
   A I _____ ª in Rome.
   B Do you _____ ᵇ for Unisports?
   A No, I _____ ᶜ. I work freelance. And _____ ᵈ?
   B I work for Unisports _____ ᵉ the marketing department.

TASK   **5** **Work in pairs and groups of three.**

1 Introduce yourself to another person in your class.
2 Introduce two people to each other.
3 Say hello to people you know.

Review

Grammar Present Simple: *do, be,* and question words

Form

We form the Present Simple with the infinitive form of the verb. For *he, she,* and *it* we add an *-s* or *-es* to the end of the verb.

Positive			Negative		
I You We They	work.		I You We They	don't work.	
He She It	works.		He She It	doesn't work.	

Question			Answer		
Do	I you we they	work?	Yes/No,	I you we they	do/don't.
Where do					work in the city centre.
Does	he she it		Yes/No,	he she it	does/doesn't.
Where does					works in the city centre.

We use *do* + verb to make questions in the Present Simple. We also use *do* in place of the verb with short answers.

Example Do you like coffee? Yes, I do. (~~Yes, I like.~~)

We put *Wh-* and *How* question words before *do* to make questions.

Example Where do you work?
How long does it take to get to work?

We can make questions with *be.*

Example Is he in a meeting?

We can also use *Wh-* and *How* question words with *be.*

Example How far is Madrid from Barcelona?

In questions with prepositions, the preposition usually goes at the end.

Examples Who do you work for?
Which university do you go to?

Use

We use the Present Simple to talk about:

Facts

Examples The meeting room is on the first floor.
How long does the journey take?

Regular activities

Examples I usually watch TV in the evenings.
What time do you have lunch?
We have a team meeting every week.

PRACTICE

1 Complete the text with the correct form of the verbs below.

be cycle go have love not have not like take work (×2)

Alberto and David both _work_ [1] for a supermarket chain. Alberto _____ [2] in the finance department and David _____ [3] a marketing assistant. They sometimes _____ [4] lunch together. David _____ [5] Italian food, but Alberto _____ [6] it. They often _____ [7] to the gym together after work. Alberto _____ [8] home. David _____ [9] a bicycle, so he _____ [10] the bus home.

2 Match the questions and answers.

1 How often do you cycle to work?
2 How many languages do you speak?
3 How much does it cost?
4 How far is it to your company?
5 How long do you have for lunch?

a Half an hour.
b About 10 kilometres.
c Every day.
d Three.
e €16.50

3 Write questions for the following answers about Luiza.

Example   She's _31 years old_.
               How old is she?

1 She lives in _São Paulo_.
2 She gets up _at 6.00 a.m_.
3 She works for _an IT company_.
4 She's _a software tester_.
5 She has _two_ computers.
6 She speaks _Portuguese and English_.
7 She goes to the cinema _once a week_.

4 Correct the mistakes. There is one mistake in each sentence.

1 Are you like playing football?
2 They doesn't have a car.
3 He goes rarely swimming.
4 What you do?
5 How much time is the lesson?

Vocabulary Talking about companies

1 Read the company profile. Are the statements true or false?

> Uniqlo is a Japanese clothes producer and retailer and its headquarters are in Tokyo. It started in 1949 and now has around 30,000 employees. It specializes in casual clothes. Uniqlo's annual revenue is $10 billion and it has stores in thirteen countries. Its global competitors include Zara, Gap, and H&M.

1 Uniqlo sells casual clothes.
2 It's a Japanese company.
3 The company started in 1994.
4 About 30,000 people work for Uniqlo.
5 Its yearly revenue is ten billion yen.
6 Uniqlo operates in thirteen countries.

2 Use the prompts to write questions for the answers about the Hershey company.

Example What *nationality is the company*?
It's an American company.

1 Where _____?
The headquarters are in Hershey, Pennsylvania.
2 What type _____?
It's a confectionery producer.
3 What _____?
It produces different kinds of chocolate and sweets.
4 How _____?
It's about 120 years old.
5 How many _____?
It employs 13,700 people.
6 Who _____?
Its main competitors are other large confectionery producers,
e.g. Mars and Nestlé.

3 Complete the sentences with the correct form of the words below.

compete   employ   manufacture   produce

Example It's a small company, with only five e*mployees*.

1 Gorenje m_____ white goods, for example fridges and washing machines.
2 There's a lot of c_____ in the electronic goods market.
3 Kellogg's is a food p_____.
4 Samsung and LG are c_____.
5 Our business is growing so I think we need to e_____ more staff.
6 Avon sells a wide range of cosmetic p_____.
7 Hasbro is a toy m_____.
8 If you have a problem at work, you should speak to your e_____.

Work skills Talking about your job

1 Eva (E) and Jakob (J) are interviewed about their jobs. Complete the questions. Then guess what their jobs are.

Example Who *do you work for*?
E I work freelance.   J I'm self-employed.

1 How many hours _____?
E Sometimes 60, sometimes none.   J Usually between 50 and 60.
2 Who _____?
E I often work with famous people.   J I work with my employee.
3 Where _____?
E I work in lots of different places.   J I work outside a lot.
4 Do _____?
E Yes, I often travel in my job.   J No, I don't.
5 What _____?
E I'm responsible for making actors look J I produce food.
   good or look right for their role.
6 Do _____?
E Yes, I love it.   J Yes, I do.

Eva's job _____   Jakob's job _____

Functions First meetings and greetings

We use the following phrases to introduce ourselves, introduce and meet other people, and greet people we know.

Introducing yourself	Hi, I'm Steve.
	Can I introduce myself? I'm Ken Martin.
Introducing and meeting someone	Rosa, do you know Tim?
	Rosa, this is Tim.
	Rosa, let me introduce you to Carol Schwarz.
	Pleased to meet you, Jason.
	Very pleased to meet you, Emma.
	Nice to meet you too, Nathalie.
Greeting someone you know	Hi, Emma.
	Hi. Great to see you.
	Good to see you, too.
	Hello, it's nice to see you again.
	How are you?
	How are things?

1 **Put the conversations in the correct order. The first line is marked for you.**

1 a Hans, this is Sunny Lee.   ___
   b No, I'm afraid I don't.   ___
   c Very good to meet you, too.   ___
   d Sunny, do you know Hans Koopman?   _1_
   e Nice to meet you.   ___

2 a Fine, thanks. And you?   ___
   b Hi, Jerry.   _1_
   c You too. How are you?   ___
   d Hi, Zol. Great to see you.   ___
   e Good, thanks.   ___

3 a No, I don't. I work for Nikon.   ___
   b Pleased to meet you, Frank. Do you work for Kodak, too?   ___
   c Mike, let me introduce you to Frank Weldon.   _1_
   d I'm in R&D.   ___
   e Oh, what do you do there?   ___

4 a Yes, it is. How are things?   ___
   b You must be Sara.   _1_
   c Fine, thanks. Busy as usual.   ___
   d Yes, it's nice to meet you in person at last, not just on the phone.   ___
   e That's right. And you're Marie.   ___

2 Celebrations

Grammar Present Continuous; Present Simple

INTRODUCTION

1 What festivals do you know about? Are there any festivals you go to or want to go to? Describe them to a partner.

2 Look at the photos. Where do you think they are? Do you know which festivals they show?

3 Read about the festivals in the pictures and answer the questions.

Are you looking for something exciting to do this year? High Flyer recommends these amazing festivals!

HIGH*flyer*

Palio di Siena is a race that takes place twice every year on July 2 and August 16 in Siena, Italy. Ten horses and riders represent ten of the seventeen contrade, or city wards. They race around the square in the centre of Siena three times. The race usually takes less than two minutes. Riders often fall off during the race.

The Snow Festival takes place every winter in Sapporo, Japan. People make ice sculptures and statues of famous people and places. They are all lit up at night and concerts take place on stages made of ice.

White Nights is an international arts festival in St Petersburg, Russia. It takes place during the summer when the sun does not set. The festival features the Scarlet Sails show which has fireworks, music, and an amazing show of ships with red sails. Around one million people usually attend the festival.

1 How often does the Palio di Siena take place?
2 How many times do the riders race round the square?
3 What do people make every year at the Sapporo Snow Festival?
4 Where do concerts often take place during the Snow Festival?
5 Where does the White Nights festival take place?
6 How many people usually attend?

Which festival would you like to go to?

4 ◉) **2.1** Petra and Craig work for Global Tours, a travel company. Listen to them talk about their current projects. Complete the sentences about Petra and Craig.

1 She is trying to find _____ .
2 She is emailing _____ .
3 He is booking _____ .
4 He is looking for _____ .

Focus

Match the tenses with the examples.

Present Simple (PS)   Present Continuous (PC)

I'm trying to find them a hotel.
The Palio di Siena horse race **takes place** twice a year.
What **are you doing**?
The race usually **takes** less than two minutes.
Do you **need** any help?

Complete the rules.

We use the _____ to talk about facts and regular events.

We use the _____ to talk about events happening now or around the present time.

We don't usually use the _____ with verbs like *be, want, need, like,* and *understand.*

We use phrases like *now, currently, at the moment, still,* and *this* (*week*) with the _____ .

We use phrases like *every* (*week*), *usually,* and *on* (*Sundays*) with the _____ .

⏵⏵ For more details and practice, go to the Review section on page 26.

PRACTICE   **5** **Complete the sentences with the correct form of the verbs in brackets.**

1   A   What _____ (you / do) at the moment?
    B   _____ (I / plan) a new tour of famous houses in London.
2   A   _____ (you / know) what Awa Odori is?
    B   Yes, _____ (it / be) a dance festival in Japan.
3   A   Have you found a place to live yet?
    B   No, _____ (I / still stay) at a friend's house.
4   A   Where _____ (be) Richard?
    B   _____ (he / be) on a business trip.
    A   Which hotel _____ (he / stay) at?
    B   _____ (he / stay) at the Continental.
5   A   What time _____ (you / get) up?
    B   At about 7 o'clock.
6   A   How _____ (your project / go)?
    B   _____ (it / go) really well, thanks.
7   A   Is John around?
    B   Yes, I think _____ (he / photocopy) some reports.
8   A   Have you finished your report yet?
    B   No, _____ (I / write) it now.

6 **Work in pairs. Student A read about Petra. Student B read about Craig on page 20.**

Petra

Petra lives and works in Florence in Italy. She speaks Italian and fluent English and German. She works part-time for Global Tours, a travel agent. It's a new company, so at the moment she is trying to develop the business and attract more customers. She thinks that Asia is a growing market so she is targeting Chinese and Korean customers. This week, she is planning a two-day tour of the Palio di Siena. Currently, she is studying for a degree in Business Studies in her spare time. She studies most weekends and doesn't have much free time.

Ask Student B questions about Craig using the prompts. Use the correct form of the verbs.

1   What / Craig / do?
2   What / he / work on / at the moment?
3   Who / Craig / live with at the moment?
4   What / he / want to do?
5   What / he / love doing?
6   Which language / he / currently study?

Craig

Craig works full-time for Global Tours. At the moment, he is booking a tour to St Petersburg. Craig is living with a friend in a small town near Florence in Italy, but he wants to move into the city when he has enough money. He loves visiting museums and art galleries and often visits the Uffizi Museum in Florence. His Italian is OK, but he wants to be fluent so he's studying in the evening. He goes to a local school twice a week.

Ask Student A questions about Petra using the prompts. Use the correct form of the verbs.

1　Where / Petra / live?
2　Which languages / Petra / speak?
3　What / she / try / develop / at the moment?
4　What / she / do / this week?
5　What / she / currently / study?
6　How often / she / study?

7　Write a short description of your job and your current project(s). Share your description with a partner.

8　How do we say the *do* words in the sentences below?

1　*Do* you know when it starts?
　No, I'm afraid I *don't*.
2　*Does* the festival start soon?
　No, it *doesn't*. It starts next month.
3　*Do* you often go to Siena?
　Yes, I *do*.
4　What sports *does* he *do*?
　He *does* karate and judo.

●)) **2.2　Listen and check.**

TASK　**9　Work in pairs. Student A look below. Student B go to page 127.**

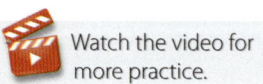
Watch the video for more practice.

Student A
Find and ask about these people in the picture: Kenichi, Mari, Dave, Paula.

Examples　What does Kenichi do?　　Is he wearing a red shirt?
　　　　　　　Is he talking to someone?

Help Student B find these people:

Paul	Sales Manager	Graham	IT engineer
Lucy	Administrator	Helen	Receptionist

Vocabulary Jobs; *make, do, have*

1 Match the jobs with the pictures.

architect   chef   electrician   hotel receptionist   journalist
optician   photographer   plumber   shop assistant   taxi driver

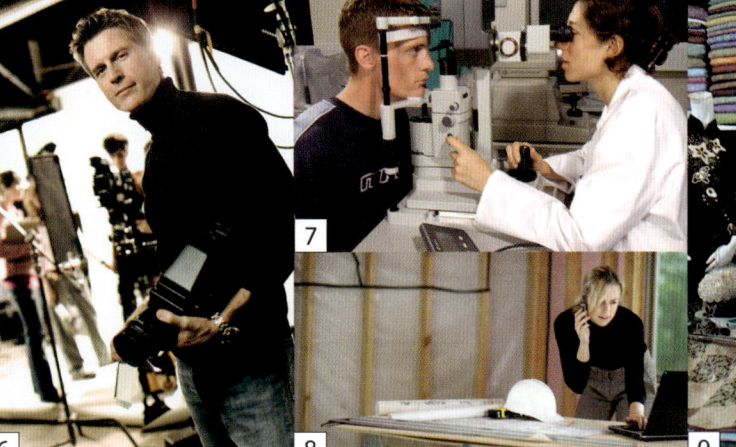

2 ◉) 2.3 Listen and mark the stress on the words in 1.

Example   a<u>r</u>chitect

3 Match the definitions with the jobs in 1.

A person who …
a   serves customers in a store or shop
b   cooks and prepares food
c   takes photos
d   designs buildings
e   takes passengers from one place to another
f   fits and fixes water pipes, drains, etc.
g   writes articles for newspapers and magazines
h   fixes lighting, wiring, etc.
i   checks people's eyesight
j   helps people check in and out of a hotel

4 ◉) 2.4 Listen to the people in 1 talk about their jobs. Which jobs are they talking about?

5 ◉) 2.4 Listen again. Add more details to the definitions in 3.

6 Work in pairs. Take it in turns to ask and answers questions about the jobs in 3. Use the details from 5 in your answers.

Example   A   What do shop assistants do?
                 B   They serve customers in a store or shop. They also check the stock and make orders.

7 Think of a person's job and what that person does every day. Describe the job to a partner and ask them to guess what the job is.

8 Which job is the odd-one-out in each list? Explain your answer.

1   plumber, optician, doctor
2   banker, accountant, designer
3   journalist, engineer, photographer
4   taxi driver, travel agent, tour guide
5   sales assistant, builder, hotel receptionist
6   computer programmer, systems analyst, teacher

9 **Match the phrases with the pictures.**

Example   make a mistake *1*

a mistake   a decision   well   (someone) a favour   a bath   fun

make   **do**   **have**

money   research   a look

10 **Add the following words to the correct word group in 9.**

a break / rest   a chance   a complaint   a good job   a good time
a phone call   a profit   an appointment   an arrangement   an idea
some exercise   trouble

11 **Complete the sentences with the verbs from 9.**

1   He _____ an idea for a new type of mobile phone.
2   Can I _____ a phone call? I need to talk to my colleague.
3   Do you think we _____ a chance of finishing in time?
4   You always _____ a really good job with your presentation slides.
5   Customers often _____ complaints about their deliveries being late.
6   We always _____ a good time at the beach when it is sunny and warm.
7   It's good to _____ some exercise at least once a day.
8   The company often does really well. It usually _____ a big profit.
9   I need to _____ an appointment to see the optician tomorrow.
10   You worked really hard this morning. You should _____ a rest.
11   She's _____ an arrangement for Anna to meet you at the station.
12   I'm _____ trouble getting to work this morning. All the trains were delayed.

12 **Work in pairs. Take it in turns to ask questions using the words in 9.**

Example   A When do you have a break at work?
             B At about 11.00 usually.

Work skills Emails 1: Parts of an email

1 **Read the email and find the following.**

1 subject
2 salutation
3 reference to previous contact
4 the reason you are writing
5 action point(s)
6 reference to attachment(s)
7 closing
8 sender's name and signature

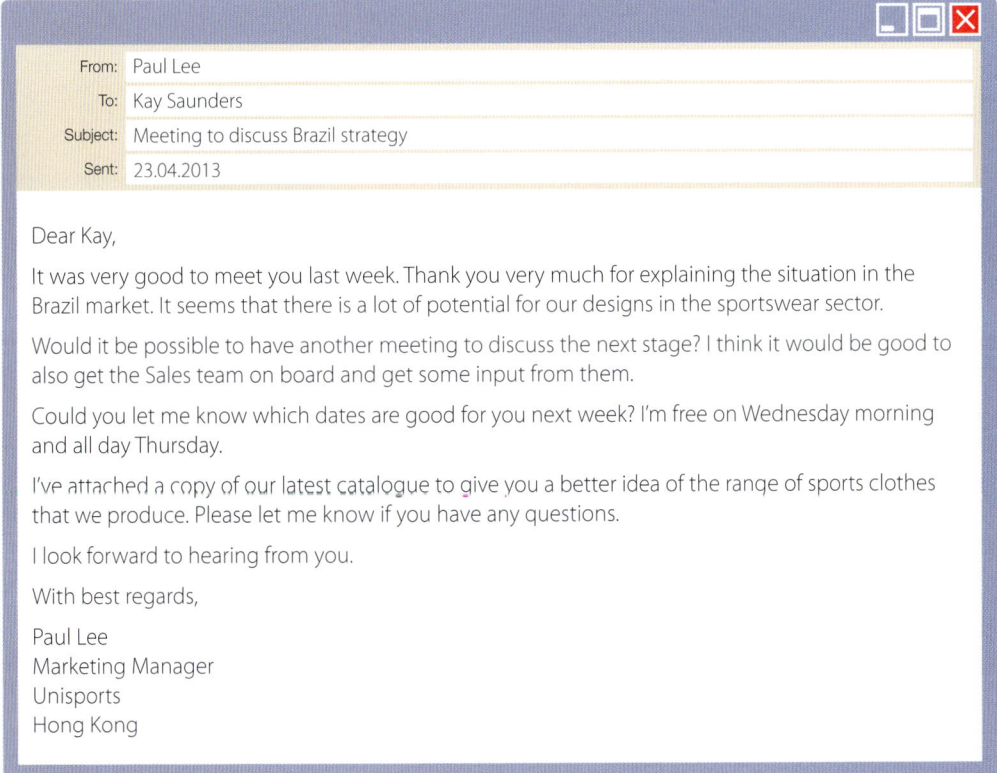

From: Paul Lee
To: Kay Saunders
Subject: Meeting to discuss Brazil strategy
Sent: 23.04.2013

Dear Kay,

It was very good to meet you last week. Thank you very much for explaining the situation in the Brazil market. It seems that there is a lot of potential for our designs in the sportswear sector.

Would it be possible to have another meeting to discuss the next stage? I think it would be good to also get the Sales team on board and get some input from them.

Could you let me know which dates are good for you next week? I'm free on Wednesday morning and all day Thursday.

I've attached a copy of our latest catalogue to give you a better idea of the range of sports clothes that we produce. Please let me know if you have any questions.

I look forward to hearing from you.

With best regards,

Paul Lee
Marketing Manager
Unisports
Hong Kong

2 **Put the following into the correct groups in 1.**

a Thanks for calling yesterday.
b I'm writing about …
c Please find attached …
d Great to see you yesterday.
e Hi Gina,
f Many thanks for your offer of help.
g Could you give me some information about …?
h Paul Rhodes
   Area Sales Manager
   Chile
i Very best
j Delivery problems
k Best regards
l I look forward to …

3 **Write Kay's reply to Paul Lee's email using these details.**

Thank Paul for email; accept the suggestion to meet again; agree that Sales should join in; suggest Thursday afternoon; thank Paul for catalogue; ask Paul which items he wants to promote in Brazil; say you look forward to meeting him; close.

Functions Talking about schedules and arrangements; *going to*

INTRODUCTION

1 Read the details of the Unisports photo shoot and answer the questions.

1 Which country is the photo shoot in?
2 How many people are going?
3 When do they arrive in Rio de Janeiro?
4 Which hotel are they staying at?
5 When does the photo shoot start?

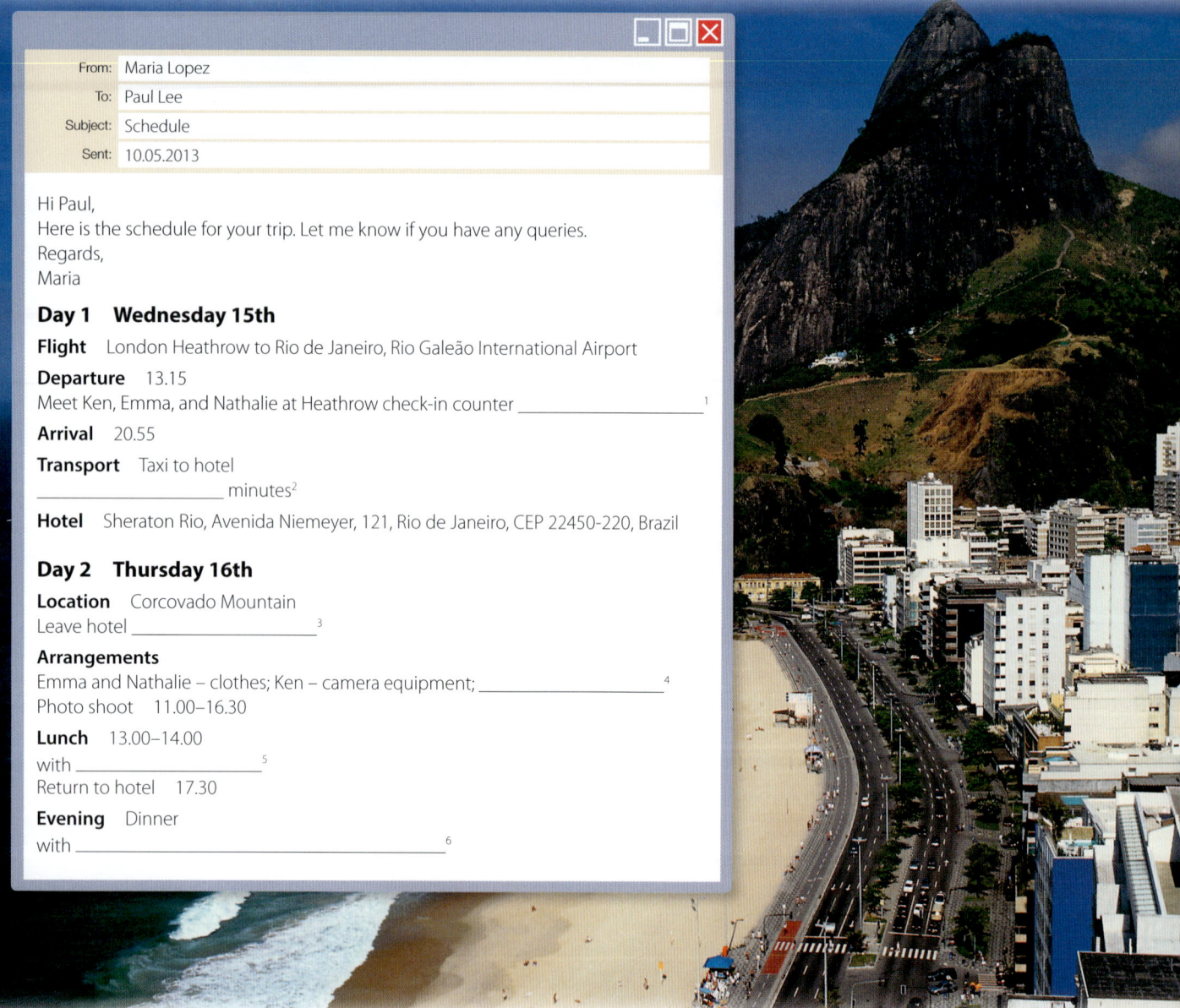

From: Maria Lopez
To: Paul Lee
Subject: Schedule
Sent: 10.05.2013

Hi Paul,
Here is the schedule for your trip. Let me know if you have any queries.
Regards,
Maria

Day 1   Wednesday 15th

Flight   London Heathrow to Rio de Janeiro, Rio Galeão International Airport
Departure   13.15
Meet Ken, Emma, and Nathalie at Heathrow check-in counter _____ [1]
Arrival   20.55
Transport   Taxi to hotel
_____ minutes [2]
Hotel   Sheraton Rio, Avenida Niemeyer, 121, Rio de Janeiro, CEP 22450-220, Brazil

Day 2   Thursday 16th

Location   Corcovado Mountain
Leave hotel _____ [3]
Arrangements
Emma and Nathalie – clothes; Ken – camera equipment; _____ [4]
Photo shoot   11.00–16.30
Lunch   13.00–14.00
with _____ [5]
Return to hotel   17.30
Evening   Dinner
with _____ [6]

2 ◄)) **2.5** Listen to the organizer explain the travel schedule to Paul Lee. Add the missing details to the schedule.

3 ◄)) **2.6** Paul calls Fabio Pérez. Complete the sentences.

1 Are you _____ for lunch on Thursday?
2 I'm really sorry, _____ I can't make lunch on Thursday.
3 Can we _____ another time?
4 How _____ Saturday?
5 When would be _____ for you?
6 Yes, that's _____ with me.

Focus

Read the examples.

The flight leaves at quarter past one.
You're all meeting at ten forty-five.
Ken's going to bring his camera equipment.

Complete the rules with the appropriate tense.

going to   Present Continuous   Present Simple

We use _____ to talk about plans and intentions.

We use the _____ to talk about fixed times, days, and dates.

We use the _____ to talk about arrangements with other people.

Put the phrases in 3 in the appropriate groups.

Change arrangement	Suggest a time	Ask when someone is free	Give a positive response	Give a negative response

⏩ For more details and practice, go to the Review section on page 29.

PRACTICE

4 Match the verb, noun, and time phrases below to make questions with *going to*.

Example   Are you going to watch television tonight?

buy	television	this year
meet	something expensive	this week
watch	another language	tonight
go on	someone for dinner	sometime
move	abroad	in the next year
study	a business trip	in the future
fly	house	in the next few months

5 Work in pairs. Take turns to ask your questions in **4**.

6 Paul Lee calls Kay Saunders. Complete the conversation with these phrases.

Are you free   *Can we arrange*   *How about*
I can't make   *that's fine*   *When would be good*

Paul Hi, Kay. It's Paul Lee.

Kay Oh hi, Paul. How are you?

Paul I'm fine, thanks. Listen, Kay, I'm sorry but _____[1] Thursday afternoon. _____[2] another time?

Kay Sure. _____[3] next week sometime?

Paul OK. _____[4] for you?

Kay Monday afternoon?

Paul Let me just check. Monday afternoon. Looks OK. What time?

Kay _____[5] at 2.00?

Paul 2.00. Yes, _____[6] with me. Let's meet at my office.

Kay OK. Great. See you Monday.

Paul Great. Have a good weekend.

TASK

7 Work in pairs. You arranged to meet your colleague next week for coffee on Wednesday. You need to change the meeting to another day. Call your colleague and try to arrange another day and time.

Student A Go to page 127.
Student B Go to page 132.

Review

Grammar Present Continuous; Present Simple

Form

We use *be* and the *-ing* form of the main verb to form the Present Continuous.

Positive			Negative		
I	'm	working.	I	'm not	working.
You We They	're		You We They	aren't	
He She It	's		He She It	isn't	

Question				Answer		
(Where)	Am	I	working?	Yes/No,	I	am / 'm not.
						'm working in the city centre.
	Are	you we they		Yes/No,	you we they	are / aren't.
						're working in the city centre.
	Is	he she it		Yes/No,	he she it	is / isn't.
						's working in the city centre.

Use

We use the Present Continuous to talk about events happening around the present time.

Examples They're preparing an important proposal.
Are you travelling much for work these days?
He's staying with his brother this week.

The following verbs are not usually used with the Present Continuous:
be, like, love, need, want, understand, prefer, know, own.
If *have* means 'own', we use the Present Simple, e.g. *She has a motorbike.*
In other situations, *have* can be used with the Present Simple or Present Continuous, e.g. *I usually have toast for breakfast, but today I'm having eggs.*

PRACTICE **1** **Match the questions with the answers.**

1 Where do you live?
2 What do you do?
3 What are you working on?
4 Where are you staying?
5 What do you do in your free time?
6 Which languages do you speak?

a At a hotel in Madrid, as I'm doing some work here.
b I speak Danish, English, and German.
c I have a small flat in Copenhagen.
d I work for a consulting company.
e A project for a Spanish telecommunications company.
f At the moment, I'm trying to learn Spanish.

2 Complete the postcard with the words below in the correct form, Present Simple or Present Continuous.

*be   drink   eat   enjoy
have   love   not get up
rain   stay   visit*

Hi

We ___*are having*___ [1] a great time! The weather's not so good – it _____ [2] usually sunny at this time of year, but now it _____ [3]! But we _____ [4] ourselves – we _____ [5] in a lovely hotel, _____ [6] until 9 o'clock, _____ [7] lovely Italian coffee, and _____ [8] the local shops, galleries, and museums. Every night we _____ [9] in a different restaurant – I _____ [10] Italian food!

See you soon!

3 Complete the questions in an interview with a rider before the Palio di Siena horse race.

1   How often _____?
     It takes place twice a year, once in July and once in August.
2   Which horse _____ in this race?
     I'm riding a beautiful horse called Elimia.
3   Which district of Siena _____?
     I'm representing the Bruco district.
4   Do _____?
     No, I live outside the city.
5   How often _____?
     I usually ride about three times a week.
6   Are _____?
     No, I'm not nervous, just excited!

Vocabulary Jobs; *make, do, have*

1 Complete the crossword with the names of different jobs.

Across

3   a person who sells something, often to other businesses
4   a person who cuts and styles people's hair
5   a person who designs buildings
7   a person who treats sick animals
8   a person who cooks in a restaurant
9   a person who fits and fixes water pipes, drains, etc.
10   a person who deals with financial accounts

Down

1   a person who assists a senior manager, e.g. making appointments, preparing documents
2   a person who deals with staff issues in a company
6   a person who sells flights and holidays

2 Select the word which is in the wrong group and add it to the correct group.

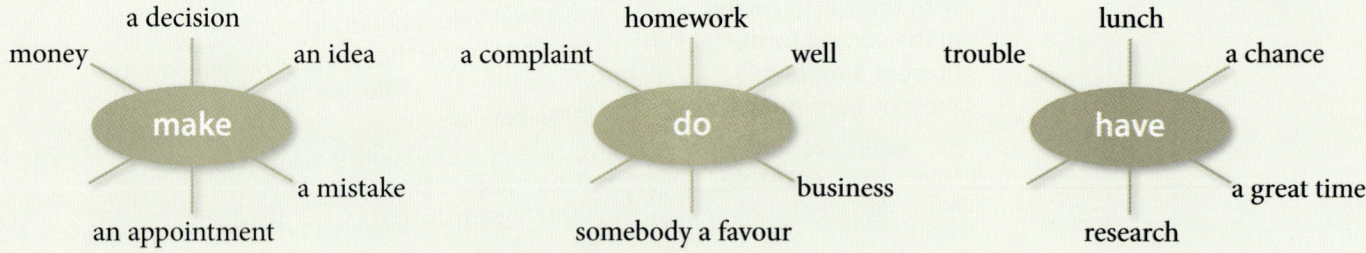

a decision
money
an idea
make
a mistake
an appointment

homework
a complaint
well
do
business
somebody a favour

lunch
trouble
a chance
have
a great time
research

3 Complete the sentences with the words below.

appointment   complaint   deal   exercise   favour   money   research   trouble   well

1 You should make your _____ to the customer service department.
2 You need to do some _____ if you want to lose weight.
3 The business is doing _____ and making a lot of _____.
4 I'd like to make an _____ for a check-up, please.
5 Before making a _____ with a new business partner, you should do some _____ into their background.
6 Could you do me a _____, please? I'm having _____ with my laptop.

Work skills Emails 1: Parts of an email

1 Put the words in the correct order.

1 forward / I / meeting / look / you / to
2 find / brochure / please / our / attached
3 about / the / writing / sales conference / I'm
4 you / send / presentation slides / could / the / me / please
5 contact / please / questions / me / any / if / have / you
6 calling / for / this morning / thanks

2 Complete the email.

From:	Steve
To:	Sylvia
Subject:	Schedule
Sent:	24.11.2013

Dear Sylvia

I_____ w_____ n_____ t_____ m_____ y_____¹ and your colleagues yesterday.

I'_____ w_____ t_____ s_____² that we can arrange German lessons for your colleagues on Mondays at 2 p.m., as requested. The trainer will be Annamarie Decker and the first lesson will be next Monday.

C_____ y_____ p_____ t_____ m_____³ which room the trainer should go to?

I'_____ a_____⁴ a training contract. P_____⁵ check and sign it and return it to me.

P_____ l_____ m_____ k_____ i_____⁶ you have any questions.

W_____ I_____ f_____ t_____⁷ working with you.

B_____ r_____⁸

Steve

Training Coordinator

Functions Talking about schedules and arrangements; *going to*

The Present Simple, Present Continuous, and *going to* are all used to talk about the future.

We use the Present Simple to talk about timetables.

Examples The plane departs at 14.20.
The meeting is on 6th December.
The train arrives at 5 o'clock.

We use the Present Continuous to talk about arrangements with other people.

Examples We're having dinner in the hotel.
She's giving a presentation at the conference tomorrow.
How long are you staying?

We use *going to* to talk about plans and intentions.

Examples They're going to discuss the problem at the next meeting.
I'm going to start exercising next week.
Are you going to visit the Pearl Tower when you're in Shanghai?

1 **Complete the emails with the correct form of the words below. Use the Present Simple, Present Continuous, or *going to*.**

bring   have   leave   meet (×2)   stay

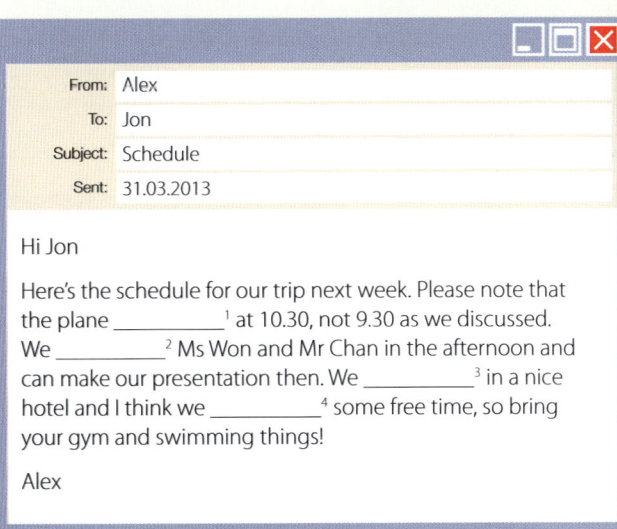

From: Alex
To: Jon
Subject: Schedule
Sent: 31.03.2013

Hi Jon

Here's the schedule for our trip next week. Please note that the plane _____ ¹ at 10.30, not 9.30 as we discussed. We _____ ² Ms Won and Mr Chan in the afternoon and can make our presentation then. We _____ ³ in a nice hotel and I think we _____ ⁴ some free time, so bring your gym and swimming things!

Alex

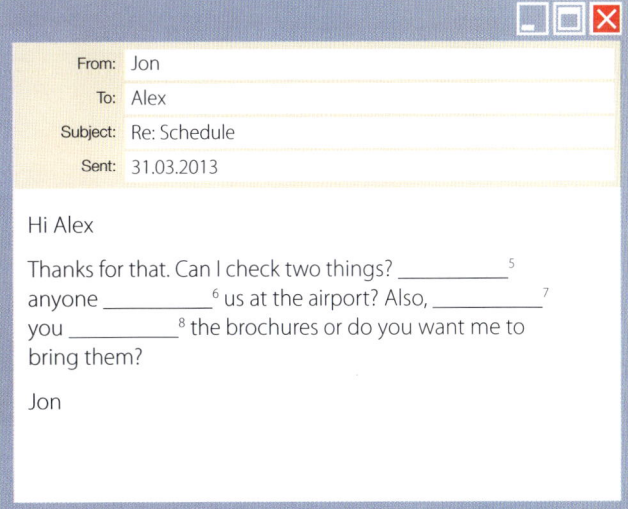

From: Jon
To: Alex
Subject: Re: Schedule
Sent: 31.03.2013

Hi Alex

Thanks for that. Can I check two things? _____ ⁵ anyone _____ ⁶ us at the airport? Also, _____ ⁷ you _____ ⁸ the brochures or do you want me to bring them?

Jon

2 **Correct the mistakes in the phone conversation. There is one mistake per line.**

Ken	Hi, Stella. I call about our lunch tomorrow.
Stella	Hi, Ken. What's problem?
Ken	Well, we've got a last-minute order, so I going to be busy with that.
Stella	No problem. Can we change another time? How about Thursday?
Ken	Sounds good. Is 12 o'clock nice for you?
Stella	Can we do it 12.30?
Ken	Sure. 12.30. On the canteen?
Stella	Yes, that's fine to me. See you then.

3 Travelling to work

Grammar Past Simple

INTRODUCTION

1 Work in pairs. Ask each other the questions.

1 What was your first job?

2 How did you find your present job? Did you travel far to find it?

2 Look at the map and photos. What do you think the story below is about?

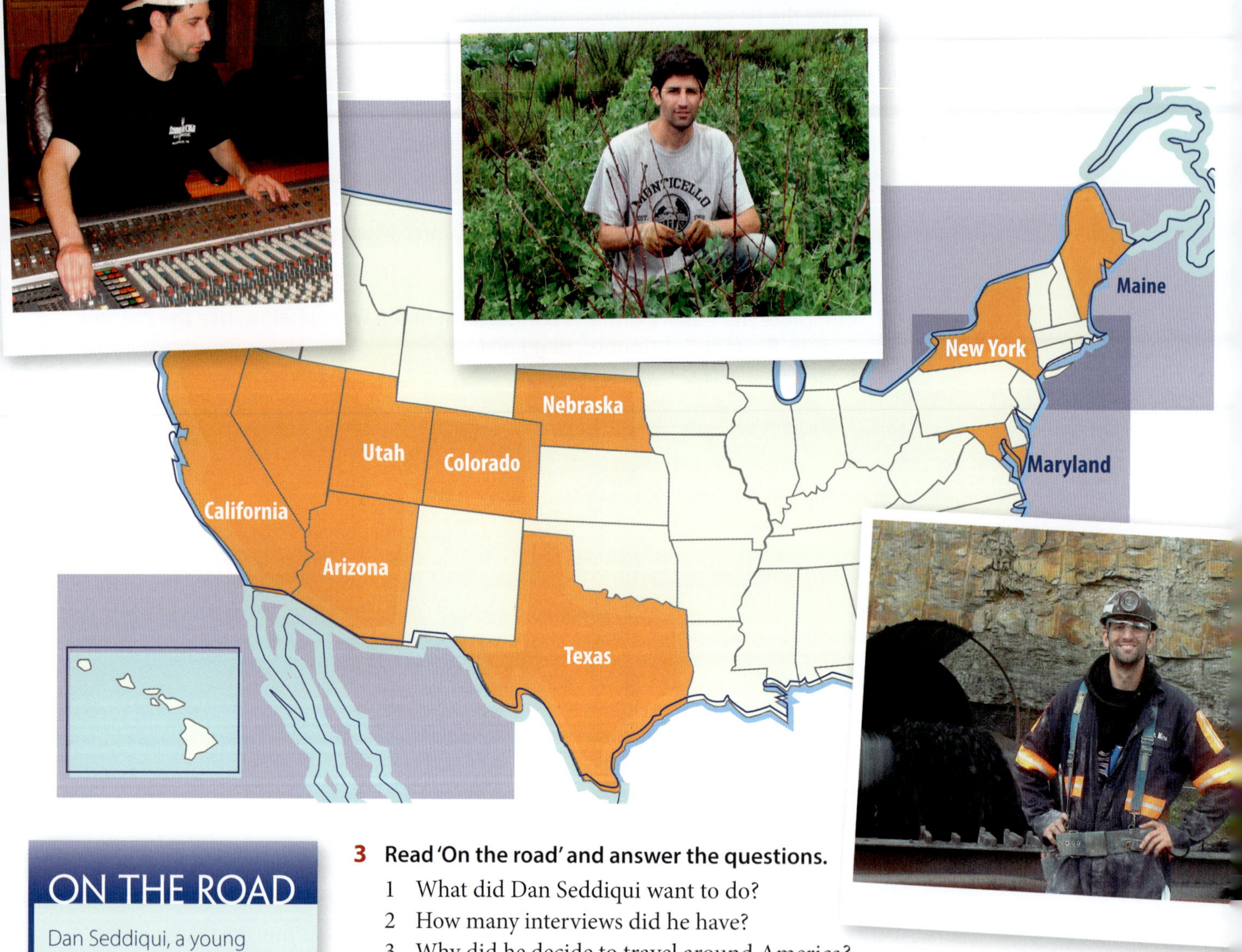

Maine

New York

Nebraska

Utah Colorado

Maryland

California

Arizona

Texas

ON THE ROAD

Dan Seddiqui, a young American from southern California, wanted to get a job. He had more than 40 job interviews and they were all unsuccessful. So he decided to travel around America by car to find work. It was a big risk and he had no idea how the journey would end.

3 Read 'On the road' and answer the questions.

1 What did Dan Seddiqui want to do?

2 How many interviews did he have?

3 Why did he decide to travel around America?

4 How did he travel?

What do you think of Dan's idea? How many jobs do you think he did?

4 •)) **3.1** Listen to the first part of the story. Answer the questions.

1 Which state did Dan go to first?

2 How long did he stay in each state?

3 How many states did he go to altogether?

4 Did he do the same job in each state?

5 How many jobs did he do altogether?

6 Was the journey a success?

5 •)) **3.2** Listen to the second part of the story. Which jobs did he do in the states highlighted on the map?

Focus

Read the examples.

Positive

He started in Utah, in the mid-west of the USA.
After that, he went north to South Dakota.
He was a wedding coordinator in Nevada.
Some of them were very well paid.

Questions	Short answers
Did he help to marry anyone?	Yes, he did.
Did he start in California?	No, he didn't.
Was he a good cook?	Yes, he was. / No, he wasn't.

Negative

He didn't do any dangerous jobs.

Complete the rules with these words.

negative   irregular   was   -ed   questions   were

We add _____ to the verb to make the Past Simple of regular verbs.

Some verb endings in the Past Simple are _____, for example *go / went, buy / bought*.

We use _____ with *I, he, she,* and *it,* and _____ with *you, we,* and *they* to form the Past Simple of *be*.

We use *did, was,* or *were* to make _____ .

We use *didn't, wasn't,* and *weren't* to make the _____ .

Choose the correct word.

We use the Past Simple for *finished / unfinished* actions and situations in the past.

⏩ For more details and practice, go to the Review section on page 38.

PRACTICE   6 Complete the table with the verbs from **3.1** and **3.2** on pages 136–137.

Infinitive	start	visit		go	work		continue	stop	marry	be	
Past Simple			got			did					forgot

7 Complete the questions. Then match the questions and answers.

1 What / your first job?
2 How / find it?
3 Did / move / to get the job?
4 What qualifications / need?
5 Did / enjoy / the job?
6 What / like / about the job?
7 Was / well paid?
8 How long / stay?
9 What job / do / after that?
10 What / favourite job?

a I needed a degree in computer engineering.
b I liked working with really smart people.
c I stayed for three years.
d Yes. It was quite hard at first, but I enjoyed it later on.
e No, it wasn't. But we did have share options.
f Yes, I did. I moved from Ohio to California.
g Next, I joined a start-up company.
h I worked as a software developer for Microsoft.
i My favourite job was my first job. It was an exciting time.
j My friend from university told me about it.

8 Work in pairs. Ask each other the questions in **7**. Think of some new questions.

9 ◉) **3.3** Listen to the words in the table and tick ✓ the *-ed* sound you hear.

	liked	stayed	started	developed	lived	wanted	asked	decided	arrived
/d/									
/t/	✓								
/id/									

10 What is a global nomad? Read and find out. Then answer the questions.

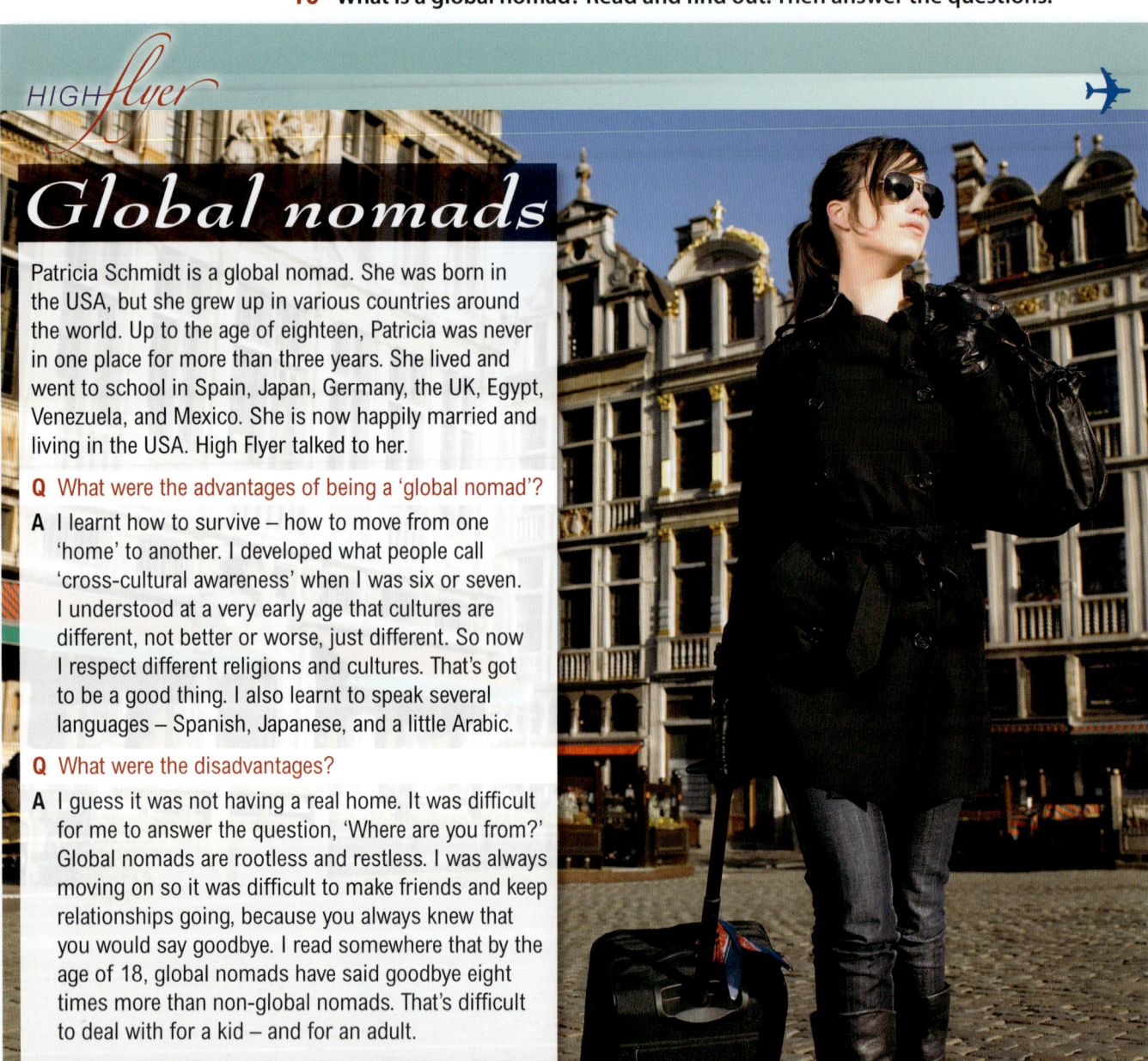

HIGH*flyer*

Global nomads

Patricia Schmidt is a global nomad. She was born in the USA, but she grew up in various countries around the world. Up to the age of eighteen, Patricia was never in one place for more than three years. She lived and went to school in Spain, Japan, Germany, the UK, Egypt, Venezuela, and Mexico. She is now happily married and living in the USA. High Flyer talked to her.

Q What were the advantages of being a 'global nomad'?

A I learnt how to survive – how to move from one 'home' to another. I developed what people call 'cross-cultural awareness' when I was six or seven. I understood at a very early age that cultures are different, not better or worse, just different. So now I respect different religions and cultures. That's got to be a good thing. I also learnt to speak several languages – Spanish, Japanese, and a little Arabic.

Q What were the disadvantages?

A I guess it was not having a real home. It was difficult for me to answer the question, 'Where are you from?' Global nomads are rootless and restless. I was always moving on so it was difficult to make friends and keep relationships going, because you always knew that you would say goodbye. I read somewhere that by the age of 18, global nomads have said goodbye eight times more than non-global nomads. That's difficult to deal with for a kid – and for an adult.

1 Where was Patricia born?
2 How often did she move to a different country?
3 What did she learn about cultures when she was young?
4 How many languages does she speak?
5 What did she find difficult as a global nomad?
6 What do global nomads do eight times more than other young people?

11 Do you know any global nomads? Would you like to be a global nomad?

TASK **12** Work in pairs. You are going to share more information about Dan Seddiqui. Student A go to page 131. Student B go to page 128.

Vocabulary Talking about travel

1 Complete the word maps using the words and phrases in the box. Choose the most appropriate word map for each word.

taxi	hire car	wildlife
cycling	resort	bed and breakfast
beach	ship, ferry	metro, underground, subway
coach, bus	campsite	package
rented flat or villa	hiking	train, TGV, Shinkansen

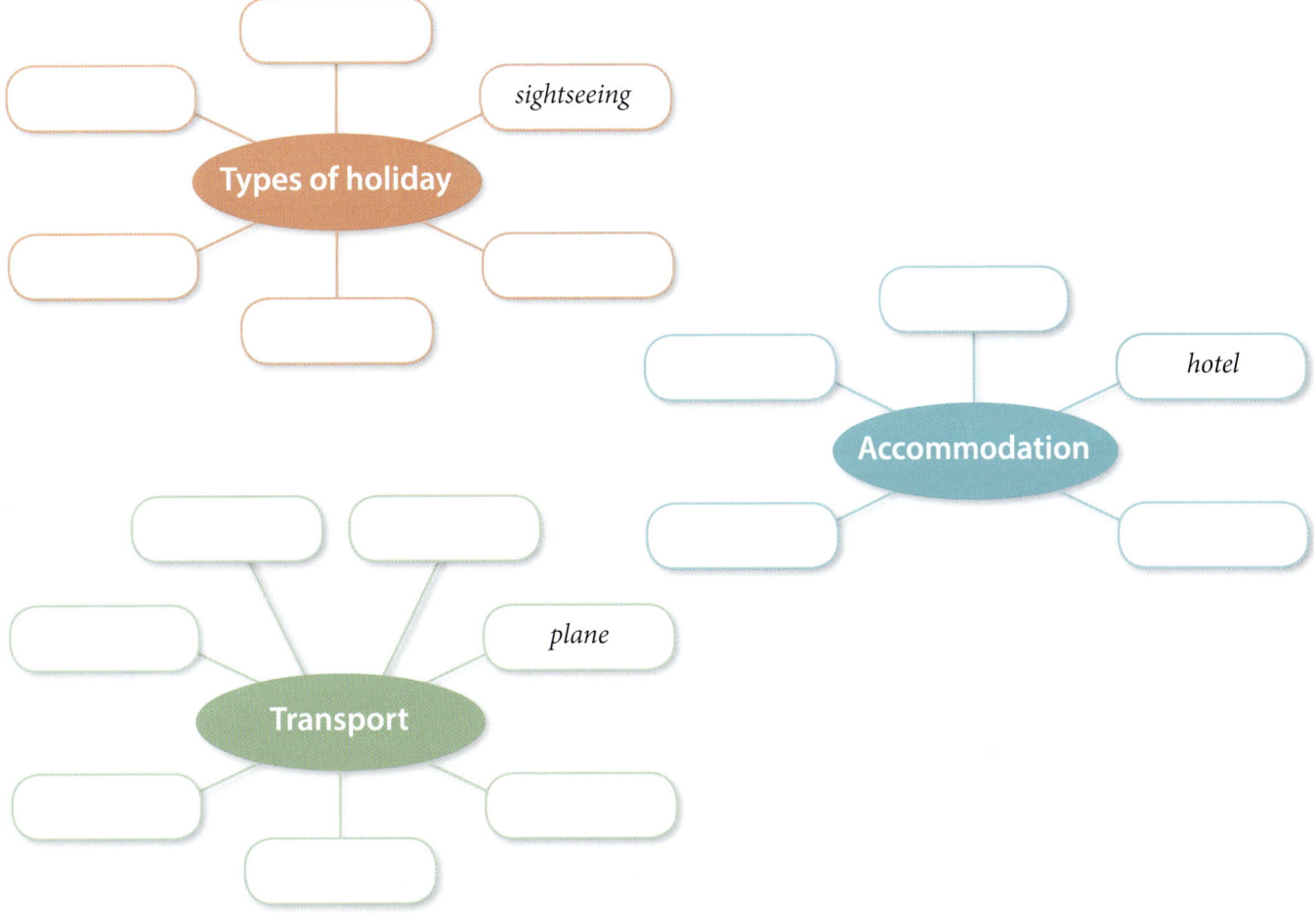

2 Match the phrases with the word maps in **1**.

1 to go on a _____ holiday
2 to go by _____
3 to stay at a _____

3 ●)) **3.4** Listen to Hana talk about her last holiday. Which things from **1** does she mention?

4 Ask a partner about a recent holiday using the vocabulary in **1**.

Examples   What type of holiday did you go on?
Where did you go?
How did you travel?
Where did you stay?
What did you enjoy doing?

5 Read the list of places where we can find travel information.

blogs	holiday programmes	online booking	social network sites
travel agents	travel guides	travel websites	

1 How do you usually book your business trips and holidays?
2 How do you usually find out about the place you are visiting?

6 Match the words in A and B. Which words do we use for air travel, train travel, or both?

A	B
1 overhead	desk
2 flight	seat
3 ticket	announcement
4 window	attendant
5 hand	locker
6 check-in	control
7 security	card
8 ticket	baggage
9 departure	ticket
10 train	lounge
11 passport	inspector
12 excess	entertainment
13 in-flight	office
14 boarding	luggage

7 Read the announcements and questions. Where and when do you usually hear them?

1 Could I see your boarding pass, please?
2 Please remain seated until the plane has come to a complete standstill.
3 The next stop will be London Paddington.
4 How much hand luggage do you have?
5 The next train arriving on platform nine will be the 10.25 from Birmingham.
6 This is a security announcement. Passengers are reminded that they must not leave baggage unattended. Any unattended baggage will be destroyed.
7 This is the final boarding call for passengers on flight VS901 to Tokyo. Please proceed to gate six immediately.
8 Did you pack your bags yourself?
9 Tickets, please.
10 Do have any sharp items in your bag?

8 Work in pairs. Talk about what you like and dislike about travelling by plane or by train. What are the advantages or disadvantages? What is your favourite way to travel?

Work skills Telephoning 1: Starting and ending a phone call

1 **How many phone calls do you make a day? Who do you usually call? How many phone calls do you get a day? Who usually calls you?**

2 3.5 **Listen to two phone conversations. Answer the questions.**

	Call 1	Call 2
1 Who answers the phone?		
2 Who is making the call?		
3 Who does the caller want to speak to?		
4 What is the call about?		

3 **Put these phrases from the two phone calls in the order you hear them.**

Call 1

a Could you hold the line? I'll put you through.
b Thanks for getting back to me.
c May I ask who's calling?
d Cathy speaking. How can I help you?
e I'm just returning your call.
f Could I speak to Alex Borini, please?

Call 2

a Listen, this is just a quick call.
b Hold on a second.
c Hi, is that …?
d Naomi's on another line.
e How are you?
f Could you ask her to call me back?
g Who's calling?

4 3.5 **Listen again and check your answers to 3.**

5 **Read the ends of the two phone calls. Which is Call 1 and which is Call 2? Who are the speakers? Give reasons for your answer.**

a
A Thanks, that's great. See you next week.
B OK. I'll call you when I get to Berlin …
A OK, bye.

b
A OK, well I think that's everything. Thank you for your help.
B My pleasure. It's good to speak to you. And good luck with the project.
A Thanks. I'll be in touch again soon. Bye.
B Bye.

6 **Work in groups of three or pairs. Practise the two conversations. Use your own names and ideas.**

Functions Asking for and giving advice

INTRODUCTION

1 **You are going to travel to a country you don't know. It's a ten-hour flight. What do you need to think about?**

Examples   food, jet lag, something to read

2 ◗) **3.6** **Ken and Emma ask a friend, Geoff, for some advice about their trip to Brazil. Listen and match Ken and Emma's questions with Geoff's answers.**

1   What should we do about jet lag?
2   What's the best way to get travel information?
3   Is there anything we need to be careful about?
4   Should we change some money at the airport?
5   Do we need to get insurance?
6   What's the best way to get around?
7   Do you think we should learn some Portuguese?

a   Yes, that's a good idea. You need to pay for a taxi from the airport.
b   Taxis are probably the best way. So you need to know the different types of taxi.
c   Yes, that's a great idea. Why don't you try something like googletranslate?
d   Yes, I think you should get travel and medical insurance.
e   You should have a look at Tripit.
f   If I were you, I'd try to sleep for an hour or two between Madrid and Rio.
g   No, not really. Rio's pretty safe. The best thing to do is check where you are going and be sensible.

Focus

Complete the table using examples from 2. Find more phrases in the script on page 137.

Asking for advice	Giving advice
What should I / we do about …?	If I were you, I'd …
What's the best way to …?	You should …
Should we …?	You need to …
_____	_____
_____	_____

❯❯ For more details and practice, go to the Review section on page 41.

PRACTICE

3 ◀)) **3.7** Listen to four messages from people in difficult situations. Where are they and what is the problem? What advice could you give them?

	Location	Problem
1		
2		
3		
4		

4 Match the advice below with the situations in **3**. Which advice do you think is the best, a or b?

A a If I were you, I'd go to a police box and explain the situation. People in Japan are really honest and if they find something, they give it to the local police. I'm sure you'll find it.

 b It could be anywhere. Why don't you go back to your hotel and check your other bags?

B a If I were you, I'd wait till you get to a town or village and signal to the driver to stop near a restaurant. Get out and go into the restaurant to ask where you are and where the city centre is.

 b I think you should wait and see where the taxi goes. Maybe the taxi driver knows a short cut.

C a OK. The best thing to do is go straight to the airline information desk and ask about hotels. Then try and find out when the hurricane is coming.

 b I'd find someone who works for the airline and ask if there are any other flights available.

D a Don't worry. Why don't you give me the client's name and I'll find their number and tell them you're on your way.

 b The best thing to do is go as fast as you can. You don't want to upset our best customer.

TASK

5 Work in pairs. Read about two problems at work. Take turns to give some advice.

1 One of my team just came into the office and said she's going to quit. She can't work with one of the team members, Bill. She says he's always late and never listens. The problem is that Bill is really popular with our biggest clients.

2 I'm printing a report on the office photocopier and find a print-out on the office printer. It has my name on it and is marked 'Confidential' in big red letters.

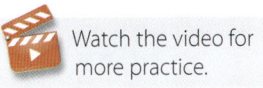

Watch the video for more practice.

Review

Grammar Past Simple

Form

We use -*ed* to form the Past Simple for regular verbs.

Examples start   started
           happen   happened
           stop   stopped

Irregular verb endings are all different. Sometimes the whole word changes.

Examples learn   learnt
           go   went
           become   became

There is a list of irregular verbs in the Pocket Book.

When a regular verb ends in a /d/ or /t/ sound, the -*ed* ending is pronounced /id/, for example *needed*, *visited*.

Positive				Negative		
I You We They He She It	worked left		(yesterday).	I You We They He She It	didn't work didn't leave	(yesterday).
I He She It	was	late		I He She It	wasn't late	
You We They	were			You We They	weren't late	

Question				Answer		
Did	I you we they he she it	work leave		Yes,	I you	did.
				No,	we they he she it	didn't.
Where did What time did				(I/You/We … worked) at head office. (I/You/We … left) at 8.00 a.m.		
(Why)	Was	I he she it	late	(yesterday)?	Yes, No,	I he she it	was. wasn't.
	Were	you we they			Yes, No,	you we they	were. weren't.
					(I was / They were … late) because of the train.		

Use

We use the Past Simple to talk about actions and situations in the past which happened at a specific time and are finished.

Examples They started the company ten years ago.
Was Noel at the conference?
Billy went on holiday to Hong Kong last year.
Olga interviewed twelve people last week.
What did you do at the weekend?

We often use the Past Simple with past time phrases, for example *last week / month / year, three years / ten minutes ago, when I was at school / on holiday.*

PRACTICE   **1** **Complete the crossword with the Past Simple form of the verbs.**

Across
2 say
3 go
5 give
7 think
8 make
10 take
12 feel
13 see

Down
1 come
3 write
4 leave
5 get
6 buy
9 drive
11 know

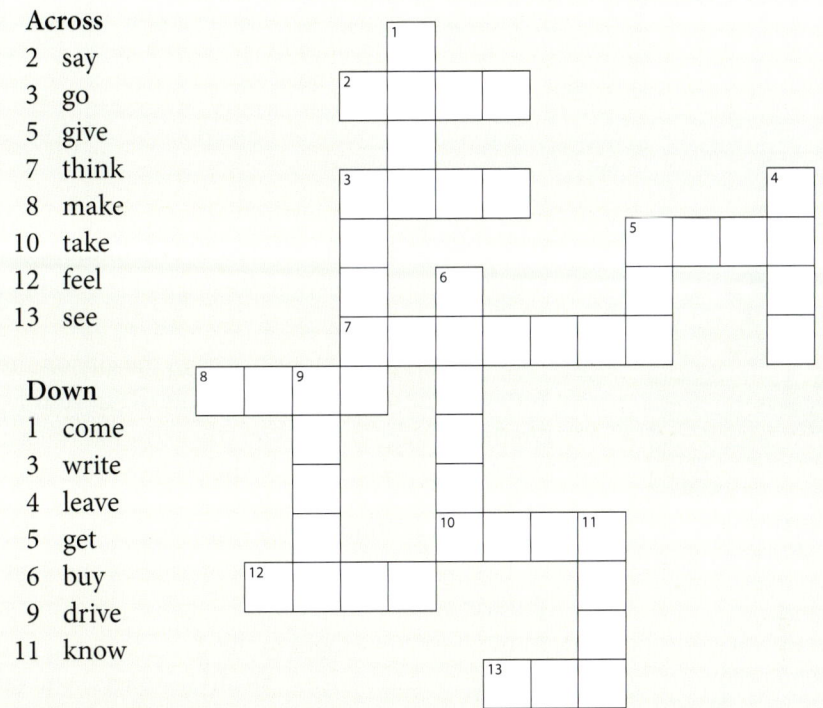

2 **Change the sentences into the Past Simple.**

Example Milo takes the train to work and arrives at 8.30 a.m.
Milo took the train to work and arrived at 8.30 a.m.

1 The meeting starts at 11 a.m. and lasts for an hour and a half.
2 Sorry, I don't have time to write the invoice because I have so much to do.
3 Sales of cinema tickets go up in winter and fall in summer.
4 Do you know what their best-selling products are?
5 Magda thinks she knows the answer, but she doesn't.
6 Terence feels very tired when he gets home.

City break in Barcelona

Sightseeing and shopping in the city of Gaudi. 3 nights in a boutique hotel for only £397, includes guided tour and taxi transfers from and to the airport.

Cycling in Scotland

Experience the freedom of two wheels and the breathtaking scenery of Scotland! 1 week organized cycle tour with bed and breakfast accommodation and bicycle hire: £545.

Vocabulary Talking about travel

1 **Look at the adverts for holidays. Are sentences 1–8 true or false?**

Family holiday in Vendée, France

Enjoy relaxing family fun on this well-equipped campsite, only four hours drive from two ferry ports. A short drive from beautiful beaches. Swimming pool and kids' club on site. Special offer on mobile home accommodation: £995 for 14 nights.

Diving in Cuba

Explore Cuba above and below the water with this holiday! 7 nights all-inclusive accommodation at the Santa Lucia diving resort with its fabulous beach. Includes 3-days' car hire and 8 dives. Only £999.

1 Only tents are available on the campsite in Vendée.
2 The campsite has entertainment for children.
3 All meals are included in the price of the diving holiday.
4 There is an additional fee to rent a car for three days on the Cuban holiday.
5 You will visit the famous places in the city on the Barcelona holiday.
6 You will take a coach from the airport to your hotel in Barcelona.
7 On the cycling holiday, you pay extra for lunch and dinner.
8 You have to hire a bike for the cycling holiday.

2 **Complete the sentences.**

1 F_____ a_____ look after passengers on a plane.
2 You have to show your b_____ c_____ at the gate when flying.
3 You wait for your flight in the d_____ l_____ .
4 H_____ l_____ means the bag(s) you take with you onto the plane.
5 You can put your bag in the o_____ l_____ on the plane.
6 To b_____ the plane means to get on the plane.

3 **Correct the mistakes.**

1 We went in a great camping holiday last summer.
2 Are you going to live in a hotel or an apartment on your trip to Prague?
3 Did you travel to London on a taxi?
4 We enjoyed to hike in the mountains.
5 We travelled with TGV and it was really fast!

Work skills Telephoning 1: Starting and ending a phone call

1 **Put the words in the correct order.**

1 hold / could / you / line? / the
2 I / who's / ask / calling? / may
3 me / getting / thanks / back / for / to
4 speak / could / Yan / I / to / please?
5 how / Marie / you? / speaking. / I / can / help
6 back? / him / you / me / to / ask / could / call

2 **Put the phone conversation in the correct order. The first line is marked for you.**

a   Just one moment. I'll put you through.

b   Good afternoon. Kangnam Supplies. How can I help you?   *1*

c   Certainly, may I ask who's calling?

d   OK, I'll pass on the message.

e   Yes, it's Marco Martin.

f   Hello. I'd like to speak to Shin Lee please.

g   Of course, can I take your number?

h   Yes, could you ask him to call me back?

i   Hello, sorry, Shin isn't at his desk. Can I take a message?

j   Yes, it's 0620-515-9374.

Functions Asking for and giving advice

We use the following phrases to ask for advice.
What's the best way to learn English?
Should I change money before we go?
Do you think we should organize a party for her?
What should we do about the noise?
Do we need to take our passports?

We use the following phrases to give advice.
(I think) you should study every day.
I (don't) think you should watch films in English.
Why don't you just take a credit card?
If I were you, I'd talk to your boss about it.
You need to check the timetable.
The best thing to do is wait.

Need is followed by *to* and a verb. *Why don't you*, *should* and *If I were you* are followed by a verb.
When giving negative advice with *I think*, we add the negative to *think* not to *should*:

Example   I don't think you should fly business class.
(~~I think you shouldn't fly business class~~).

1 **Match the advice with the three situations.**

1   I'm going on a business trip to Washington next week and I've just noticed that my passport has expired.

2   I've got an interview for a new job next Tuesday at 10 a.m. What should I do about taking the time off work?

3   I'm going to visit my family in Germany soon and I'm really nervous about flying with my nine-month-old baby son.

a   You should tell the truth.

b   Why don't you take lots of toys and snacks with you!

c   The best thing to do is phone the passport office and ask if they have an express service.

d   You should try not to worry – he'll be fine!

e   If I were you, I'd book half a day's holiday. Say you have a doctor's appointment.

f   I think you should explain the situation to your boss as soon as possible.

g   Why don't you ask your family to visit you instead.

h   You should ask the interviewer for an early morning or late afternoon interview instead?

i   You need to find a colleague who can go in your place.

4 Objects and designs

Grammar Passives: Present Simple, Past Simple

INTRODUCTION

1 **What sort of objects do people collect? Why? Do you collect anything?**

2 **Look at the objects below and put them in order of value.**

3 **Read the article about the objects in 2. Were your guesses correct?**

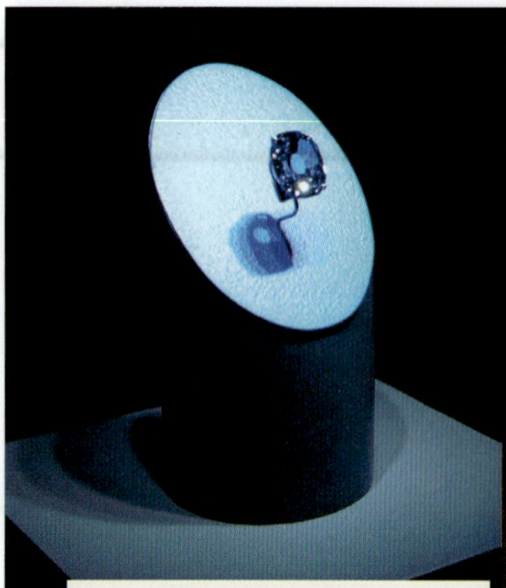

Wittelsbach-Graff Diamond

Leonardo da Vinci's *Codex*

Edvard Munch's *The Scream*

Collectors' items

This 35.56-carat diamond is known as the ***Wittelsbach-Graff*** Diamond. The stone was found in India about 400 years ago, and was owned by many famous people, including King Philip IV of Spain. It was purchased by the London jeweller, Laurence Graff, for $23.4 million in 2008.

The ***Codex*** was written by Leonardo da Vinci about 500 years ago. Bill Gates, the founder of Microsoft, bought the ***Codex*** in 1994. The pages were scanned into digital image files and a CD-ROM version was released by the digital image licensing company Corbis in 1997. The ***Codex*** is put on public display once a year in a different city around the world. At $30.8 million, it is the most expensive book in the world.

The Scream was painted by Edvard Munch in 1893. Four versions of the picture were produced. Versions of the painting were stolen twice, from the National Gallery and from the Munch Museum in Oslo, Norway. This painting was sold for nearly $120 million in 2012.

4 **Are the statements true or false?**

1. The diamond was found in South Africa.
2. It was owned by a Spanish king.
3. *The Codex* was sold by Bill Gates.
4. A digital version was produced.
5. *The Scream* was painted by Édouard Manet.
6. The painting was stolen four times.

5 4.1 **Listen to the stories of two other objects and answer the questions.**

1. What are the objects?
2. What are they worth?
3. Why are they worth so much?

6 **What do you think of these objects? Are they worth the money people paid for them? Do you know any other objects that are very valuable?**

Focus

Read the examples of the Passive.
Present Simple
The *Codex* is put on public display once a year.
Past Simple
The *Codex* was written by Leonardo da Vinci about 500 years ago.

Choose the correct words to complete the rules.

We form the Passive with *be / do* + past participle.
We use the Passive to focus on the *object / doer (agent)*.
We use the active form to focus on the *object / doer (agent)*.
We use *by / for* before the agent.

▶▶ For more details and practice, go to the Review section on page 50.

PRACTICE

7 Find the Passive form of these verbs in the article in **3**.

find	own	paint	produce	purchase	put
release	scan	steal	write	sell	

How many examples of the Passive can you find in **4.1** on pages 137–138?

8 Complete the texts with the correct form of the verbs in brackets. What do you think the names of the things described are now?

Auction Web

Auction Web _____¹ (start) in 1995 in California by a French-born Iranian computer programmer called Pierre Omidyar. One of the first items that _____² (sell) was a broken laser pointer for $15. Today, it's the biggest online auction company in the world.

Brad's Drink

Brad's Drink _____³ (create) by Caleb Bradham, a pharmacist from North Carolina, USA in 1893. It _____⁴ (make) of carbonated water, sugar, vanilla, rare oils, pepsin, and cola nuts. In 1898, it _____ ⁵ (give) a different name because of the nuts in the recipe. A new 'Diet' version _____⁶ (introduce) in 1964. This drink _____⁷ (sell) in over 200 countries around the world.

Sphairistike

The game of 'sphairistike' _____⁰ (Invent) in England by Major Walter Wingfield in 1874. It _____⁹ (play) on grass using a ball, a net, and two rackets. It _____¹⁰ (watch) and _____¹¹ (play) all around the world by millions of people. The most famous championship _____¹² (hold) at Wimbledon every summer.

9 Read about two more brand names.

Student A Go to page 128.
Student B Go to page 132.

Can your partner guess the brand.

10 Do you know any products, cities, or people that were originally called something different? Why were the names changed? How did these names change?

11 Look at the logos. Can you find the following?

1 a short hidden arrow
2 a number
3 a peacock
4 a smile symbol
5 the company name written five times

12 •)) **4.2** Listen to an advertising executive talk about the process of designing logos. Answer the questions.

1 What does a logo do?
2 What is interesting about the Amazon arrow?
3 What is the main feature of a great logo?
4 Where can we find logos?
5 What are the three stages of producing a logo?

13 Which logos or brands do you like? What do you like about them?

TASK 14 Work in pairs. Student A's part of the products quiz is below. Student B go to page 132.

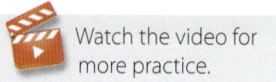
Watch the video for more practice.

Here are the clues for your quiz. Read them to your partner and ask them to guess what the answer is. The answers are on page 129.

1 It's a musical instrument. It's usually made of brass. It was invented by Adolf Sax.
2 It's a type of material used to make jeans. The name comes from the French town of Nîmes.
3 It's a famous mobile phone maker. It's named after a town in Finland.
4 It's a brand of sports shoe. It is made in Germany. It was named after an African animal.

Vocabulary Describing people and objects

1 How would you describe yourself? How would you describe your favourite possession?

2 ●)) **4.3** Listen to people describing their colleagues. Tick ✓ the words and phrases they use.

about 30 (years old)	*ambitious*	*tall*	*friendly*
good at languages	*hard-working*	*talkative*	*medium-height*
sense of humour	*shy*	*smart*	*wears a suit*

3 Put the words in **2** into these groups.

	Facts	Personality	Appearance
Lena			
Bill			
Michelle			

4 Put these phrases in the appropriate groups in **3**. Use the phrases and your own ideas to describe Damian and Keiko.

about five foot four
easy-going
long black hair
brown eyes
good at problem solving
married
dresses casually
hard-working
quiet
dresses smartly
likes sports
short brown hair

5 ●)) **4.4** Listen and write the short forms of the verbs in these sentences.

1 He has got dark hair.   _____

2 Which one is Bill?   _____

3 Yes, that is her.   _____

4 She is very friendly.   _____

5 Who is coming to the meeting?   _____

Practise saying the sentences.

6 Complete the table with details about a colleague at work, a friend, and a member of your family.

	Facts	Personality	Appearance	Hobbies
1				
2				
3				

7 Work in pairs. Share details about the people in **6** with your partner.

8 •)) **4.5** Listen to people talking about their favourite bags and watches. Which objects are they talking about?

a

b

c

d

e

f

9 •)) **4.5** Listen again and complete the sentences.

Object 1

1 It's very light. It _____ 66 grams.
2 It _____ how fast you are running.
3 It's got a _____ face.
4 The strap is black and green and _____ plastic.

Object 2

5 It's got a grey strap about 120 _____.
6 It's got a _____ to make it easy for carrying.
7 It's _____ people who need to carry books and papers.
8 It's made of _____.

10 Make sentences about the other bags and watches using the words below.

blue face	canvas	convenient	everyday	expensive
ladies	leather	round	steel	

11 Match the words on the left with their opposites on the right.

1	small	a	not useful, useless
2	casual	b	inefficient
3	black	c	weak
4	easy to use	d	large, big
5	expensive	e	heavy
6	comfortable	f	formal
7	useful	g	white
8	efficient	h	difficult to use
9	tough	i	uncomfortable
10	light	j	cheap, reasonably priced

12 Put the adverbs in the correct order from most to least.

a bit   not very   extremely   pretty   quite   very

13 Work in pairs. Talk about some of your favourite people and objects.

Work skills Meetings 1: Stages of a meeting

1 Match the stages of a meeting with the expressions in the speech bubbles.

> Good morning, everyone.

| 1 Welcoming | → | 2 Introductions | → | 3 Starting the meeting | → | 4 Stating the aim of the meeting |

| 8 Introducing the final agenda item | ← | 7 Moving to a new item | ← | 6 Asking people to contribute | ← | 5 Introducing the first agenda item |

| 9 Asking for questions | → | 10 Confirming action points | → | 11 Thanking people | → | 12 Finishing the meeting |

| 13 Confirming date of next meeting |

> a Could everyone check their sales figures after the meeting and get back to me?

> b The first item on the agenda is 'Sales trends in Europe'.

> c The main aim today is to review our recent sales performance.

> d Has anyone got any questions?

> e Gina, would you like to talk about Italy?

> f Shall we make a start?

> g We meet again at the same time next week.

> h Thank you very much for your ideas and suggestions.

> i The last item for today is …

> j That's all for today, I think.

> k Let's introduce ourselves.

> l So let's move on to the next item on the agenda.

2 ◉)) **4.6** Listen to the extracts from a meeting and check the order.

Functions Asking for and giving opinions; agreeing and disagreeing

INTRODUCTION

1 **Look at the design samples for Unisports' new outdoor wear range. Work in pairs or small groups. Choose designs for combinations of the following.**

Example   I think *a* would work for the men's market in the UK for hiking.

Country	Brazil	UK	
Gender	Men	Women	Unisex
Age group	16–18	18–25	25+
Activity	hiking	beach	casual evening
Season	winter	summer	

2 ◉)) **4.7** **Listen to the sales director Charles Ward, Laura Mancini, and her team discussing the new Unisports designs. Number the designs in the order you hear them discussed.**

3 ◉)) **4.7** **Are the statements true or false? Listen again and check your answers.**

1   Pietro works with Laura.
2   The first item on the agenda is swimwear.
3   The designs are for the UK and Brazilian markets.
4   George likes the first design.
5   Tiffany doesn't like design number two.
6   Everyone generally agrees about the designs.

4 **Complete the sentences. Use the script on pages 138–139 to help you.**

1   What _____ about the first design, number one?
2   How _____ about age group?
3   _____ it's a bit old?
4   Really? Don't _____ it's mainly for beachwear?
5   I see _____ , but it could work for hiking or maybe cycling.

Focus

Complete the table with these phrases.

I see your point, but …   I think …   Absolutely!   Don't you think …?

Asking for opinions	Replying
What do you think about …? How do you feel about …? _____	I'm not sure, but … Yes, I do. / No, I don't. _____
Agreeing	**Disagreeing**
I think you're right. I totally agree. _____	Do you think so? No, I don't think so. _____

▶▶ For more details and practice, go to the Review section on page 52.

For more details and practice, go to the Review section on page 52.

PRACTICE

5 Complete the exchanges with the two possible phrases.

Do you think   Don't you think   How do you feel   What do you think

1 **A** _____ the design will work for the 16–18 age group?
   B I'm not sure, but it looks a little old to me.

2 **A** _____ about the short-sleeved shirt?
   B I think it's a great design.

3 **A** _____ about the new product launch?
   B I'm sure it'll be a great success.

4 **A** _____ the design is a bit boring?
   B No, I don't think so. It looks quite modern.

6 What sort of clothes do you wear at work? Would you like to wear different clothes?

TASK

7 Your company thinks all staff should wear formal clothes every day. Some staff disagree and want to wear casual clothes in the office. Discuss the idea in groups and come to a decision.

Example **A** What do you think about the idea of staff wearing formal clothes?
   B I don't agree with it. I think … How about you?
   A I think it's a …

Review

Grammar Passives: Present Simple, Past Simple

Form

We form the Passive with *be* + past participle.

	Positive	Negative
Present Simple	Dinner is served at 7 p.m. Ferraris are made in Italy.	Dinner isn't served after 8 p.m. Ferraris aren't made in France.
Past Simple	She was paid 300 dollars. The paintings were stolen a year ago.	She wasn't paid 500 dollars. The paintings weren't stolen yesterday.

	Questions	Short answers
Present Simple	Is dinner served in the restaurant? Are credit cards accepted? Why is he invited? Where are the meetings usually held?	Yes, it is/No, it isn't. Yes, they are/No, they aren't.
Past Simple	Was the conference organized well? Were the speakers paid? Where was the conference advertised? How much were the speakers paid?	Yes, it was/No, it wasn't. Yes, they were/No, they weren't.

Use

We use the Passive when we focus on the action or object, not on the agent (the person or thing that did the action) or when we don't know who or what the agent is.

If we want to include the agent in a passive sentence, we use *by*.

Example   The accident was caused by a drunk driver.

The Passive is more frequently used in formal or written English than in informal or spoken English.

Example   Smoking is forbidden (on a written sign).
You can't smoke here (spoken).

In spoken English, we sometimes use *they* and the active, instead of the Passive.

Example   They opened the new bridge last week.
(The new bridge was opened last week.)

PRACTICE   **1   Change the sentences from active to passive.**

Example   They make iPhones in China.
iPhones are made in China.

1   The management introduced a new security system last month.
2   Somebody cleans the office every day.
3   Somebody stole my new motorbike.
4   They always check tickets on the train.
5   When did someone invent the microscope?
6   They published a new edition of the book last year.

2 Choose which of the sentences below should not use the passive form and change them to the active form.

1 A new car was bought by my sister.
2 Charles Darwin was born in Shrewsbury, UK in 1809.
3 Fresh fruit and vegetables are bought by us for our lunch menu every day.
4 A great new restaurant for dinner was found by them.
5 The new business centre was designed by an international team of architects.
6 Sales data will be released at the end of the month.

3 Complete the questions for the answers.

Example   When were you born?
           I was born in 1985.

1 When _____?
   The new shopping centre was opened last spring.
2 Where _____?
   The empty bottles are taken back to the factory.
3 Where _____?
   It was made in the Philippines.
4 Why _____?
   The road is closed because of an accident.
5 How much _____?
   $22 million was spent on the new headquarters.

Vocabulary Describing people and objects

1 Match the questions and answers.

1 What does he look like?
2 What colour hair has he got?
3 What's he like?
4 What does he like doing?

a He's friendly and has got a good sense of humour.
b He's quite short and wears glasses.
c He's interested in films and he often goes to the cinema.
d He's got light brown hair.

2 Which words are in the wrong group?

Facts:	Personality:	Appearance:
divorced	ambitious	easy-going
a dentist	fair-haired	tall
dresses smartly	shy	has a beard
in her forties	outgoing	medium-build
retired	quiet	blonde

3 **Complete the product reviews with the words below.**

big	comfortable	convenient	delicious	easy to use
expensive	leather	reasonably-priced	small	tough

Urban stylze Bag

I love this bag! A casual bag for everyday use. It's made of _____¹, long-lasting _____². The size is perfect – _____³ enough for all my stuff! It looks great, and is also light and _____⁴ to carry. Best of all, it's very _____⁵ so it doesn't break the bank.

Noir Coffee Machine

I got this as a present for my parents and they love it! It makes a variety of absolutely _____⁶ coffees. The design is stylish and _____⁷ enough to fit easily into the kitchen. My parents really like the fact that it is _____⁸, especially because you can take the water tank out to fill it up, which is very _____⁹. It was a bit _____¹⁰, but well worth the price.

Work skills Meetings 1: Stages of a meeting

1 **Correct the mistakes.**

  a Now, let's move on to the next instruction on the agenda.
  b Shall we do a start?
  c Thank you very much to your ideas and suggestions.
  d Good afternoon. Let's introduce us.
  e Could everyone look their figures after the meeting and get back to me?
  f Olga, do you like to start?

2 **Number the sentences in 1 in the order of stages of a meeting.**

Functions Asking for and giving opinions; agreeing and disagreeing

Asking for opinions	Giving opinions
What do you think about …? How do you feel about …? Do you think …?	I think … I'm not sure, but … Yes, I do. / No, I don't.
Agreeing	**Disagreeing**
Absolutely! I think you're right. OK. I totally agree.	Don't you think …? Do you think so? I see you point, but … No, I don't think so.

What do you think about …? and *How do you feel about …?* are followed by *-ing* or a noun.

Examples What do you think about reducing our prices?
What do you think about the new designs?
How do you feel about visiting Australia?
How do you feel about the style?

1 Read the conversation and decide if the sentences below are true or false.

Harumi   So what does everyone think about launching a kids range? Frank, would you like to start?

Frank   I think it's a great idea. People always want to spend money on nice stuff for their kids.

Yuko   Absolutely. Research shows that parents spend more on their kids than on themselves.

Mei   I find that hard to believe. And remember – the economy isn't good right now. People haven't got much money to spend.

Frank   I see your point, but our brand is really strong, so I think we should grow.

Harumi   Don't you think we should focus on our success – high quality adult casuals?

Yuko   I don't think so. There's a market for high quality kids' casuals too. And I know some great designers for kids' clothes.

Harumi   Hmm, I'm still not sure. Perhaps we should start with some market research?

Frank   Yes, definitely. And how do you feel about meeting some designers?

Harumi   OK. That's a good idea.

1   Harumi doesn't ask for everyone's opinion.
2   Yuko disagrees with Frank.
3   Mei disagrees with Yuko.
4   Frank doesn't understand what Mei says.
5   Harumi thinks they should only sell adult clothes.
6   Frank thinks they should do some market research first.

2 Complete the conversation.

David   So, h_____ d_____ y_____ f_____ a_____[1] the new website? Personally, I think it's a big improvement.

Frida   A_____[2]! It looks fantastic and the online shopping is really easy to use.

Karl   D_____ y_____ t_____ s_____[3]? I think it's a bit too colourful and with too many things on one page. It's difficult to read.

David   I d_____ t_____ s_____[4]. I don't have any problems reading it. And the colours are part of our image.

Frida   T_____ r_____[5], David. It's important that the website shows our bright, modern image. D_____ y_____ t_____ s_____[6], Karl?

Karl   OK, I s_____ y_____ p_____[7], but I'm still n_____ s_____[8] about it. I liked the old website.

5 Resources

Grammar Countable and uncountable nouns

INTRODUCTION

1 Does your country have any of these natural resources?

forests oil diamonds gas farming land copper/iron/gold

Can you name some countries which are famous for these resources?
Which resources are difficult to find or extract?

2 Read the article about a mining accident in Chile and answer the questions.

1 Which metal is important to Chile's economy?
2 What is it used for?
3 Where in Chile is the San José mine?
4 How many miners were trapped?
5 How long did it take to rescue them?

The 33

Copper is one of Chile's main resources with exports worth $3 billion. There are a lot of copper mines in the northern part of the country such as the Andina, Chuquicamata, and El Abra mines. The copper industry is an important source of revenue and jobs. Copper is used in computer circuit boards, wiring, and other electrical devices.

The San José copper mine is located deep in the Atacama Desert, in northern Chile. It is a very hot, dry, and dangerous place to work. In August 2010, 33 miners were trapped in the 121-year-old mine. The miners were working 600 metres underground when their path became blocked. It took seventeen days to discover their location, and it took another 52 days to drill a hole and bring the miners to the surface. None of the miners were injured and all of them survived.

3 •)) **5.1** Listen to a journalist report on the story. Tick ✓ the words you hear.

food	information	space
biscuits	vitamins	treats
milk	cereal	music
tinned fish	pears	magazines
peaches	apples	cigarettes
oranges	calories	exercise
water	fresh air	ladders

4 ◉) **5.1 Listen again and complete the sentences.**

1 How _____ food did they have?
2 Each day, they had _____ biscuits, _____ milk, _____ tinned fish, and _____ peaches.
3 They also had _____ water.
4 Their families didn't have _____ information at first.
5 At first, the doctors gave them _____ vitamins.
6 How _____ calories a day did they have?
7 There wasn't _____ fresh air.
8 They had _____ space.
9 Did they have _____ treats?
10 There weren't _____ ladders in the mine.

Focus

Which of the words in 3 are countable and which are uncountable?

Countable nouns, e.g. cigarettes
Uncountable nouns, e.g. food

Complete the rules with *countable* or *uncountable*.

_____ ¹ nouns have a singular and a plural form.

_____ ² nouns do not have a plural form.

We use *the* with countable and uncountable nouns.

We only use *a* or *an* with _____ ³ nouns.

Use the sentences in 4 to help you complete this table. Put a ✓ in the appropriate boxes.

		some	any	a lot of / lots of	(how) much	(how) many	a few	a little
Countable	positive	✓						
	negative							
	question							
Uncountable	positive							
	negative							
	question							

◉ For more details and practice, go to the Review section on page 62.

PRACTICE   **5 Choose the correct words to complete the sentences.**

1 The miners didn't have *many / much* food before the rescuers discovered them.
2 The miners drank *a little / a few* water every day.
3 There was *a lot of / many* space in the mine.
4 To keep healthy, the miners took *a little / a few* vitamins every day.
5 How *many / much* miners were in the mine? There were 33.
6 The miners sent *information / informations* to the surface using notes.
7 At first, they didn't have *any / some* music.
8 They ate *some / any* cereal and *some / any* pears.
9 The rescuers sent down *lots of / much* cigarettes.
10 There weren't *many / any* ladders in the mine.

6 Make questions using *How* for the sentences in 5.

Example   1   *How* much food did the miners have before the rescuers discovered them?

7 These words can be countable and uncountable. Put the correct word and form into the sentences.

business/es coffee/s exercise/s paper/s room/s space/s sport/s time/s

1 SMBs are small to medium-sized _____ .
2 To get fit, you need to do lots of _____ .
3 There isn't enough _____ in my bag for a laptop.
4 How many _____ did you try calling him?
5 The best _____ in the world is made in Jamaica.
6 Have you got any _____ for the printer? The tray is empty.
7 There are three meeting _____ for this week's seminars.
8 Football and rugby are my favourite _____ .

8 Use the other form of the words in **7** to make a new sentence.

1 My desk is covered with books and _____ .
2 There were plenty of empty _____ in the car park.
3 _____ is big business, especially the Olympics.
4 Have you got any _____ to read this report?
5 Exports are up and _____ is booming.
6 Doing vocabulary _____ every day helps you remember more words.
7 The room was so small that there was only _____ for two people.
8 Could I have two _____ , please and a pain au chocolat?

9 ◀)) **5.2** Listen to *High Flyer* magazine ask top executive, Josh Kantner, about his work habits. Are the statements true or false?

1 Josh doesn't get many calls or emails.
2 He never switches off from work.
3 He has an iPad and a laptop.
4 He doesn't go on many business trips.
5 He gets a lot of exercise.
6 He doesn't eat much fast food.
7 He drinks a lot of coffee.
8 He gets a lot of days' holiday a year.

What do you think of Josh's work habits? How could he improve them?

10 Write a question about each topic. Use *how much* or *how many*.

Examples How many hours do you work a week?
How much free time do you have at the weekend?

1 hours / work a week?
2 free time / at the weekend?
3 emails / send a day?
4 exercise / a week?
5 time / Internet or social network sites?
6 days holiday / year?
7 sleep / have a night?
8 people / talk to in a day?
9 coffee / drink every day?
10 hours / spend travelling to work?

Watch the video for more practice.

TASK 11 Ask people in your class your questions in **10**.

Vocabulary Word groups; quantity

1 **Match the lists of items 1–12 with the group names.**

cereal   drink   fuel   entertainment   fruit   information
mail   material   ~~money~~   print media   sport   transport

1	_money_	note	coin	cent
2	_____	gas	coal	oil
3	_____	pineapple	banana	grape
4	_____	wood	plastic	iron
5	_____	fact	statistic	number
6	_____	running	golf	tennis
7	_____	letter	envelope	stamp
8	_____	tea	juice	coffee
9	_____	car	truck/lorry	van
10	_____	maize/corn	wheat	rice
11	_____	newspaper	magazine	book
12	_____	film	DVD	TV show

2 **Which group names in 1 can be countable (C)? Add your own words to the groups.**

3 **Complete the sentences with words from 1. Add an *s* where necessary.**

1 I've only got a ten-pound _____ in my wallet.
2 _____ is processed to make a variety of chemicals and fuel.
3 1.5 billion _____ are eaten every day.
4 Most chopsticks are made from _____ or _____ .
5 _____ show that most people don't get enough sleep.
6 She likes outdoor _____ like football and rugby.
7 I got a _____ from my bank, but I don't want to open it.
8 It's better to buy real fruit rather than fruit _____ .
9 Cycling is a very cheap form of _____ .
10 _____ is grown in many countries including China, India, Indonesia, Vietnam, and Japan.
11 The sales of e-_____ are growing very quickly.
12 Cinema numbers are dropping because more people are watching _____ online.

4 Match the counter with the uncountable item.

Example a sheet of paper

1	sheet	a	oil
2	plate	b	mineral water
3	jar	c	bread
4	slice	d	sugar
5	litre	e	tape
6	bottle	f	information
7	packet	g	petrol
8	gallon	h	paper
9	metre	i	food
10	piece	j	coffee

5 Work in small groups. Do the quiz.

1 How many apples do we eat globally a day?
   a 1 million   **b** 5 million   **c** 1 billion

2 How much oil is produced every day?
   a about 800 barrels   **b** about 8,000 barrels
   c about 80,000 barrels

3 How much information can we store in our brain?
   a 2.5 million gigabytes   **b** 250 gigabytes
   c 25 gigabytes

4 How many tweets are put up every day on Twitter?
   a 1 million   **b** over 200 million   **c** 50 million

5 How many people live in these cities?
   1 New Delhi   2 Tokyo   3 Paris
   a about 37 million   **b** about 10 million
   c about 22 million

6 How many miles of roads are there in the USA?
   a 400,000 miles   **b** 4 million miles
   c 40 million miles

7 How many babies are born a day in the world?
   a 180,000   **b** 280,000   **c** 380,000

8 How much energy is used per person every day in these areas?
   1 the USA   2 Africa   3 the UAE
   a about 0.7 units   **b** about 7 units
   c about 11 units

Work skills Presentations 1: Basic staging and signposting

1 ●)) **5.3** **Listen to these extracts from a presentation by a health adviser to a group of employees. Answer the questions.**

   1   What three areas is the speaker going to talk about?

   2   What can people do after the presentation?

   3   Do you agree with the speaker's conclusion that a good diet and plenty of exercise makes us happier people?

2 **Do these signposting phrases come in the introduction (I), in the middle (M), or in the final part (F) of the presentation?**

   1   Now I'd like to move on to …

   2   Today I'm going to talk about …

   3   That brings us to the final part of the presentation.

   4   I'm happy to take questions at the end of the presentation.

   5   I'd like to make some general conclusions.

   6   At this point, I'd like to hand over to my colleague.

   7   I've divided my presentation into three areas …

   8   First of all, thank you all for coming.

   9   To sum up …

  10   Good morning.

  11   Thank you for listening.

3 ●)) **5.3** **Listen again. Check your answers to 2.**

4 **Work in groups of three. You are going to prepare a short presentation on sport and exercise opportunities in the place or region where you are working / studying.**

   1   Decide on the key areas you are going to talk about (e.g. the range of facilities available, how much they cost, how you get there, the type of person they suit).

   2   Organize the different parts of the presentation, and decide who is going to talk about what.

   3   Decide when you will use the different 'signposting' phrases.

   4   Make notes for the presentation, but do not read from a script.

5 **Listen to each group's presentation. Note down the signposting phrases that they use. Which group uses the most?**

Functions Eating out; requests

INTRODUCTION

1 When you eat out, how do you decide where to go? Add your ideas to the list.

location   price   type of food

2 ◉)) **5.4 Paul, Emma, Ken, and Nathalie meet at the check-in counter at Heathrow Airport. Listen to them choosing a restaurant and answer the questions.**

1 What does Ken think of the Italian restaurant?
2 Does Paul want to eat a snack or a full meal?
3 Is the place that serves sandwiches expensive?
4 What sort of food can't Emma eat?
5 Does Paul know where the restaurant is?

3 ◉)) **5.5 Listen to Paul and his colleagues at the restaurant. Match the people with their orders.**

1 Nathalie   a   sparkling mineral water, fish and chips
2 Emma   b   cranberry juice, classic burger
3 Ken   c   caffè latte, grilled chicken salad
4 Paul   d   caffè latte, potato soup

4 ◉)) **5.6 Complete the sentences. Then listen and check your answers.**

1 _____ have a table by the window?
2 _____ a caffè latte, please.
3 _____ a cranberry juice.
4 Some mineral water, _____ . Sparkling.
5 _____ the grilled chicken salad?
6 _____ just ask? Does the soup have any gluten in it?
7 We're in a bit of a hurry so _____ bring the bill now?
8 _____ any bread?

PRACTICE **5** **Complete the sentences with one of the words below or leave it blank.**

a any some the

1 Could I have _____ bill, please?
2 Could you bring me _____ more water, please?
3 Could I have _____ seat somewhere quieter?
4 Have you got _____ vegetarian dishes?
5 Could I see _____ menu?
6 Can I pay by _____ credit card?
7 Could you ask the chef if there are _____ nuts in this dish?
8 Could I have _____ fork, please?
9 Have you got _____ cloth? I've spilt some water.
10 Could you bring us _____ dessert menu, please?

TASK **6** **Work in pairs. Practise ordering food and drink using the phrases and menu below.**

A Would you like a starter?
B Yes, please. I _____.
A And for your main dish?
B Could _____?
A And what would you like to drink?
B I'd _____.
A Yes, of course.

MENU

Starters
Garlic bread 3.50
Soup of the day 3.90
Prawn cocktail 4.20

Mains
Classic burger 6.50
Classic burger with cheese 6.90
Grilled chicken salad 7.50
Tuna sandwich 4.50
Fish and chips 7.25

Drinks
Mineral water *Still / Sparkling* 2.00
Juice *Orange / Grapefruit / Cranberry* 2.50
Tea 2.25
Coffee 2.25
Caffè latte 2.90

Review

Grammar Countable and uncountable nouns

Form

Countable nouns have a singular and plural form.
Example   company, companies

Uncountable nouns only have a singular form.
Example   music, information

Use

Countable

We use *the* with both singular and plural forms.
Examples   The visitors are in reception.
The new sales manager starts today.

We use *a* and *an* with the singular form.
Example   I've got a new job.

We use *some* and *a lot of / lots of* with countable nouns in positive sentences.
Examples   We have a lot of new customers.
We had some problems last week.

We use *any* and *many* with countable nouns in questions and negative sentences.
Examples   We didn't have any complaints last week.
Do you have any pens?
They don't work many hours a week.
How many invitations did you send?

Uncountable

We do not use *a* or *an* with uncountable nouns. We use *the* with uncountable nouns and the singular verb form.
Example   The equipment is rather old.

We use *some* and *a lot of / lots of* with uncountable nouns in positive sentences.
Examples   We have a lot of work this week.
He has some good news for you.

We use *any* and *much* with uncountable nouns in questions and negative sentences.
Examples   We don't have any money.
Do you have much time tomorrow?

Some nouns can be countable or uncountable, depending on whether they have a general or specific meaning.
Examples   You should do more exercise (general). I do special exercises for my back every day (specific).
There isn't enough room for everybody (general). There are three rooms in my flat (specific).

PRACTICE

1 Put these words in the correct box: countable, uncountable, or both.

advice	business	coffee	equipment	furniture	ice cream
information	luggage	money	motorbike	music	news
printer	room	song	space	sport	suggestion
suitcase	table	traffic	weather		

countable	uncountable	both

2 Complete the conversation with the words below.

a lot of   any   many   much   some

A There isn't _____[1] time before the conference, so let's check everything now.

B OK. Do we know how _____[2] people are coming?

A Yes, 54. What about the food and drink?

B The hotel is preparing that. They organize _____[3] conferences, so they know what to prepare.

A OK, good. And do we need _____[4] special equipment?

B No, the hotel has a projector in the conference room, and we'll take our own laptop. We should also remember to take _____[5] company brochures.

A OK, I think that's everything.

3 Correct the mistakes.

1 My boss gave me some great advices.
2 Sorry, we don't have some tea.
3 Do you usually do many exercise?
4 I read an interesting news this morning.
5 How much employees are there in your company?
6 Can you help me, please? My luggages haven't arrived.

Vocabulary Word groups; quantity

1 Find the odd-one-out in each list 1–6. Then write the group name.

cereal   fuel   mail   material   print media   sport

					Group name
1	swimming	football	iron	golf	_____
2	DVD	magazine	newspaper	book	_____
3	wood	coal	plastic	wool	_____
4	letter	photo	stamp	envelope	_____
5	oil	gas	tea	coal	_____
6	wheat	coffee	rice	corn	_____

2 Use counters to describe the items 1–8.

Example   1 a sheet of paper

3 Read the conversation and decide if the sentences below are true or false.

Doctor	You need to change your diet. How much water do you usually drink a day?
Ken	Uh, I usually have juice at breakfast, and lots of water in my coffee – about six or eight cups of coffee a day, so that's a lot of water.
Doctor	Six or eight cups of coffee? That's far too much. You should have a maximum of two cups of coffee a day, and drink at least two litres of mineral water. You don't put sugar in your coffee, do you?
Ken	Well, usually only one or two spoons.
Doctor	No sugar! And that means no cakes or biscuits either!
Ken	OK, but I can have fruit, can't I? I love bananas.
Doctor	Fruit is good, but to lose weight you shouldn't have more than five pieces of fruit a day.
Ken	Right.
Doctor	And, you need to eat less bread – only two slices a day. And you should eat lots more vegetables, especially green vegetables – try to eat them at every meal.
Ken	OK, I'll eat more vegetables, then.

1 The doctor advises Ken to eat less bread and sugar and eat more vegetables.
2 Ken rarely drinks juice.
3 Ken usually drinks a lot of water.
4 The doctor advises Ken to drink two glasses of mineral water a day.
5 Ken takes sugar in his coffee.
6 The doctor advises Ken to have three bananas a day.
7 The doctor advises Ken to have two loaves of bread a day.
8 The doctor tells Ken he should eat green vegetables at breakfast.

Work skills Presentations 1: basic staging and signposting

1 Put the words in the correct order to make signposting phrases.

1 listening / thank / for / you
2 divided / presentation / into / I've / my / areas / three
3 move / like / I'd / now / to / on to
4 about / I'm / today / to / talk / going
5 questions / have / any / anyone / does
6 to / final / moving / my / on / point
7 conclusions / make / like / I'd / some / to / general
8 all / thank / all / for / you / first / coming / of

2 Complete the presentation extracts with the phrases in 1.

Good morning. _____¹ _____² staff motivation.
_____³: what is motivation, why it is important, and how we can improve it. So, what does motivation mean …?
_____⁴ why it is important …
_____⁵, how can we improve motivation?
_____⁶ Motivation is directly connected with productivity and that means profits. The best ways to improve motivation are …
That brings me to the end of my presentation. _____⁷
_____⁸

Functions Eating out; requests

We make requests with *Could you* + verb when the speaker wants the listener to do something.

Example   Could you spell your name, please?

We use *Can / Could I* + verb when the speaker wants something or wants to do something.

Example   Could I have the chicken salad, please?
Can I just ask?

We use *I'd like* + verb/noun to explain what we want.

Examples   I'd like two tickets to the city centre, please.
I'd like to reserve a table for four, please.

We also use these phrases in a restaurant:

Ordering food and drink
I'll have the tuna salad, please.   *A cappuccino, please.*

Asking about a dish on the menu
Does the soup have any gluten in it?   *Is there any meat or fish in the salad?*

Asking about food that is not on the menu
Do you have any vegetarian dishes?   *Have you got anything for small kids?*

1   Put the words into the correct box.

apple pie	bill	cheesecake	chicken noodles
cloth	crisps	croissant	espresso
fish and chips	fruit tea	ice cream	knife and fork
lemonade	menu	muffin	sandwich
seafood pizza	spaghetti bolognese	sparkling water	steak and salad

Things in a restaurant	Main courses	Desserts	Snacks	Drinks

2   Match the sentence halves.

1	Have you got	a	some more bread, please?
2	Could I have	b	by credit card?
3	Can I pay	c	two mozzarella and tomato sandwiches, please.
4	I'd like	d	to order anything else?
5	Would you like	e	any kids' dishes?

3   Complete the conversation.

Waitress   Are you r_____ t_____ o_____[1]?

Filipe   Yes, I'_____ h_____ t_____[2] chicken noodles, p_____.

Luis   I_____ t_____ a_____[3] meat in the soup of the day?

Waitress   No, i_____ v_____[4].

Luis   OK, I'_____ l_____[5] that then. And, c_____ I h_____
s_____[6] bread with it?

Waitress   Of c_____[7]. W_____ w_____ y_____ l_____
t_____ d_____[8]?

Luis   A_____ o_____ j_____[9] for me, please.

Filipe   And a beer f_____ m_____[10], please.

Waitress   OK, I'll bring the drinks now.

6 Street life

Grammar Comparisons

INTRODUCTION

1 What do professional people want when they live and work in a city? Discuss the question using the ideas below. Add your own ideas to the list.

shopping   eating out   parks   public transport   safety   weather

2 Read the text. Match the cities with the paragraphs. Which city would you like to live in?

Dubai   Shanghai   Zurich

Great cities

1 Would you like to wake up every morning to views of the Alps, fresh air, and fresh coffee and croissants? Would you like ski slopes on your doorstep, and a city full of museums and cafés?

2 Is your idea of perfection a stroll along the beach at the end of a day's work, followed by a round of golf? Or maybe a day's shopping in one of the world's largest shopping malls.

3 Would you like a meal in a trendy roof-terrace restaurant overlooking the waterfront and the futuristic district of Pudong? Or perhaps take a walk around the beautiful Garden of Peace?

3 ◗)) **6.1** Listen to a *High Flyer* report comparing Zurich with Shanghai and Dubai. Choose the correct word to complete the sentences.

1   Zurich is *smaller / bigger* than Shanghai and Dubai.
2   Zurich has the *worst / best* transport system.
3   Dubai is the *coldest / hottest* city in the summer.
4   Shanghai has a *wider / smaller* range of shops and department stores than Zurich.
5   Dubai has one of the *most expensive / biggest* shopping malls in the world.
6   Dubai is the *least / most* modern city.
7   Shanghai is the most *expensive / interesting* city.
8   Zurich is *an older / a younger*, more *traditional / modern* city.

Focus

Complete the table with the types of adjectives 1–6.

two syllables not ending in -y   one syllable   irregular adjectives
three or more syllables   two syllables ending in -y
one syllable ending in consonant + vowel + consonant

Type of adjective	Example	Comparative	Superlative
1	large	larger	largest
2	wet	wetter	wettest
3	happy	happier	happiest
4	crowded	more / less crowded	most / least crowded
5	interesting	more / less interesting	most / least interesting
6	good bad far	better worse further	best worst furthest

Examples   Shanghai is bigger than Zurich.

Zurich is more traditional than Dubai.

Dubai is the hottest of the three cities.

Shanghai is probably the most interesting city.

We can also use an adverb + noun + *than*.

Example   Zurich has fewer shops than the other two cities.

▶▶ For more details and practice, go to the Review section on page 74.

PRACTICE

4 **Put the adjectives into the correct categories in the table above.**

small   fast   efficient   cold   hot   famous
wide   modern   quick   exciting   traditional

5 **Choose the correct adjective below to complete the sentences. Use the information in 3 to help you.**

big   bad   cold   fast   good   modern   old   small   tall

1   Dubai is _____ than Zurich, but _____ than Shanghai.
2   Shanghai has the _____ train system in the world.
3   Dubai has _____ traffic jams than Zurich.
4   Zurich is the _____ city in the winter.
5   The _____ place for duty-free shopping is Dubai.
6   Zurich is a _____ city than Dubai.
7   The Burj Khalifa, the world's _____ building, is in Dubai.
8   Shanghai has one of the _____ department stores in the world.

6 **Work in pairs. Take it in turns to ask questions about the sentences in 5.**

Example   A   Is Zurich bigger than Dubai?
              B   No, it isn't.

7 ●)) **6.2 Listen to a businesswoman talk about the three cities and answer the questions.**

1   Why did Fiona like Shanghai?
2   What does Fiona not like about Zurich?
3   What did Fiona say about clothes shopping in Shanghai?
4   What type of shopping areas does Fiona mention?
5   How does Fiona compare the cost of living in Zurich and Shanghai?

8 **Work in pairs or small groups. Discuss the cities or towns that you like and explain why you like them.**

9 Complete the sentences about other cities using the correct form of the adjectives in brackets.

1 Seoul has the second _____ urban population in the world. (large)
2 Shopping on Fifth Avenue in New York is _____ than on the Avenue des Champs Elysées in Paris. (expensive)
3 Tokyo has one of the _____ subway systems. (complicated)
4 Mexico City is _____ than San Francisco. (hot)
5 London has the _____ department store in the world. (famous)
6 Florence has _____ tourist attractions than Rome. (good)
7 Madrid is the _____ city in Spain. (big)
8 Copenhagen has one of the _____ restaurants in the world. It's called Noma. (good)
9 Vancouver is _____ with young professionals than Montreal. (popular)
10 Mumbai is the _____ city in the world. (crowded)

10 Work in pairs. Exchange the information about the three cities below. Then make comparisons about them.

Student A Look at the table below.
Student B Go to page 129.

Watch the video for more practice.

		Zurich	Dubai	Shanghai
1	Distance from airport to city centre by taxi	15 kilometres	12 kilometres	
2	A one-room apartment in city centre to rent		$1,950	$725
3	Pay (hourly rate)	$144		$17
4	Shopping mall	Einkaufszentrum Glatt 43,000 m²	The Dubai Mall 502,000 m²	
5	Internet speed	20 mbps*		Less than 1 mbps
6	Five-star hotels		74	140

*mbps = megabits per second

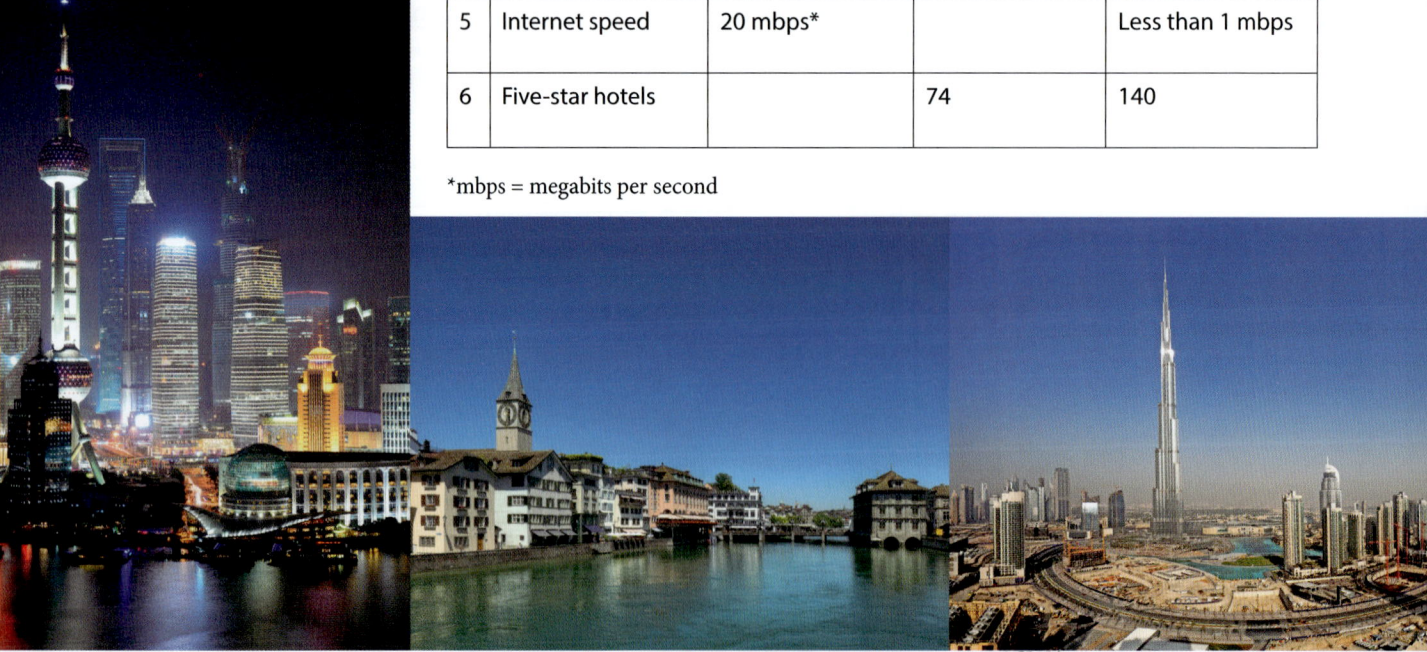

TASK 11 Work in small groups. Each choose a city you know well. Give the city a rating 1 (high) to 4 (low) for the features you listed in **1**.
Example I would give Tokyo a 1 for eating out.

Now compare your cities and agree on your ratings. Describe the final outcome.
Example Tokyo has the best restaurants, but London has the most parks.

Vocabulary Talking about cities

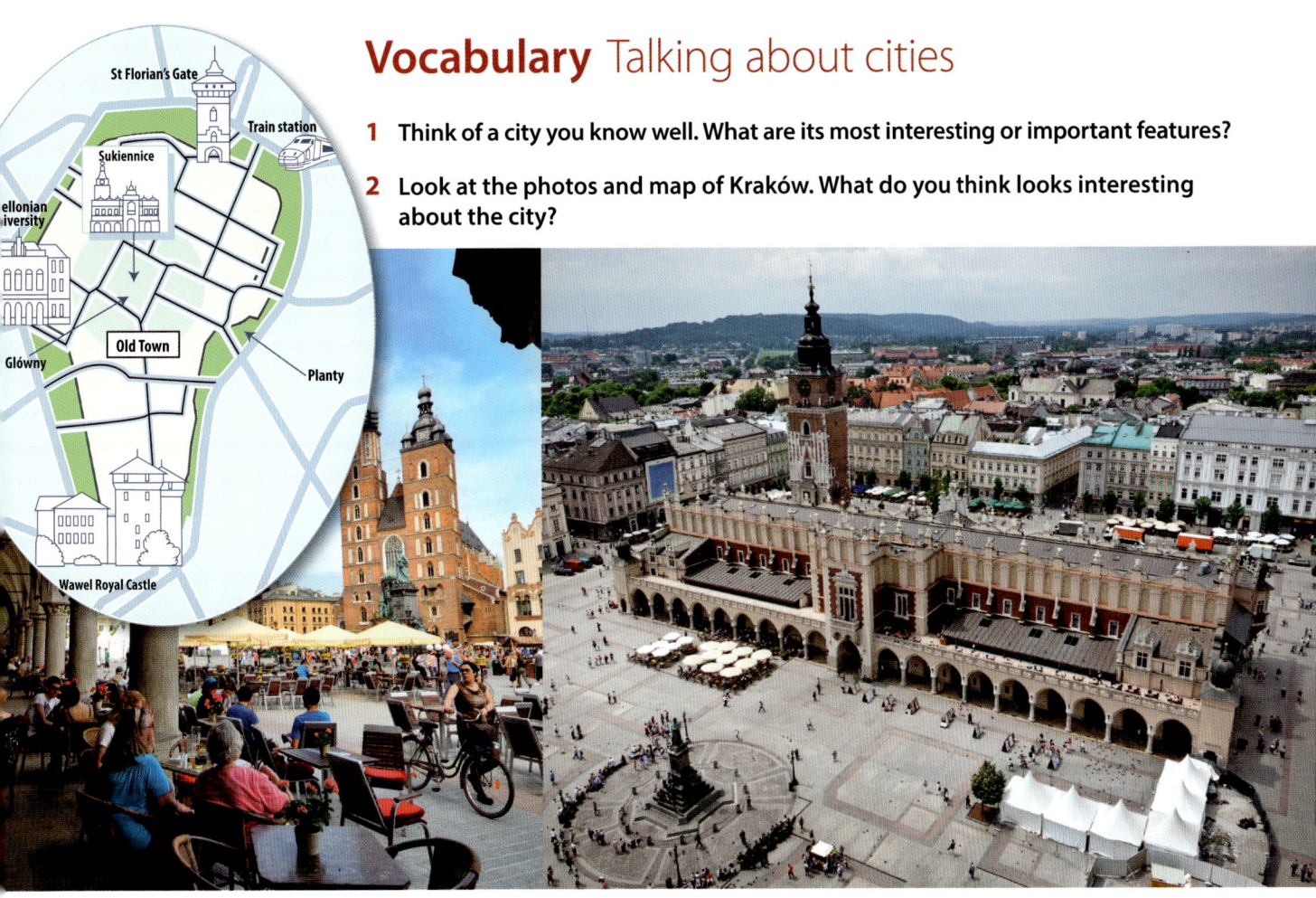

1 Think of a city you know well. What are its most interesting or important features?

2 Look at the photos and map of Kraków. What do you think looks interesting about the city?

3 Read the guide to Kraków and find the places on the map.

Lovely Kraków

Kraków is a beautiful city in the southern part of Poland. In the centre of Kraków is the Old Town, which is surrounded by a park called the Planty. In the middle is Rynek Główny, the main market square. Most of the city's central area is a pedestrian zone.

Many of the important buildings are in the Old Town, including the Jagellonian University, St Mary's Basilica in the main square and St Florian's Gate. Outside the city walls, and just to the south by the river, is the royal castle called Wawel.

Public transport is based on a network of trams and bus lines which run between 5 a.m. and 11 p.m. Local trains connect some of the suburbs to the city centre. Tickets are available from newspaper kiosks and ticket machines at stops, or you can buy them from the driver.

Kraków's airport is 11 km west of the city. Direct trains run between Kraków Główny train station and the airport. The journey takes about 15 minutes. The city centre is about a 20-minute walk south-west of the station.

The Polish currency is the złoty. There's a cash point and a currency exchange office in the main train station building, and you can also find them around town. The city is full of interesting places to shop – a covered market, shopping malls, and a wide variety of shops and stores, including bookstores and art galleries. The most interesting of these is Cloth Hall or Sukiennice, which is said to be the first shopping mall in the world.

4 Read the guide again and answer the questions.
1 What is in the centre of Kraków?
2 Can people drive in the city's central area?
3 Where is Wawel Castle?
4 What types of public transport do people use?
5 In which three ways can you buy a train ticket?
6 How far is the airport from the city centre?
7 How can you get money in the train station?
8 Where is the most interesting place to go shopping?

5 Match the words in A and B to make noun phrases.

Example art gallery

	A	B
1	art	machine
2	train	mall
3	cash	transport
4	city	kiosk
5	currency	train
6	direct	point
7	newspaper	zone
8	pedestrian	centre
9	public	exchange
10	shopping	gallery
11	ticket	line

6 Complete the sentences with phrases from **5**.

1 Changing your money at a _____ office can be expensive.
2 People interested in modern Polish art visit places like the Barbara Kraków _____ .
3 It is much safer walking in a _____ than an ordinary street.
4 You can buy magazines, tickets, drinks, and sweets at a Polish _____ .
5 The most convenient place to get money is at a _____ .
6 Kraków has about 137 _____ connecting various parts of the city.
7 One of Kraków's main _____ , Galeria Krakowska, has about 270 different types of brand shops.
8 You can buy daily or seven-day tickets from the _____ .
9 Kraków's _____ system includes trams, buses, and local trains.
10 _____ between the two main stations in Kraków run every 15 to 30 minutes.

7 6.3 Listen to Alex, a tour guide, explain about Kraków to two visitors. Are these statements true or false?

1 Alex says the tram is the best way round the Old Town.
2 Paul and Lisa live outside the city centre.
3 Lisa is planning to go to Vienna.
4 Kraków isn't an expensive place to live.
5 Hotels are the best places to exchange money.
6 The castle gets very crowded in the summer.
7 Florian Street is only good for sightseeing.

8 Imagine that friends are visiting a town/city near you next month. Tell them some useful facts about the city.

Work skills Telephoning 2: Answering the phone

1 **Work in pairs. Discuss the questions.**

1   What reasons are there for someone not to answer the phone?
Example   They are in a meeting.

2   When do you ask a caller to wait?
Example   You need to connect them to the person they want to speak to.

3   When is it not a good idea to answer the phone?
Example   When you are in a cinema.

2 ◆)) **6.4** **Listen to three phone calls. Tick ✓ the sentences you hear.**

Call 1

1   Do you mind if I take this?
    Is it OK to answer this call?

2   I can't speak right now.
    It's difficult to talk at the moment.

3   Can I call you back?
    Can I phone you later?

Call 2

4   Can you call me back urgently?
    Can you return my call as soon as possible?

Call 3

5   Can you put me through to Mr Myers?
    I'd like to speak to Mr Myers, please.

6   Can I ask who's calling?
    Could you tell me your name?

7   Could you hold on a moment?
    Please hold.

8   He's on another call at the moment.
    His line is busy.

9   Do you want to hold or shall I ask him to call you back?
    Would you like to wait or do you want him to return your call?

10 I'll give him your message.
    I'll see he gets your message.

3 **Practise the three situations using the alternative phrases in 2 and the script on page 141.**

Functions At a hotel

1 Work in pairs and discuss the questions.

1 How do you usually choose a hotel?
2 How do you make a booking?
3 What do you need when you check in?
4 How do you pay?

2 ◉) 6.5 Listen to the Unisports group check in at their hotel in Rio de Janeiro and answer the questions.

1 How many nights are they staying?
2 How many rooms did they book?
3 What time can they have breakfast?
4 Does the hotel have Internet access?
5 What is Paul going to ask the concierge about?
6 What time is the taxi coming to pick them up?

3 ◉) 6.5 Listen again and complete the sentences.

1 We'd like to _____ .
2 Could I have _____ , please?
3 Could you fill out _____ , please?
4 Breakfast is included in the _____ .
5 Are you all on one _____ ?
6 I hope you enjoy _____ .

4 ◉) 6.6 Listen to the members of the group call from their hotel rooms. Number the situations in the order you hear them.

a ordering a snack   ☐
b complaining about the air conditioning   ☐
c asking for a wake-up call   ☐
d complaining about the bed linen   ☐

5 ◉) 6.7 Paul checks out. Listen to the conversation. Are the statements true or false?

1 There is a problem with Paul's room charge.
2 Paul didn't use the minibar last night.
3 There is a problem with Paul's credit card.

Focus

Match the phrases with the following situations.

Are you all on one credit card?   Do you have a business centre?
Breakfast is included in the room rate.   I'm calling about the air conditioning.
Could I have your passports, please?   We'd like to check in.

Arriving at reception	
Asking for identification	
Giving information	
Asking about facilities	
Asking about payment	
Complaining about something	

▶▶ For more details and practice, go to the Review section on page 77.

6 Match the two parts of the conversations, 1–6 and a–f.

1 I'd like to order some drinks.
2 I can't get the shower to work.
3 Could I see your credit card, please?
4 Is there anything else I can help you with?
5 The carpet in my room is very dirty.
6 Are you staying for two nights?

a I see. Have you tried the tap on the left?
b Yes, of course. Here it is.
c Certainly, sir. What would you like?
d I'm very sorry to hear that, sir. I'll get someone to clean it immediately.
e Yes, that's right.
f Yes, could you tell me how to get to the beach from here?

7 Work in pairs. Practise checking in and checking out.

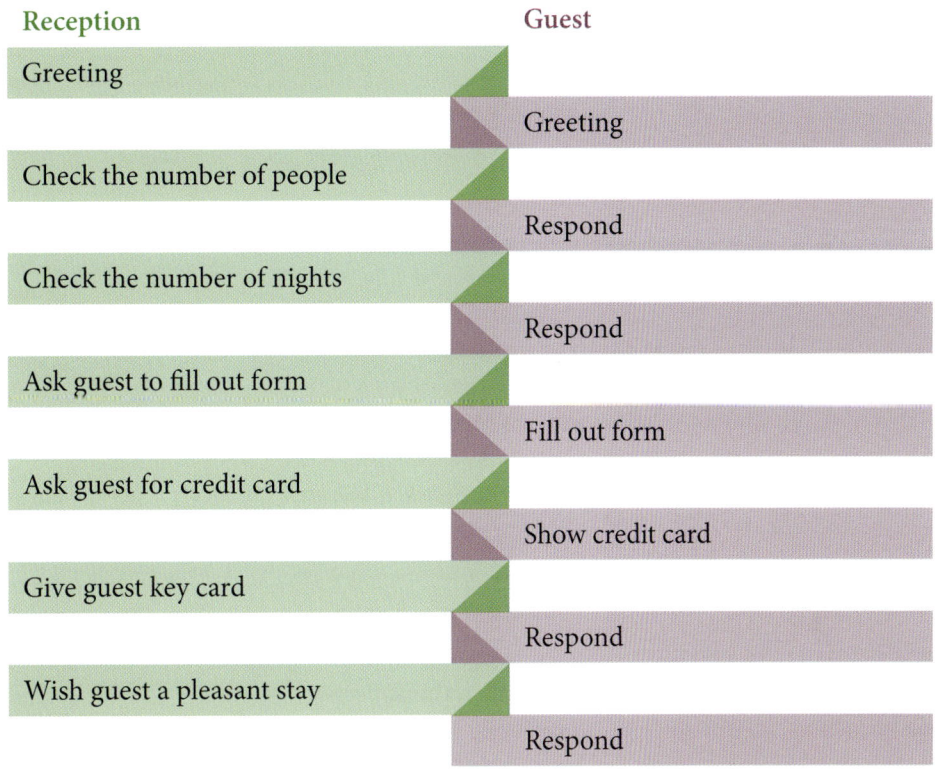

Reception	Guest
Greeting	
	Greeting
Check the number of people	
	Respond
Check the number of nights	
	Respond
Ask guest to fill out form	
	Fill out form
Ask guest for credit card	
	Show credit card
Give guest key card	
	Respond
Wish guest a pleasant stay	
	Respond

8 Work in pairs. One of you is a guest and one of you is the receptionist. Have conversations based on the pictures.

Review

Grammar Comparisons

Form

We form comparisons with -er, -est, more, most, less, and least. There is also a group of irregular adjectives.

Type of adjective	Example	Comparative	Superlative
1 one syllable	large	larger	largest
2 one syllable ending in consonant + vowel + consonant	wet	wetter	wettest
3 two syllables ending in -y	happy	happier	happiest
4 two syllables not ending in -y	crowded	more / less crowded	most / least crowded
5 three or more syllables	interesting	more / less interesting	most / least interesting
6 irregular adjectives	good bad far	better worse further	best worst furthest

Use

We can show a stronger comparison by using *much*.
Computers are much cheaper than in the past.
Our new office is much more modern than our old one.

When describing superlatives, we have to use *the* or a personal pronoun in front of the superlative adjective.
That was the best dinner I've ever had. We don't want to lose our biggest client.

We can also use *one of* + superlative + plural noun to show that there are more than one of the superlative items.
This is one of our newest products.
Shanghai is one of the most exciting cities in China.

PRACTICE **1 Rewrite the sentences.**

Example Using public transport is usually cheaper than driving.
Driving is usually more expensive than using public transport.

1 Our profits were higher last year than this year.

_____

2 I think modern art is more interesting than traditional art.

_____

3 Travelling by plane is faster than travelling by train.

_____

4 Orly airport is closer to Paris than Charles de Gaulle airport.

_____

5 Shanghai has a bigger population than Beijing.

_____

6 More people are working at home these days than in the past.

_____

2 Read the restaurant reviews and complete the conversation. Use the words below in the correct comparative or superlative form.

cheap   expensive   far   quiet   traditional   wide

Berg
Restaurant Berg is a fantastic restaurant located high above the city, with beautiful views of the city, lake, and mountains. A wide menu includes Swiss and international dishes. **$$$**

Maison Blanc
Maison Blanc is a trendy Moroccan restaurant not far from the city centre. It has friendly service and excellent Moroccan food. **$$**

Roter Hahn
Roter Hahn is a traditional restaurant serving quality Swiss specialities. It's popular with tourists and usually busy so reservations are recommended. **$**

Lily So, where shall we go for dinner? Maison Blanc sounds interesting.

Theo I'd prefer something _____¹. I'd like to try Swiss food while we're here.

Peter OK, it says Roter Hahn is good and traditional. And it's _____² of the three, so why don't we go there?

Lily But it also seems to be very busy and touristy. I'd prefer somewhere _____³.

Theo Well, there's also Berg, but it is _____⁴.

Peter And it's _____⁵ than the other two – it's up a mountain!

Lily It sounds lovely, though. Great views, and there's a _____⁶ choice of food – Swiss and international.

Theo True. Let's go there then.

Peter OK. Now where can we get a taxi?

Vocabulary Talking about cities

1 Complete the crossword.

Across

2   something tourists buy to remember their holiday

7   a place where you use your card to get money

8, 10   a place with a lot of shops

12   a tourist activity – looking at famous places

Across, down

16, 3   a place where you can exchange money

Down

4, 2   a place where trains arrive and leave

5, 13   a place where you can look at paintings

6, 1   a place on the street where you can buy newspapers and magazines

9, 11   an area where you can't use a car

15, 14   buses, trains, trams, underground

2 Match the tourist information questions and answers.

1	Where can I buy a tram ticket?	a	There's a currency exchange on the corner, or you can go to a bank.
2	Where's the best place to buy some presents for my family?	b	There are some good food stalls in the market.
3	What's the fastest way of getting to the airport?	c	There's an interesting modern art gallery nearby.
4	Where can I exchange some money?	d	Either at a ticket machine or a newspaper kiosk.
5	The weather's terrible. Can you recommend something for me to do?	e	I recommend either the market for traditional presents or the shopping mall for something more modern.
6	Is there anywhere to park the car in the city centre?	f	Yes, we have a number of tours you can choose from.
7	Are there any cheap places to eat near here?	g	A taxi is usually fastest, but there's also a train.
8	Can I book a sightseeing tour?	h	No, you can't even drive there, as it's a pedestrian zone.

Work skills Telephoning 2: Answering the phone

1 Put the phone conversations in the correct order.

1   a   Sorry, she's out of the office today. Can I help?
     b   Hello, can I speak to Rachel Blair, please?
     c   No, that's OK. I'll try her mobile.

2   a   Of course, speak to you later.
     b   Sorry Bob, can I call you back later? I'm in the middle of something.
     c   Sorry, is it okay if I take this call?

3   a   Sorry, he's not at his desk. Would you like to leave a message?
     b   Hello, it's Pat Jalbuena speaking. Could I speak to Serkan Yilmaz, please?
     c   Of course, I'll see he gets your message.
     d   Yes, could you ask him to check my email, please?
     e   Thanks very much.

2 Complete the questions for the answers.

1   Can _____ calling?
    Yes, it's Jamie Flowerdew.

2   Can _____ Ms Till, please?
    Just one moment. I'll connect you.

3   His line is busy. Do _____ message?
    No, thanks. I'll call back later.

4   (ringing phone)
    Sorry, do _____ take this?
    No, please go ahead.

5   Shall _____ you back?
    Yes, please. He can contact me on my mobile phone number.

Functions At a hotel

We use the following phrases at a hotel.

Arriving at reception
I'd / We'd like to check in.
Hello, I'm Bruno Bianco. I've booked a room for two nights.
Can you fill out this form, please?

Asking for identification
Could I have your passport(s), please?

Giving information
Breakfast / Internet / Use of the gym is included in the room rate.
The restaurant / business centre / sauna is on the second floor.
Dinner is served from 6 until 9 p.m.

Asking about facilities
Is there a swimming pool?
Do you have a shop?
Where's the cocktail bar?

Asking about payment
Are you all on one credit card?
Could I have your credit card, please?

Complaining about something
The carpet / bathroom / sheets and pillows is / are dirty.
I can't change the temperature with the air conditioner / set the alarm clock / turn on the television.
The shower / television / air conditioning isn't working.

1 **Put the phone conversations in the correct order.**

1. a Yes, please. Could you book it for two o'clock?
   b Thank you.
   c How can I help you?
   d There's a bus from just around the corner or you can take a taxi. I can book one for you if you like.
   e Yes, of course. I'll do it now.
   f I'd like to know how to get to the beach.

2. a Certainly. It'll be with you soon.
   b Good evening, room service.
   c Steak and green salad please, and an orange juice.
   d I'd like to order dinner. Is it too late?
   e Thanks.
   f No, we serve until midnight. What would you like?

3. a 227.
   b Hello, my air conditioning isn't working and it's really hot in the room.
   c Thanks.
   d Hello, reception.
   e Sorry to hear that Madam. I'll send an engineer up straight away. Which room are you in?
   f OK, the engineer will be there in about five minutes.

The sound of music

Grammar Present Perfect; Past Simple

INTRODUCTION   **1**   Can you put the pictures of the items below in order of oldest to most recent?

AT THE SPEED OF SOUND

The way we listen to music has changed many times. The first recording of a human voice was in 1860, with the French folk song 'Au Clair de la Lune'. Soon, recordings became more widely available on Edison's phonograph cylinders and then on gramophone records called 78s. In the early 1930s, 45rpm singles, and 12-inch vinyl long-playing records, or LPs, took over. 'Rock Around the Clock', released in 1955, was the first single to sell more than a million copies in the UK.

In 1963, when Philips introduced the audio cassette, music became more mobile. This trend continued when Sony introduced the Walkman in 1979. Shortly afterwards, in 1982, Sony also introduced the digital compact disc and ten years later, the less successful minidisc. However, the minidisc was important as the first device to allow people to record and store music digitally.

Music has been available online since the early 2000s. In 2003, iTunes was launched in the USA, and two British record companies, HMV and Virgin, have sold music online since 2005. In ten years, the sales of digital singles have gone from zero per cent to 98 per cent of all singles sales. The Black Eyed Peas' song 'I Gotta Feeling' has sold over 7,500,000 downloads, and UK customers alone have spent more than £1,000,000,000 on online music since 2004. On the downside, however, Virgin Megastore have recently closed stores in the UK, Ireland, Spain, the USA, Canada, and Japan.

2   **Work in pairs. Ask each other the questions.**

1   How do you buy and listen to music?
2   What did you buy or listen to last month?
3   How many of the items in **1** have you bought or listened to?

3   **Read the article about the way we listen to music. Check your answer to 1.**

4   **Answer the questions.**

1   When was the first voice recording made?
2   What was the first single to sell more than one million copies in the UK?
3   How long has digital music been available?
4   What was special about the minidisc?
5   How much money have British consumers spent on online music?
6   What negative effect has downloading music had on the music business?

5   ◉)) **7.1   Listen to Susie and Jon talk about how they buy and listen to music. Answer the questions.**

1   Has Susie bought a CD recently?
2   Has Jon ever downloaded music?
3   What are Jon and Susie going to do?

Focus

Read the examples. Are the sentences in the Past Simple or Present Perfect?

a Music has been available online since the early 2000s.

b In 1979, Sony introduced the Walkman.

c I've bought lots of albums online.

d Soon, recordings became more widely available on Edison's phonograph cylinders.

Which tense do we use to talk about the following?

1 an event at a definite time in the past

2 a situation that started and finished in the past

3 a situation that started in the past and continues to the present

4 an event or series of events at an indefinite time in the past

Complete the rules.

We form the Present Perfect with _____ + _____ .

We form questions in the Present Perfect with _____ + subject + _____ .

We form negatives in the Present Perfect by putting *not / n't* after _____ .

Which of these word groups do we use with the Past Simple or Present Perfect?

just, since, so far, yet

in 1963, last week, a year ago, when?

▶▶ For more details and practice, go to the Review section on page 86.

PRACTICE

6 Choose the correct verb in these exchanges.

1 A Have you ever bought an LP?

   B Yes, I *did / have*.

2 A How many shops have closed down where you live?

   B I think three shops *closed / have closed* down so far.

3 A Did your family have a gramophone player when you were a child?

   B Yes, we *had / 've had* a huge wooden one.

4 A Have you subscribed to iTunes yet?

   B Yes, I *have joined / joined* a few months ago.

5 A Did you throw away all your old LPs?

   B No, I *didn't / haven't*. I gave them to a friend who collects records.

6 A How long have you had your MP3 player?

   B I *had / 've had* it for ages.

7 A *Did you download / Have you downloaded* any music last week?

   B Yes, I downloaded two songs on Friday.

8 A White Denim are on tour at the moment. *Did you see / Have you seen* them?

   B Not yet. I'd like to see them next week.

7 Write the questions for these answers.

1 Q _____

   A I bought my first single in 1978.

2 Q _____

   A I've had my CD player for about fifteen years.

3 Q _____

   A Yes, the number of downloads has increased dramatically.

4 Q _____

   A No, the record company made a loss last year.

5 Q _____

   A No, I've never been to a music festival.

6 Q _____

   A 45s were popular in the 50s and 60s.

8 **Work in pairs. Ask your partner about the following.**

their favourite track or record
a live concert
the first record they remember hearing
the album or single they've owned the longest
their first CD / MP3 / record player

9 **You are going to hear an interview with the lead singer of a new band. Complete the interview questions using the verbs in brackets.**

1. When ________ you ________ the band? (start)
2. ________ any band members ________ since you started? (change)
3. How many live gigs ________ you ________? (play)
4. How ________ you ________ the band at first? (promote)
5. ________ you ________ an album yet? (record)
6. When ________ you ________ using social media sites? (start)
7. ________ many people ________ to your EP online? (listen)
8. What ________ your reviews ________ like so far? (be)

10 7.2 **Listen to the interview and check your questions in 9.**

11 7.2 **Listen again and correct the band's answers.**

1. Last year, when we were all living in Liverpool.
2. No, we've had the same line-up for 16 months now.
3. So far, we've played three gigs in London and we did a mini tour of the USA, which was six gigs.
4. We started a website which we've updated quite a lot since.
5. No, not an album. But we recently recorded an EP, which came out two months ago.
6. We went on Facebook at the same time as the EP came out. You can hear and buy the tracks online.
7. Yes, our best track has had over 10,000 plays, which is really great.
8. We've had a really poor response from most people.

12 **Work in pairs. Do the band interview using the questions and answers in 9 and 11.**

TASK **13** **What do you know about these people and products?**

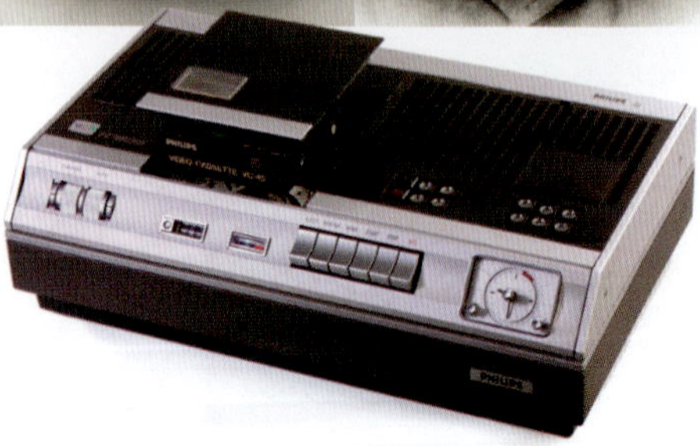

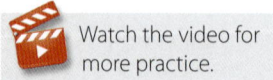

Watch the video for more practice.

Work in pairs. Take it in turns to ask and answer questions about the companies using your notes.

Student A Go to page 129.
Student B Go to page 133.

Vocabulary Talking about changes and trends

1 Read the facts about the music industry and match them with the correct graphs.

1 Music downloads rose sharply in the first quarter, and remained at 10,000 units in the second quarter.

2 Sales of CDs fell steadily at the beginning of the year, and then recovered slightly in April.

3 Digital single downloads increased by 12% in the first half of the year.

4 Company profits peaked at $34.7 million in June.

5 There was a dramatic decrease in unemployment last year from 7% to 2.7%.

6 There was a rise in production costs between April and June, followed by a slight fall between July and September.

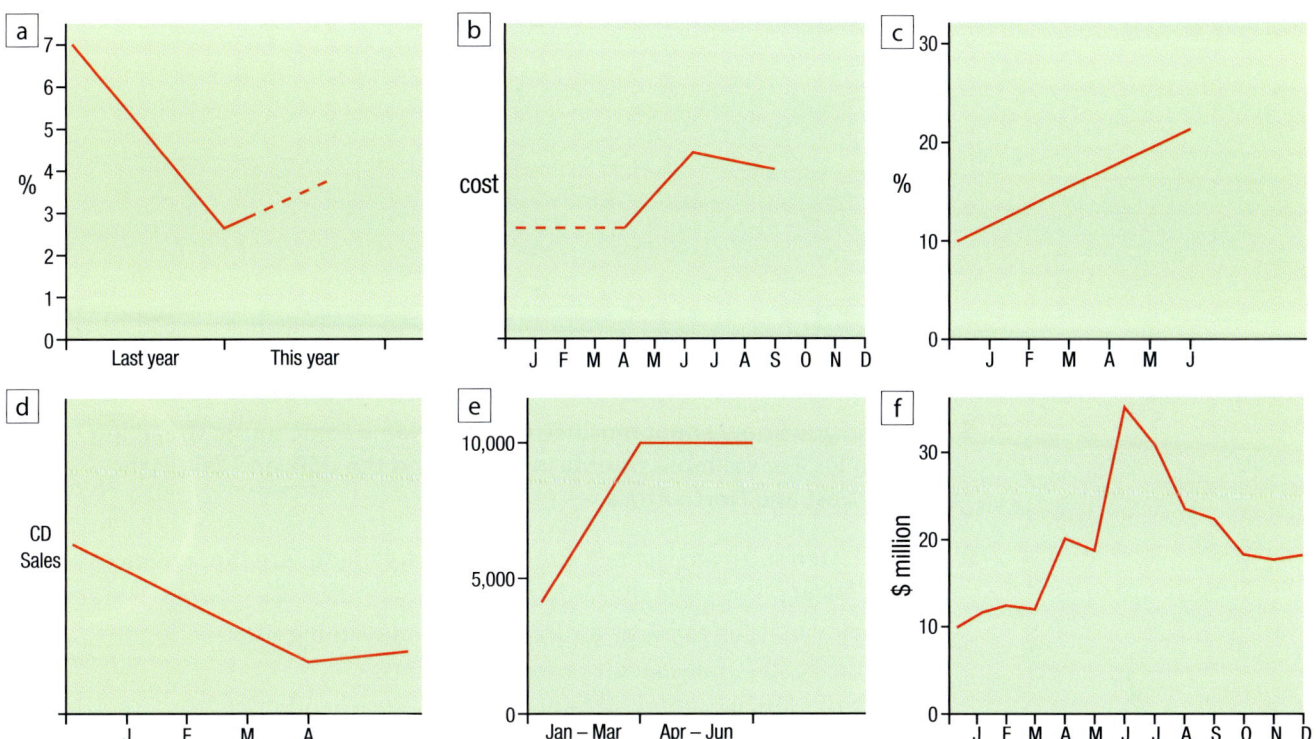

2 Complete the sentences with the correct preposition below.

by   to (x2)   at (x2)   in (x2)   from   of

1 Sales went up _____ 11% _____ £15.4 million.

2 Inflation remained stable _____ 2%.

3 There was a steady decrease _____ production costs in July.

4 Exports fell _____ 1,000 units _____ 920 units a month.

5 Monthly revenue peaked _____ $340,000.

6 There was a rise _____ 2.5% _____ salaries.

3 Change the sentences into the verb or noun form.

Example   verb   Sales of CDs *rose* slightly last month.
                noun   There was a slight *rise* in CD sales last month.

1 There was a sharp fall in the number of tourists in November.

2 Inflation has increased slightly so far this year.

3 The value of the dollar decreased from 0.67 to 0.62 pounds sterling.

4 The number of hours I work each week has risen sharply.

5 There has been a slight drop in the number of unemployed.

6 The EBC share value rose to 235.09.

7 There has been a steady increase in company profits in the first quarter.

8 The number of new recruits fell steadily last month.

4 Complete the report on digital music sales using the phrases below. Put the verbs in the Past Simple. Then complete the graph.

decrease   remain   peak   rise dramatically   fall steadily

We started the year with digital music downloads at €100 million. During Quarter 1, sales _____¹ to €95 million. In Quarter 2, sales _____² at around €94-95 million. In Quarter 3, during the summer music festival season, the number of downloads _____³ from €95 million to €140 million and finally _____⁴ at €150 million. In Quarter 4, sales _____⁵ by €20 million and ended the year at €130 million. So far this year, sales have risen slightly and are now at €135 million.

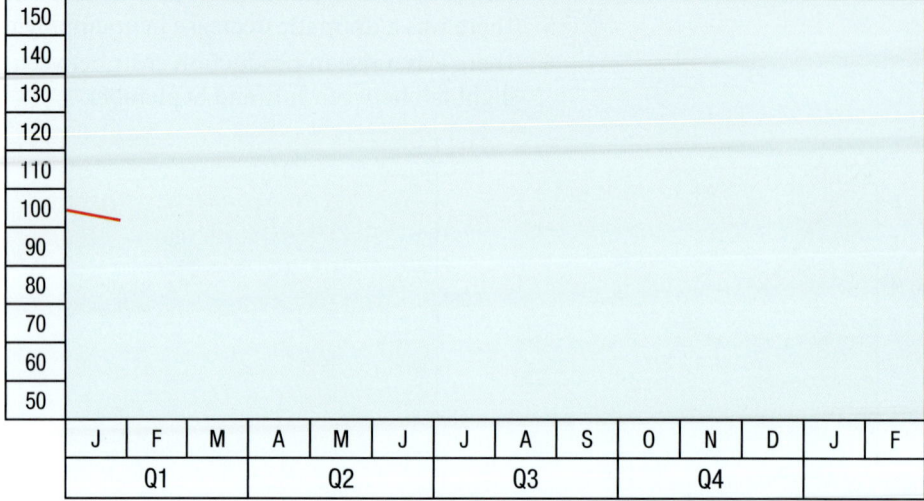

5 What do you know about music streaming? Name some music streaming companies. For example, Spotify in Europe and the USA, and Yala in the Middle East and North Africa.

6 ◉)) **7.3** Listen to an analyst talk about music streaming. Are the sentences true or false?

1 People can listen to music for free on music streaming sites.
2 All music streaming sites have advertisements.
3 A lot of musicians think streaming services are a good thing.
4 The number of digital downloads has gone up over the last few years.
5 The number of people listening to music online has gone down.
6 People use Facebook and Twitter to tell friends about music.

7 Work in pairs. Take it in turns to describe your graph and draw your partner's graph.

Student A   Describe the graph on the left below. Use the empty graph on the right to draw Student B's graph.
Student B   Go to page 130.

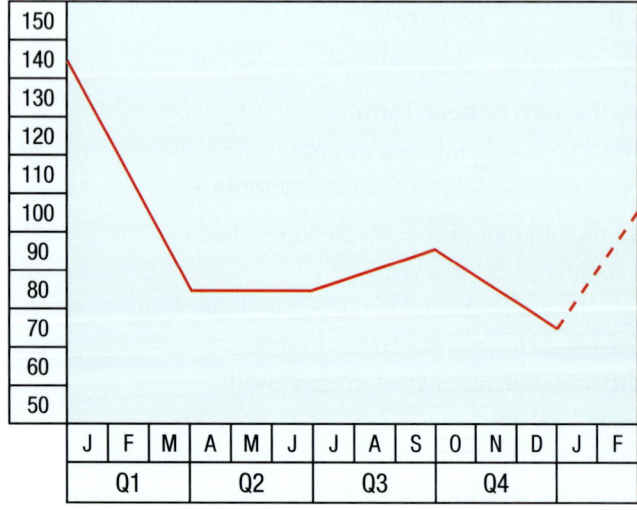

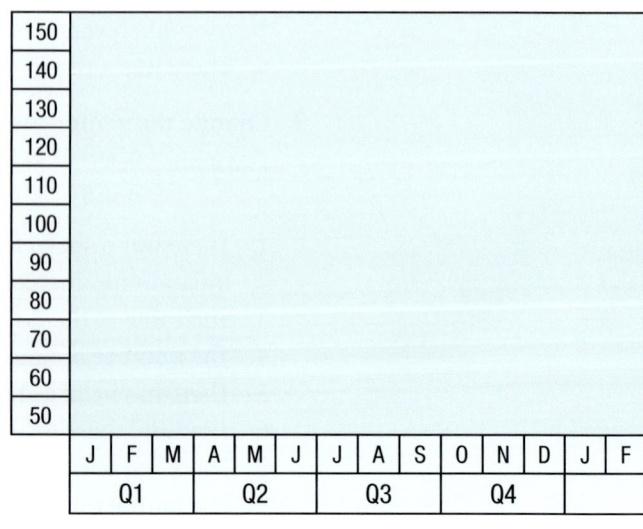

Work skills Presentations 2: Using PowerPoint; presentation tips

1 Read the guidelines on making PowerPoint slides. Which do you agree with?

Make the heading as big as possible.
Include a maximum of five lines, with five words per line.
Use a mix of fonts and sizes.
Put the key information on the last line of the slide.
Include long quotes so that your audience can read them.
Use plenty of animation to keep your audience awake.
Use simple charts and graphs.
Make your slides look attractive with lots of photos.

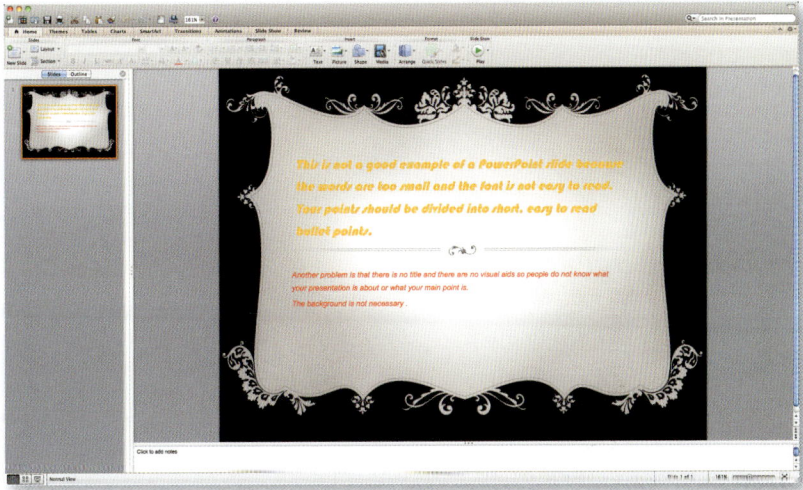

2 Read the tips for giving a presentation and put them in the appropriate group.

Before	During	After

1   Decide the main aim of the presentation.
2   Check your equipment.
3   Keep eye contact with the audience.
4   Give the audience a chance to ask questions.
5   Find out who the audience are and what they want to hear.
6   Practise as much as possible.
7   Look at your notes only when you need to.
8   Decide where you are going to stand and where you are going to move.
9   Tell the audience if they can ask questions during the presentation.
10 Prepare your slides and notes as early as possible.
11 Keep the presentation simple.
12 Check the time regularly.
13 Keep your energy levels up.
14 Give the audience your contact details.

3 Prepare a short presentation on one of the following topics:

- How many hours you worked recently
- How much you spent each month this year
- The amount of travelling you do

Functions Job interviews

INTRODUCTION

1 **Unisports are recruiting a Sportswear Product Manager. János Bogrács has applied for the position. Read the job requirements and János' CV. What relevant experience and qualifications does he have?**

Job requirements

- 5+ years' experience in the sportswear business
- Knowledge of product development process
- University degree in a related area
- Strong presentation skills

- Ability to prepare business performance reports
- Ability to travel internationally at least twice a year
- Proficiency in Microsoft Office suite
- Experience with project data management

János Bogrács

Nationality	Hungarian
Address	Herzogenaurach, Germany
Marital status	Married, two children

Work experience

2009–present	Adidas Assistant Product Manager Herzogenaurach, Germany
2006–08	Kappa Sportswear Product Design Executive
2004–05	Kappa Sportswear Data management assistant Turin, Italy

Education

2001–04	Degree in Business Studies, London School of Commerce
1997–2000	RF Secondary School, Budapest. Key subjects: Chemistry, English, and German
1989–97	MB Primary School, Budapest

2 **Answer the questions using the information in the CV.**

1 How long has János worked in the sportswear business?
2 When did he start working in Germany?
3 What is his degree in?
4 Has he worked in Italy?
5 When did he graduate from university?

3 •)) **7.4 Listen to János' interview and complete the sentences.**

1 _____ any other courses since you graduated?
2 It really _____ me manage larger teams and _____ my communication with team members.
3 I _____ to most of Europe, either on holiday or for business.
4 You _____ any languages on your CV.
5 I _____ English at school and Italian while I was at college.

Focus

Read the examples 1–3 from the interview and match each one with its function a–c.

1 I haven't done much travelling recently. I've been pretty busy with my job and looking after my family.
2 I did a course when I was promoted in 2011 to Assistant Product Manager.
3 So far, I've lived in four countries.

a to talk about experiences up to the present
b to talk about recent activities
c to talk about past events in a career

Read the example sentences and complete the rule with *for* and *since*.

I have lived / lived there for six years.
I have worked here since 2012.

We use _____ with a period of time and _____ with a point in time.

▶ For more details and practice, go to the Review section on page 89.

PRACTICE

4 Choose the correct words to complete the interview.

A Have you ever worked in Spain?
B Yes, I *have / did*[1]. I've *got / got*[2] a job there last year.
A Where *have you worked / did you work*[3]?
B I've *worked / worked*[4] in a ski resort in the Pyrenees.
A How long did you work there?
B I worked there *for / since*[5] three months.
A And what do you do now?
B I am a skiing instructor in New Zealand.
A When *did you learn / have you learnt*[6] to ski?
B I first *learnt / have learnt*[7] to ski about six years ago.
A How long *were you / have you been*[8] in New Zealand?
B I *have been / was*[9] there since May this year.
A *Have you ever worked / Did you ever work*[10] in Canada?
B I *didn't work / haven't worked*[11] there yet, but I'd like to in the future.
A What's *been / was*[12] your best experience as a ski instructor so far?
B I *really enjoyed / have really enjoyed*[13] watching people learn how to ski.

TASK

5 Work in pairs. One of you has applied for the job at Unisports. One of you is the interviewer. Ask and answer questions using the prompts below. Add some more questions. If the answer is 'Yes', ask for more details.

- Work in the sportswear industry
- Do any marketing / sales
- Give any presentations
- Study any other languages
- Travel on business
- Manage a large project

Review

Grammar Present Perfect; Past Simple

Form

We form the Present Perfect with *have / has* + past participle. We often use the contraction of *has* and *have* when we speak.

Statement

I You We They	have ('ve) have not (haven't)	worked. gone.
He She It	has ('s) has not (hasn't)	

Question			**Short answer**		
Have	I you we they	worked? gone?	Yes/No,	I you we they	have/haven't.
Has	he she it			he she it	has/hasn't.

How long have you worked there?
Where has she gone?

Use

In general, we use the Present Perfect to link the past and the present:

1 to talk about a situation that started in the past and continues to the present

Example   They've been married for 30 years.
                    He's lived there for a month.

2 to talk about an event or series of events at an indefinite time in the past.

Example   I've visited 10 different countries.
                    Have you ever tried Indonesian food?

We use the Past Simple to refer to an event at a specific time in the past.

Examples   They got married 30 years ago.
                    He moved to Washington in September.

Time expressions

Present Perfect	**Past Simple**
for, since, just, yet, so far, already, ever, never	in 2010, two weeks ago, yesterday, last winter

PRACTICE   **1   Complete the text with the words below.**

just   last week   yet   six months ago   so far

I've _____¹ graduated in chemistry and I'd like a job in research. I haven't found one _____², although I started looking for jobs _____³, before I finished university. I've applied for about twenty jobs _____⁴. I went to two very good interviews _____⁵, so I'm hoping I'll get a job offer soon!

2 Choose the best options to complete the questions and sentences.

1 *Have you ever learnt / Did you learn* to play a musical instrument?
No, unfortunately, I *wasn't / haven't been* interested in music when I was younger and these days I don't have time.

2 *Have you downloaded / Did you download* any new music recently?
Yes, *I've downloaded / I downloaded* a Rihanna album yesterday.

3 *Have you bought / Did you buy* LPs when you were a kid?
No, I'm not that old! *I've bought / I bought* cassettes.

4 *Have you ever been / Did you go* to a concert?
Only to some very small ones in my local town. *I've never been / I didn't go* to a big concert.

5 *Have you ever sung / Did you sing* karaoke at the party last night?
Yes, *I've sung / I sang* three songs – I was great!

6 *Have you ever met / Did you meet* a famous singer or musician?
Actually, *I've chatted / I chatted* to a British pop singer in a pub once, but I forgot to ask for his autograph.

3 Use the information in the table to make sentences (Past Simple or Present Perfect) about the young cello player, Laura van der Heijden.

1997	Born in England
2001	Starts learning the recorder
2003	Starts learning the piano and cello
2005	Joins the Royal College of Music
2010	Wins the Swiss National Youth Music Competition
2011	Wins the Marjorie Humby Competition and Beckenham Musician of the Year Competition
2012	Wins Woking Young Musician of the Year and BBC Young Musician Competition

1 Laura van der Heijden _____ in 1997.
2 She _____ in 2001.
3 She _____ in 2003.
4 She _____ since 2005.
5 She _____ three instruments.
6 She _____ four big competitions, including the BBC Young Musician Competition.

Vocabulary Talking about changes and trends

1 Complete the table.

Verb	Past Simple	Present Perfect	Noun
go up / down	went up / down	have gone up / down	–
increase			
decrease			
rise			
fall			
grow			
drop			
level off			
peak			
remain stable			

2 Using the information in the graph, decide if the sentences are true or false. Correct any sentences which are false. Imagine it is now the end of December.

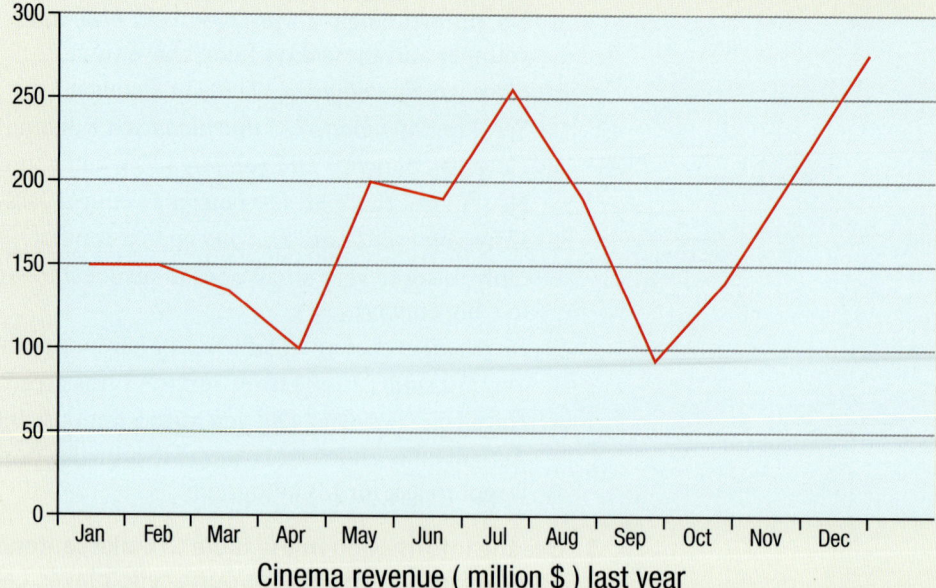

Cinema revenue (million $) last year

1   Revenue peaked in December.
2   Revenue was higher in June than in May.
3   Revenue has increased continuously since August.
4   Revenue fell slightly from July to September.
5   Revenue decreased steadily from February to April.
6   Revenue has grown slightly since September.

3 Complete the sentences using the information in the graph and the words below.

by   in   of   remained stable   sharply   slightly

1   There was a second peak _____ cinema revenue in July.
2   Revenue _____ between January and February.
3   Revenue fell _____ between May and June.
4   Revenue increased _____ between April and May.
5   Revenue grew _____ almost $200 million between September and December.
6   There was a decrease _____ $50 million between February and April.

Work skills Presentations 2: Using PowerPoint; presentation tips

1 Complete the presentation tips with the words in the box.

breathe   check   decide   find out   give   keep (× 3)   practise   prepare   read   use

1   _____ the presentation simple.
2   _____ your equipment before the presentation.
3   _____ simple charts and graphs.
4   _____ your slides and notes as early as possible.
5   _____ your energy levels up.
6   _____ who the audience are and what they want to hear.
7   _____ as much as possible.
8   _____ the audience time to read what's on your slides.
9   _____ the main aim of the presentation.
10 Don't _____ your presentation.
11 _____ eye contact with your audience.
12 If you are nervous, _____ deeply and try not to speak too quickly.

Functions Job interviews

The Present Perfect is often used to talk about experiences up to the present (when we don't specify the time of the experience).

Examples I've met a lot of interesting people in my job.

He's been a software engineer, a nurse, a sales assistant, and a dog-walker.

I've never learnt a foreign language.

We can use *Have you ever …?* to ask about general experience.

Examples Have you ever ridden a motorbike?

Has she ever been late for work?

We also use the Present Perfect to talk about recent activities.

Examples The R&D department have just developed a new type of watch.

Have you been busy?

She's just got a new job.

We often use *for* and *since* with the Present Perfect to answer the question *How long …?*

We use *for* with a period of time and *since* with a point in time.

Examples He's been unemployed for six months / since June.

I've been ill for three days / since Tuesday.

1 **Complete the email with the verbs in brackets in the Past Simple or Present Perfect.**

From: János
To: Sven

Hi Sven

How are you? And how are the rest of the team? Busy as usual, I imagine.

So, I _____¹ (start) my new job just over a month ago, and I _____² (have) lots of interesting experiences already! I _____³ (make) three presentations, _____⁴ (take part) in a management training course, and I _____⁵ (just get back) from a business trip to Brazil. We _____⁶ (have) a lot of meetings there, but I also _____⁷ (do) some sightseeing – it's a fantastic country! Now I have to start studying Portuguese.

Trina and the girls are enjoying life back in London. I hope your family are well. _____ you _____⁸ (find) a new flat yet? Please remember to come and visit if you're in London some time.

All the best
János

2 **Complete the questions in the interview.**

1 How long / worked / for Seymourpowell?

I've been there for almost five years now.

2 What / learn / there?

Hmm, a lot I think – a lot about design, about dealing with customers, and about working with other people.

3 Where / work / before?

Seymourpowell was my first job after graduating, although I did have some holiday jobs when I was a student.

4 ever / manage / a team?

No, but I have a lot of experience of working in a team, so I think I could learn.

5 What / know about / our company / before coming to this interview?

Well, I knew that you were one of the top product design companies in Europe, and that you have grown a lot in recent years. That's one of the reasons I wanted to work for you.

8 Doing the right thing

Grammar Modals and related verbs

1 Read these cultural tips for working and living in India. Do you think they are true or false?

1 Generally, you *don't have to* wear formal clothes to work.
2 You *have to* get to meetings exactly on time.
3 You *mustn't* interrupt someone senior talking in a meeting.
4 In a traditional company, you *don't have to* address your boss as 'Sir' or 'Madam'.
5 In a modern company, you *can* call your boss by their first name.
6 If you work for a company in India, you *must* speak Hindi.
7 You *should* leave a little food on your plate at the end of a meal.
8 You *shouldn't* shake hands with a person of the opposite sex.
9 *Don't* say 'Thank you' after a clerk hands you your grocery bag.
10 You *should* tip hotel and train station porters.

2 ◉)) **8.1** Sreenath Aravind talks to two friends about working in India. Listen and check your answers to **1**.

Focus

Put the italicized verbs in 1 into these categories.

Meaning	Example
It's necessary / important to	
It's important not to	
It's a good idea to	
It's not a good idea to	
It's not necessary to	
It's OK / possible to	
It's not OK / possible to	

▶▶ For more details and practice, go to the Review section on page 98.

3 Match the countries with the rules and tips for exchanging business cards. One tip may match more than one country.

India   Japan   Spain   UK

1 *It is important not to* write on the back of a business card.
2 *It is OK to* keep business cards in your pocket.
3 *It is important not to* use your left hand to give and receive business cards.
4 *It is not necessary to* translate your business cards into Hindi.
5 *It is a good idea to* place the business cards on the table in front of you in the order people are seated.
6 *It is necessary to* treat someone's card with respect and take time to read the information.
7 *It is important not to* put a card straight into your card case.
8 *It is a good idea to* include your degree or other qualifications on your card.

Explain the rules for exchanging business cards in your culture or a culture you know well.

4 Replace the highlighted phrases in **3** with 'you' and an appropriate verb.

Example   You mustn't write on the back of a business card.

5 ◁)) **8.2** Listen to people talking about travel rules and tips. What do they say about the following?

Heathrow airport	**Tokyo taxi**
passport	cash
bottled water	tipping
laptop	getting out of the taxi
sharp objects	map and address
bottles	fare

What are your tips for taking a taxi where you live?

6 Read the text. Which country do you think is being described? Discuss the questions below.

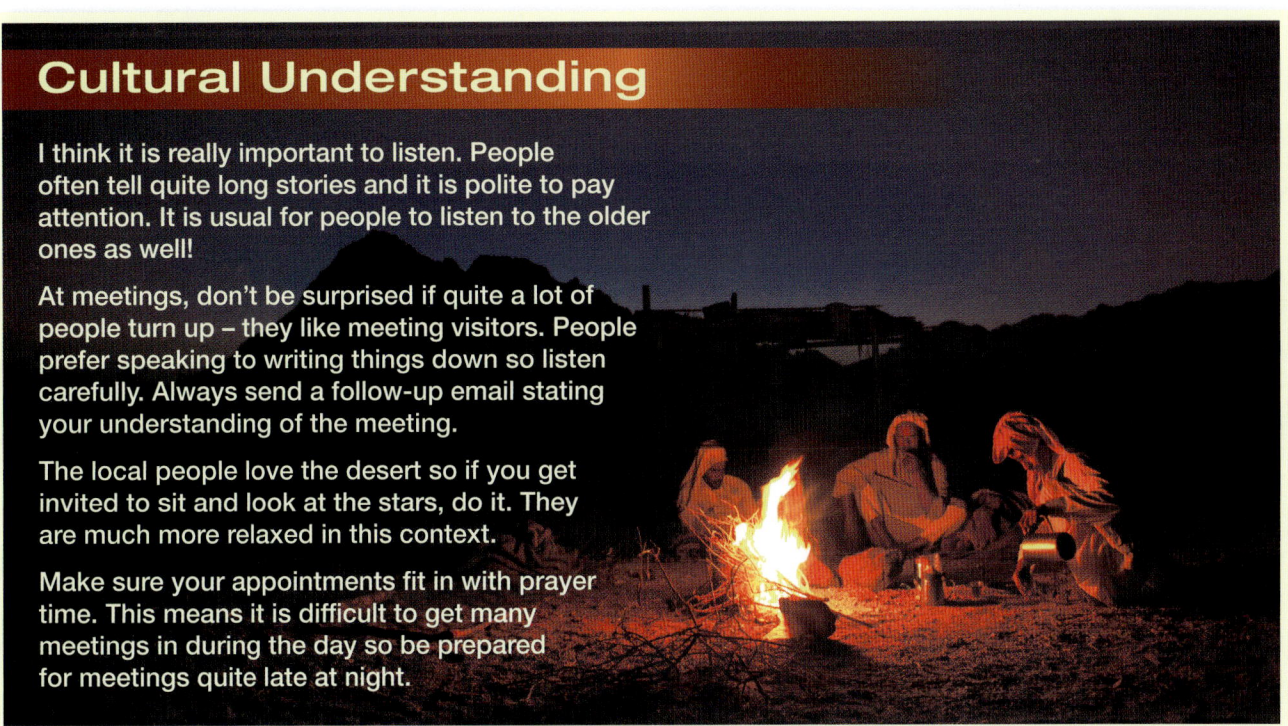

Cultural Understanding

I think it is really important to listen. People often tell quite long stories and it is polite to pay attention. It is usual for people to listen to the older ones as well!

At meetings, don't be surprised if quite a lot of people turn up – they like meeting visitors. People prefer speaking to writing things down so listen carefully. Always send a follow-up email stating your understanding of the meeting.

The local people love the desert so if you get invited to sit and look at the stars, do it. They are much more relaxed in this context.

Make sure your appointments fit in with prayer time. This means it is difficult to get many meetings in during the day so be prepared for meetings quite late at night.

How important is listening in your culture?
Are there strict rules about who attends a meeting?
Do you have any favourite customs or events?

7 **What are the challenges when you relocate to another country? Think of ideas for these topics.**

accommodation   education   money   culture

8 **8.3 Listen to Hazel Masterson, the manager of an international recruitment agency, talk about working abroad. What does she say about the topics in 7?**

9 **8.4 Listen to these positive and negative sentences. Are there any differences in the way we pronounce the vowels in the verbs in italics?**

Watch the video for more practice.

1 You *must* let people finish speaking.
  You *mustn't* interrupt someone senior talking in a meeting.
2 People *do* arrive late for meetings.
  You *don't* have to get to meetings exactly on time.
3 You *should* let the taxi driver close the door.
  You *shouldn't* try to close the taxi door yourself.
4 You *can* wear casual clothes at home.
  You *can't* wear casual clothes in the office at the weekend.

Practise saying the sentences.

TASK **10** **A business colleague is coming to work in your country for a year. Prepare some tips for them using this list.**

speaking the language
clothes
keeping time
talking in meetings
addressing seniors
greetings and business cards
gift giving
eating
physical contact

Example You should learn a few phrases like 'Buongiorno'.

11 **Take turns to ask and talk about the tips in 10.**

Example **A** Should I learn the language?
B You don't have to, but you should learn a few phrases like 'Buongiorno'.

Vocabulary Career paths

1 ◉)) **8.5** **Listen to Gina Prentiss talk about her career and answer the questions.**

1 What sort of company did Gina want to work for?
2 What was unusual about her visa situation?
3 What sort of training did she get?
4 How long did she stay with the company?
5 What did she do after she left the company?
6 What is the current situation with her business?

2 **Match the sentences with the different parts of the career path below.**

a The company offered me the job.
b I had an interview.
c I signed the contract.
d I transferred to another branch.
e I saw a job advertisement.
f I got my first promotion after a year.
g I finished my three-month probationary period.
h I did a training course.
i I applied for the job.
j I graduated from school / college.
k I started work.

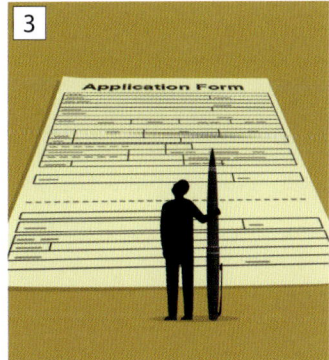

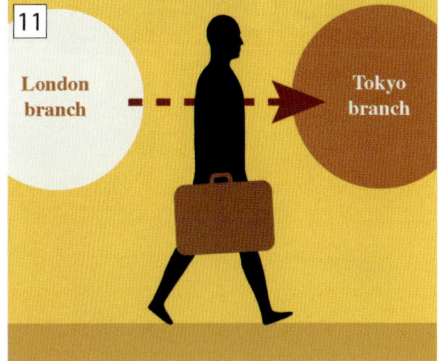

3 How similar are the stages in **2** to the first stages in your career? In what ways are they different?

4 Read about the first stage of a career and add your own ideas.

1 What do you need to do when you apply for a job?
write a letter
send in your CV

_____

2 What does a company usually expect from a candidate?
qualifications

_____

3 What sort of contracts are there?
full-time
part-time

_____

4 What details does a contract give you?
hours of work
salary

_____

5 What does a job description tell you?
reporting lines (who your manager is, who you manage)
your responsibilities

_____

6 What benefits do companies offer their employees?
health care
pension

_____

5 Work in pairs. Discuss the pros and cons of these alternative career paths.

1 work as a freelancer   2 start your own business   3 go abroad to work

Work skills Meetings 2: Turn-taking and turn-giving

1 You are in a meeting and you want to say something. Which of the following would you do or not do?

put your hand up

stand up

cough

point at someone

make eye contact with the person who is speaking

wait until you are asked

2 ●)) 8.6 Listen to a meeting about training for people going overseas. Tick ✓ the expressions you hear.

Turn-taking / Interrupting
May I?
Sorry …
Excuse me …
Sorry to interrupt, but …
Could I just say …
I'd just like to …

3 You are leading a meeting. How do you let other people speak or stop people from talking too much?

4 ●)) 8.7 Listen to a later part of the meeting. Tick ✓ the expressions you hear.

Turn-giving
Paula, what do you think?
Any comments, Karl?
How about you, Ted?
John?
Sorry, Charles, could you let …

5 Work in small groups. Discuss the topic 'Rules in the workplace'. One person leads the discussion. Everyone in the group takes turns to speak. Anyone can interrupt. Use the expressions in **2** and **4**.

Functions Invitations and offers

INTRODUCTION

1 8.8 **Emma King is visiting some friends in Rio de Janeiro. Listen to the conversation and complete the questions.**

1 Would you like ________________?
2 Would you like to ________________?
3 Would you like us ________________?
4 ________________ pick you up at your hotel at about 2.00.
5 Would you like to ________________?

2 8.9 **Listen and complete Emma's responses. Which response is negative?**

1 Yes, I'd love ________. Thanks.
2 I'd love ________.
3 Yes, ________. It sounds great.
4 ________. That's perfect.
5 I'd love to, ________ I've promised to meet Ken on Sunday.

Focus

Complete the phrases with the correct form.

me / us + to + verb   *noun*   *to + verb*   *verb*

Invitation	Would you like …?
Offer	Would you like …?
	Would you like a / some …?
	I'll …

Which responses can we use with invitations and offers?

I'd love to.
I'd love some / one.
I'd love to, but …
Thank you very much. / Thank you. / Thanks.
Thanks for the offer, but …
Yes, please.

Which responses are negative?

For more details and practice, go to the Review section on page 101.

3 **Match the invitations and offers with the responses.**

1 Would you like to go sailing at the weekend?   a   I'd love one.
2 Would you like a glass of water?   b   I'd love to, but I get seasick.
3 Would you like me to get a ticket for you?   c   Thanks for the offer, but
4 Would you like some chocolate?   I've ordered a taxi.
5 Would you like me to give you a lift?   d   I'd love some.
6 Would you like to go shopping on Saturday?   e   I'd love to.
                                                 f   Yes, please.

4 **Work in pairs. Make and respond to offers in these situations.**

1 Student A has just arrived at Student B's company after a long journey.
2 It's 12.30. Student A hasn't had lunch yet.
3 You are in the company canteen. Student A says they left their wallet in your office.
4 Student A needs to send an email to their company but they can't get a signal on their smartphone.
5 Student A needs to get to the airport.

5 **Work in pairs. Read the conversation. Use the prompts below to have similar conversations.**

A Do you like modern art?
B Yes, I do.
A Would you like to visit the Niterói Art Museum on Saturday?
B I'd love to.

films   Japanese food   pop music   reading novels   shopping   swimming

6 **Work in pairs. Have similar conversations to 5 but give a polite negative response.**

7 **Work in pairs. A friend is going to visit you in your home town. Take turns to invite your partner to do something, and make offers to make their stay more enjoyable.**

Review

Grammar Modals and related verbs

Form

Here is a table of common modal and related verbs.

Necessary / Very important to	must have / has to	I must finish this before I go home. You have to show your passport at the border.
Important not to	mustn't Don't	You mustn't be rude to the customers. Don't spend more than the budget.
Not necessary to	don't have to doesn't have to	We don't have to work overtime.
Good idea to	should	You should check your emails before you send them.
Not a good idea to	shouldn't	We shouldn't increase our prices.
Possible to	can	You can use my office if you want.
Not possible to	can't	You can't park here.

We don't use *to* after modal verbs.
Examples She can't ~~to~~ speak Japanese.   He should ~~to~~ study more.

Have and *has* are followed by *to*.
Example   I have to finish my email before I go home.
            Do you have to work at the weekend?

We add *not* or *n't* (not *don't* or *doesn't*) to make a modal verb negative.
Examples You shouldn't phone him until after 9 a.m.
            He can't drive.

To make questions with modal verbs, we put the modal before the subject.
Examples Can I park here?   Where can I park?

We usually use *have to* instead of *must* for questions.
Example   Do I have to take my passport?

Use

We use modal and related verbs to talk about how to do the right thing or behave correctly in social and work situations.
We can also use the imperative to give advice.
Examples Don't forget to take your passport.
            Introduce yourself to your new colleagues.

We use a polite tone of voice so that these forms do not sound too direct.

PRACTICE

1 Read the guide to writing a successful CV. Complete the sentences below the guide using a modal or related verb.

Writing a successful CV

- It is very important that your CV looks professional.
- It is a good idea to start with your personal details: name, address, telephone number, and email address.
- It isn't necessary to include your date of birth.
- It is a good idea to use one kind of font.
- It's OK to add a photo, but it's a good idea to look smart.
- It is important not to make up qualifications or write about experience you don't have.

1 Your CV _____ look professional.
2 Your personal details _____ come first.
3 You _____ write your age on your CV.
4 You _____ use a variety of fonts and styles in your CV.
5 You _____ put a photo of yourself on your CV.

2 Complete the sentences for the situations. Use the verbs in brackets and the correct form of the verbs below.

arrive   borrow   check   go   register   sit   tell

Example   The party is a surprise for Greta. (must)
            You mustn't tell Greta about the party.

1 Andrew is meeting visitors at the airport, but has forgotten what time they arrive. (should)
   He _____.
2 I've forgotten to bring a pen. (can)
   You _____.
3 My boss doesn't like anyone to be late for meetings. (must)
   You _____.
4 Flo wants to take an exam. The deadline for registration is 20th February. (have to)
   She _____.
5 The workshop is optional for employees (don't have to).
   Employees _____.
6 Sorry, this table is reserved (can't).
   You _____.

3 Write questions for the answers using the verbs below.

can (× 2)   have to   need   should (× 2)

Example   Do I have to get a receipt?   Yes, you have to get a receipt.

1 _____?
   No, you don't have to wear a uniform, but you should wear formal clothes.
2 _____?
   Yes, you must take your driving licence with you.
3 _____?
   No, you shouldn't eat in the office. You can eat in the kitchen or the café.
4 _____?
   You should ask for Mr Hunt.
5 _____?
   You can go home at 7.30.
6 _____?
   No, you mustn't take any company files out of the building.

Vocabulary Career paths

1 Match 1–8 with a–h to make sentences or questions.

1	Please sign	a	probationary period.
2	I'm going on a cultural awareness	b	work?
3	I think we should give him	c	the contract.
4	When can you start	d	the job yet?
5	I'm nervous – I've got an	e	a promotion.
6	In the summer, I'm going to transfer	f	course.
7	There is a six-month	g	interview tomorrow.
8	Have you applied for	h	to the Stockholm office.

Work skills Meetings 2: Turn-taking and turn-giving

1 Complete the conversation.

Abi So, it seems we need to rethink how we find new employees. Sam, w_____ d_____ y_____[1] think?

Sam Yes, I think we need to start advertising, for example …

Chandra S_____ t_____ i_____[2], but didn't we do that before?

Abi Yes, but it was a long time ago.

Mike C_____ I j_____ s_____ t_____[3] if we do advertise, we have to think very carefully about …

Chandra I think using our own …

Abi S_____[4], Chandra, c_____ y_____ l_____ Mike f_____[5]?

Chandra Sorry, Mike?

Mike Well, I j_____ w_____ t_____ s_____[6] that we don't want to spend time on the wrong sorts of people, so we have to choose where we are going to advertise carefully. I think our website would be enough.

Abi Hmm, I don't think that reaches enough people. I think we should try a recruitment agency. H_____ a_____ y_____[7], Will?

Will Yes, I think advertising is too much work. Using a recruitment agency means that they will do some of the work for us.

Mike M_____[8] I? We have to remember that it will be much more expensive.

Abi True, but I think it'll be worth it if we get the right kind of people quickly. A_____ c_____[9], Chandra?

Chandra I think it sounds like a good idea, and I know a good one. Shall I contact them and get some more information?

Abi Yes, please Chandra. Good idea.

Functions Invitations and offers

We use the following phrases to make and respond to invitations and offers.

Invitations
Examples   Would you like to visit our factory tomorrow?
            Would you like to go swimming this afternoon?

Accepting an invitation
Examples   I'd love to.
            Yes, that sounds good, thanks.

Rejecting an invitation
Examples   I'd love to, but I've got another appointment tomorrow.
            Thanks for the invitation, but I'm afraid I can't swim.

Offers
Examples   Would you like a drink?
            Would you like some dessert?

Offering to do something for someone
Examples   Would you like me to phone the restaurant for you?
            Would you like us to get tickets for you?

Accepting an offer   **Rejecting an offer**
Examples   I'd love one / some, thanks.   *Examples*   Thanks, but I'm full.
            Yes, please. Thanks.   Thanks for the offer, but I've
                                                          already got tickets.

1 Put the lines of the conversations in the correct order.

1   a   Would you like any milk or sugar?
    b   I'd love one.
    c   You must be tired after your journey.
    d   Thanks.
    e   I'm a little bit tired. It's the six-hour time difference.
    f   Sure. Here you are.
    g   Would you like some coffee?
    h   Just one sugar, please.

2   a   I'd love to.
    b   Would you like me to pick you up from your hotel?
    c   I really like Thai food.
    d   Thank you.
    e   Would you like to go to a restaurant for dinner this evening?
    f   Thanks. That would be great.
    g   What kind of food do you like?
    h   Great, there's a Thai place near the office. I'll book us a table.

2 Complete the conversations using the prompts.

1   A   like / go shopping?
    B   I / love
2   A   like / me / call a taxi?
    B   Thanks / offer / but / I / walk.
3   A   like / some cake?
    B   Thanks / I / full.
4   A   I / give / you / lift / to / airport.
    B   Thanks. / perfect.
5   A   like / us / translate / you?
    B   Yes, please.

9 Start-ups

Grammar Past Continuous; Past Simple

INTRODUCTION

1 Work in pairs. Discuss the questions.

Which social media sites do you use?

What do you use them for? Here are some ideas.

Facebook™   finding out what other people are doing

Twitter™   telling people about events

Flickr™   sharing information and photos with friends

What do you know about the people in the photos?

Facebook™

Facebook is a social networking service used to exchange messages. You can also create common-interest user groups, and pages for events and organizations.

Mark Zuckerberg had the idea for Facebook in 2003 while he was studying at Harvard University. The original name was Facemash. At the same time, three other students, Cameron and Tyler Winklevoss and Divya Narendra, were working on a similar site called HarvardConnection.com. Zuckerberg was working on his idea, when Cameron and Tyler asked him to help them with their website. For a while, Zuckerberg worked on both projects. The Winklevosses believed that while Zuckerberg was working for them, he used some of the HarvardConnection ideas to build his own site.

In 2004, Zuckerberg launched Thefacebook and within the first month, more than half of the undergraduate students at Harvard were using the site. The name later changed to Facebook and became hugely popular.

In 2012, Facebook had over 900 million active users and the average Facebook user had over 200 friends.

2 Read the article about Facebook. Answer the questions.

1 Who started Facebook?

2 What was Harvard Connection? Whose idea was it?

3 What did Cameron and Tyler Winklevoss think Zuckerberg did?

4 Was Facebook successful at first?

5 How many Facebook users were there in 2012?

3 Work in pairs. Discuss the questions.

1 Do you think Facebook will continue to be popular? Why?

2 Which websites are competition for Facebook? Which are the most popular social media sites in your country?

Focus

Read the example sentences and answer the questions.

1 Mark Zuckerberg had the idea for Facebook in 2003 while he was studying at Harvard University.
2 At the same time, three other students … were working on a similar site called HarvardConnection.com.
3 Zuckerberg was working on his idea, when Cameron and Tyler asked him to help them with their website.

a Which verbs describe an activity that was in progress in the past?
b Which verbs describe a completed action in the past?

Are the verbs in the Past Simple or Past Continuous?

How is the Past Continuous formed?

Which tense do we often use with the following adverbs?

a while, meanwhile _____
b when, then _____

We do not use the Past Continuous with state verbs, e.g. *have, be, like*.

⏩ For more details and practice, go to the Review section on page 110.

PRACTICE

4 Are these sentences about the article in **2** true or false? Correct any false sentences.

1 Mark Zuckerberg was studying at Yale University when he started Facebook.
2 The original name for Facebook was Facemash.
3 Zuckerberg met the Winklevosses while they were studying at Harvard.
4 Cameron and Tyler Winklevoss were helping Zuckerberg build his website.
5 Zuckerberg was working on two sites at the same time.
6 Cameron and Tyler were happy when Thefacebook was launched.
7 A lot of students were using Zuckerberg's site a month after the launch.

5 Work in pairs. Take turns to check the answers in **4**.

Example   **A** Was Mark Zuckerberg studying at Yale University when he started Facebook?
            B Yes, he was. / No, he wasn't. He was studying at …

6 Complete the sentences with the correct form of the verbs in brackets.

1 He _____ (watch) YouTube videos in the office when his boss _____ (come) in.
2 Business _____ (not / go) very well, when we suddenly _____ (get) a huge order in from a new company.
3 The company _____ (start) a Facebook page and a blog because they _____ (try) to attract new customers.
4 When I _____ (meet) my wife, I _____ (work) in a beach café.
5 While I _____ (try) on shoes in Harrods, David Beckham _____ (walk) in.
6 When I _____ (discover) Flickr, I _____ (not / have) a digital camera.
7 Where _____ (you / work) when you _____ (get) a job with Facebook?
8 When I _____ (arrive) home, Hannah _____ (upload) photos and Nick _____ (cook) dinner.
9 I was thrilled when we _____ (win) the €1,500 lottery because, at the time, Jon _____ (look for) a new job.
10 Kit Dotcom _____ (start) Megaload while he _____ (live) in Hong Kong.

7 •)) **9.1 Listen to the sentences. How are *was* and *were* pronounced?**

1 He was living in Hong Kong.
2 Was he living in Hong Kong?
3 They were working together.
4 Were they working together?
5 The company was making a lot of money.
6 Was the company making a lot of money?

Listen again and practise saying the sentences.

8 •)) **9.2 Listen to Zita talk about using social media sites for work in an interview with *High Flyer* magazine. Answer the questions.**

1 Which websites did she use?
2 How did these social media sites help Zita's work?

9 How do companies use social media sites? Give some examples.

10 Work in pairs or small groups. Take turns to ask and answer about the following.

Example Where were you living when you left school?

When you left school
When you started your first job
When you met your partner
When you met a famous person
When you fell in love for the first time
When you had a fantastic idea
When you last went on a great holiday

TASK 11 Work in pairs.

Student A Read the article below.
Student B Go to page 130. Read the text about a social media site.

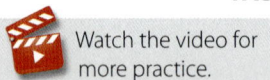
Watch the video for more practice.

TWITTER™

In 2006, a group of developers were working for a podcasting company, Odeo Inc. in San Francisco. The group needed some new ideas so they divided into small brainstorming teams. Jack Dorsey, who was studying at New York University at the time, joined one of the teams.

They went to the local park to talk. They were eating Mexican food and playing on a slide, when Jack Dorsey had the idea of sharing short messages with other people. Everyone thought it was a great idea. The team developed the idea and Twitter was launched in July 2006. By 2012, there were 140 million active users sending over 340 million tweets a day. Jack Dorsey later became the company CEO.

Ask your partner about Flickr, another online company.

Example When did Flickr start?
Who started it?
What were they doing at the time?

Vocabulary Staying in and going out

1 **What do you do in your free time? Add your ideas to the two groups below.**

Staying in	Going out
watching TV	going for a walk

2 **Which verbs do we use with the activities below?**

do   get   go   have

(my / your) homework
a drink / takeaway / break
lunch
for a run / walk / bike ride / drive
out for a meal
ready / up / dressed
shopping
some exercise
the washing / washing-up
to a concert / friend's house
to bed
to the cinema / gym

3 **Work in pairs. Have short conversations using the prompts below and phrases from 2.**

A I've been using the computer all day.
B You should go for a walk.
A Good idea.

I need some new shoes.　　*I'm bored.*　　*I'm not very fit.*
I'm really hungry.　　*I'm really tired.*　　*I'm thirsty.*
I've got an exam tomorrow.　　*I've had a huge lunch.*

4 **Work in pairs. Ask your partner when or how often they do the activities in 2.**

5 ◉》 **9.3** Listen to Kara and Jack discussing how Kara can improve her lifestyle. Tick ✓ the *get* phrases they use.

	Kara	Jack
get fit		
get up earlier		
get home late		
get a bike		
get into my jeans		
get better		
get angry		

How could you improve your lifestyle?

6 Match the games with the balls.

American football	baseball	basketball	cricket	golf
pool	rugby	soccer / football	table tennis	tennis

1 _____ 2 _____ 3 _____ 4 _____ 5 _____

6 _____ 7 _____ 8 _____ 9 _____ 10 _____

7 Which games in **6** do we play with these items?

bat   club   cue   racket

8 Which verb do we use with the sports in **6**? What do these sports have in common?

9 Put these sports into the correct verb groups.

aerobics	badminton	cycling	gymnastics	hiking	hockey
judo	running	sailing	skiing	squash	swimming

Do	Go	Play

10 Work in pairs. Ask your partner about the sports they do and/or watch.

Example   **A** Which sports do you do?
              B I play tennis and I go running.

11 Imagine you have a week that you can do what you want, meet who you want, go where you want, spend as much money as you want. What would you do?

Work skills Emails 2: Problems and solutions

1 **Read the four emails and put them into pairs in the correct order.**

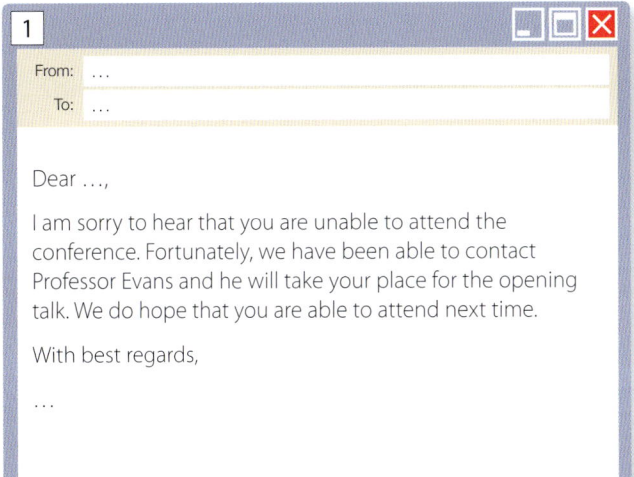

1

From: ...
To: ...

Dear ...,

I am sorry to hear that you are unable to attend the conference. Fortunately, we have been able to contact Professor Evans and he will take your place for the opening talk. We do hope that you are able to attend next time.

With best regards,

...

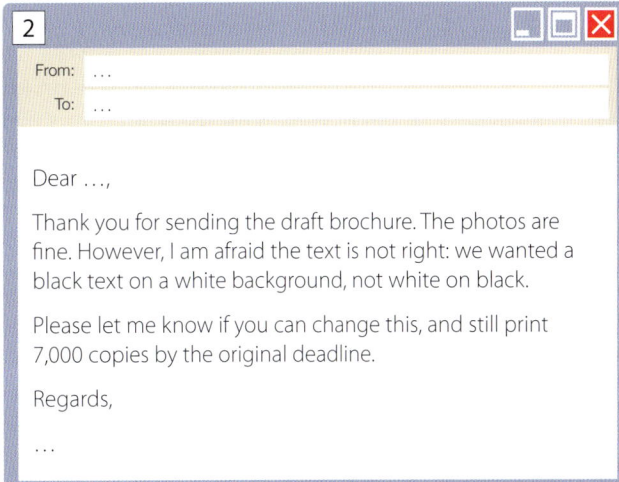

2

From: ...
To: ...

Dear ...,

Thank you for sending the draft brochure. The photos are fine. However, I am afraid the text is not right: we wanted a black text on a white background, not white on black.

Please let me know if you can change this, and still print 7,000 copies by the original deadline.

Regards,

...

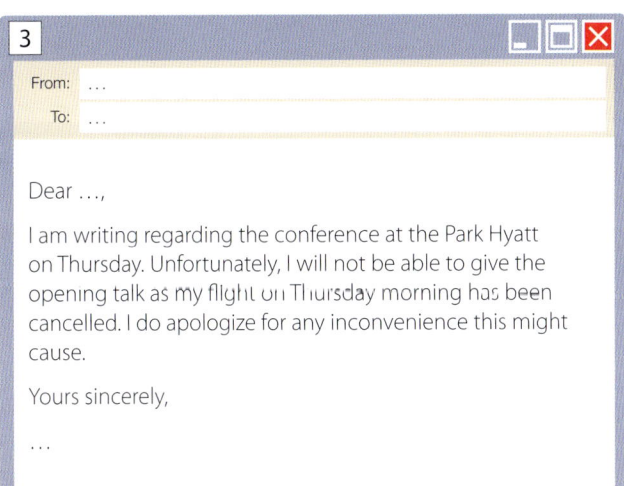

3

From: ...
To: ...

Dear ...,

I am writing regarding the conference at the Park Hyatt on Thursday. Unfortunately, I will not be able to give the opening talk as my flight on Thursday morning has been cancelled. I do apologize for any inconvenience this might cause.

Yours sincerely,

...

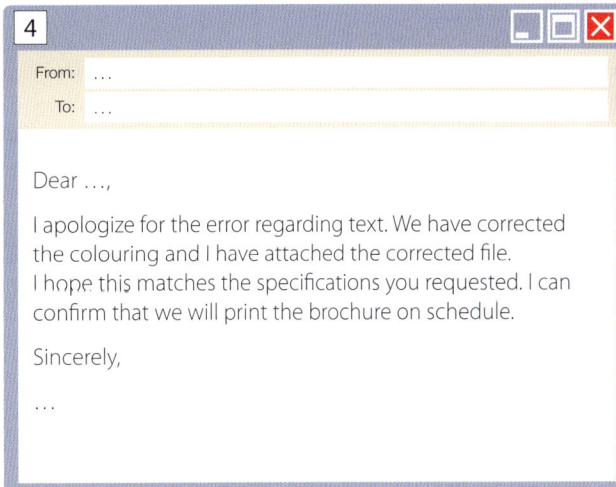

4

From: ...
To: ...

Dear ...,

I apologize for the error regarding text. We have corrected the colouring and I have attached the corrected file. I hope this matches the specifications you requested. I can confirm that we will print the brochure on schedule.

Sincerely,

...

2 **Read the emails again and answer the questions.**
1 What are the two problems described?
2 How are the problems resolved?
3 Which phrases are used to:
   - give good news?
   - give bad news?
   - apologize?

3 **Work in pairs. Write an email using the information below. Give your email to your partner and write a reply to your partner's email.**

A
Stayed at hotel last week. Booked room on Internet with view of Eiffel Tower. Room faced another building, no view.

B
Giving a workshop tomorrow. Laptop stolen yesterday. No backup files. Cannot attend.

Functions Making suggestions

1 ◉) **9.4** Unisports has problems at their distribution centre. Listen to the distribution manager, Mike Webber, talking to his colleagues. What are the two problems?

2 Imagine you are on Mike's team. What suggestions can you think of to help? Discuss your ideas in small groups.

3 ◉) **9.5** Listen to the second part of the meeting and compare your ideas.

4 Which suggestions do they finally choose? Why?

1 Get the materials from another supplier
2 Use a cheaper alternative
3 Postpone introducing this line
4 Get in touch with the transport people
5 Contact the outlets
6 Send an email to the shops and the transport people

5 ◉) **9.6** Listen and complete the extracts from the meeting.

1 Tamara   What about _____ ?
    Mike   Yes, that's a possibility.
2 Ed   Why don't we _____ ?
    Mike   That's a good idea.
3 Mike   How about _____ ?
    Tamara   I'm sorry, but I don't think that will work.
4 Mike   We could _____ .
    Tamara   Absolutely not.
5 Mike   Let's _____ .
    Ed   OK. Let's do that. I can do that now.
6 Mike   I suggest we _____ .
    Tamara   Good idea, Mike.

6 Tick ✓ the positive responses in **5** and put a cross ✗ next to the negative responses.

Focus

Look at the suggestion phrases in 5. Which ones are followed by the infinitive of the verb without *to*, and which are followed by the *-ing* form of the verb?

⏩ For more details and practice, go to the Review section on page 113.

7 Choose the correct form of the verb in these sentences.

1 Why don't we *go / going* out for something to eat?
2 Next time we have a team-building event, we could *go / going* hiking.
3 Let's *cancel / cancelling* all meetings, and communicate online instead.
4 How about *watch / watching* a film in English next time?
5 What about *have / having* our next English class in a café?
6 I suggest we *finish / finishing* the class now!

8 Work in small groups. Make the suggestions to each other from **7** and respond appropriately. If you disagree, offer an alternative suggestion.

9 Work in small groups. You work with Mike and some other problems below have come up. In groups, use the idea prompts, or any other ideas you have, to make suggestions. Agree on the best one(s).

Problem 1

One of the trucks has broken down near the Spanish border. The delivery will be 24 hours late.

Ideas: *phone the transport company / phone the shops / cancel the delivery / find another driver / …*

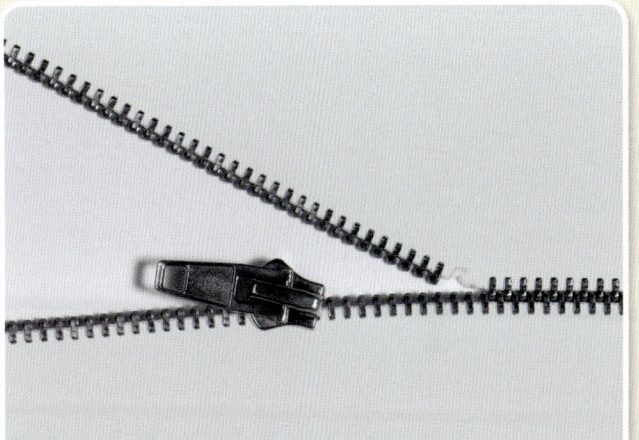

Problem 2

You have received an email to say that the tents delivered last week have faulty zips.

Ideas: *sell them at a discount / throw them away / get them back to the distribution centre in Brussels / arrange for someone locally to repair them / …*

Problem 3

Two shops in Slovenia and two shops in Croatia have received the wrong deliveries. They have been mixed up.

Ideas: *ask the shops to arrange the exchange themselves / contact the transport people to collect and redeliver / tell the shops to try to sell the goods at a 10% discount / tell the shops to keep the goods, and order extra supplies / …*

Review

Grammar Past Continuous; Past Simple

Form

We form the Past Continuous with *was* or *were* and the *-ing* form of the verb.

Statement		
I He She It	was wasn't	working.
You We They	were weren't	

Question			Short answer		
Was	I he she it	working?	Yes / No,	I he she it	was / wasn't.
Were	you we they			you we they	were / weren't.

Where was he working?
Why were they working there?

Use

We use the Past Continuous to talk about an action that was in progress at a particular time in the past.

Example   This time last year we were planning our expansion project.

We also use the Past Continuous to talk about the background to another action in the past. We use *when* to introduce the action in the Past Simple.

Example   I was living in London when I decided to start my own business.

We can also use *while* to introduce the action in the Past Continuous.

Example   While I was living in London, I decided to start my own business.

We use the Past Continuous to talk about two actions that were in progress at the same time in the past.

Example   Terry was showing some visitors around while Dawn was pouring drinks for the other guests.

We can also use *meanwhile* or *at the same time* to talk about two things happening at the same time.

Example   Sales were increasing. Meanwhile / At the same time, the company was making people redundant.

We use the Past Simple to talk about completed actions in the past, about long-term situations in the past, about repeated actions or events in the past, and to talk about a sequence of activities.

Examples   We finished the lesson early.
I studied hard when I was a student.
I got to the office, made some coffee, opened the mail, and started work.

PRACTICE

1 Match 1–5 with a–e to make sentences.

1 I was giving the presentation   a when the system crashed.
2 I was preparing the invoice   b when I got the idea for my own
3 I was driving to her office   business.
4 I was showing the room to a guest   c when the fire alarm went off.
5 I was working for a supermarket   d when she phoned to cancel the
                                   meeting.
                                   e when I saw a mouse in the corner.

2 Complete the sentences with the words below.

at the same time   meanwhile   then   when   while (× 2)

1 Did you talk to Klaudia about the new plan _____ you were having lunch?
2 I worked all day and _____ I had to take work home as well.
3 She was trying to phone me _____ that I was trying to phone her.
4 He studied hard and got top grades at college. _____ , he was working at a
   bank and starting his own business.
5 _____ I got to the shop, lots of customers were already waiting outside.
6 Prices were rising _____ salaries remained the same.

3 Complete the conversation with the correct form of the verbs in brackets.

Lou   Did I tell you about the time I _____¹ (meet) Michael Jackson?

Greg   No, Michael Jackson! Really?

Lou   Yeah, I _____² (live) in Budapest.

Greg   Budapest? What _____ you _____³ (do) there?

Lou   I _____⁴ (study) at the Business School for a semester. Anyway,
           one day I _____⁵ (go) down to the big record shop in the city centre
           to buy a CD.

Greg   A Michael Jackson CD?

Lou   No, George Michael actually, but that's not the point. So, I _____⁶
           (walk) to the store, when I _____⁷ (see) that there were lots of people
           around, and they _____⁸ (shout) Michael Jackson, Michael Jackson,
           Michael Jackson …

Greg   And _____⁹ (can) you see him?

Lou   No, but when I _____¹⁰ (get) to the store, there were security men
           outside the door and I _____¹¹ (cannot) go in. Michael Jackson
           _____¹² (be) inside!

Greg   What _____ he _____¹³ (do)?

Lou   He _____ just _____¹⁴ (look) around, _____¹⁵ (dance) a bit.
           So, I _____¹⁶ (wait) outside. Lots of people _____¹⁷ (wait). But
           when he _____¹⁸ (come) out, his security guards were all around
           him, and he just _____¹⁹ (disappear)!

Greg   So you _____ actually _____²⁰ (not meet) him then?

Lou   No, but I _____²¹ (stand) really close when he _____²² (come)
           out!

Greg   And what _____ he _____²³ (look) like?

Lou   Well, it was difficult to see his face, because he _____²⁴ (wear) a hat
           and sunglasses and a scarf.

Greg   So you didn't see much at all!

Vocabulary Staying in and going out

1 Complete the conversation with the correct form of the verbs below.

do (× 4)   get (× 5)   go (× 7)

Maria   So, what are you _____ [1] at the weekend?

Sara   I'm _____ [2] to a friend's house tonight, and then it's the usual – I've got to _____ [3] the housework, the washing, my homework, _____ [4] shopping, and I should _____ [5] to the gym.

Maria   Why don't you _____ [6] something different? How about _____ [7] to the cinema with me?

Sara   Thanks, but I've got so much to _____ [8]. Anyway, there's nothing I want to see.

Maria   A concert then?

Sara   Mmm, maybe, but don't we need to _____ [9] tickets in advance?

Maria   Maybe, and they're usually quite expensive. OK, what about _____ [10] out for a meal? There's a new restaurant I'd like to try.

Sara   Sounds nice, but I'm on a diet. I need to _____ [11] into my summer clothes.

Maria   OK, how about _____ [12] for a bike ride? That way we can _____ [13] some exercise and have fun. I need to _____ [14] fit too.

Sara   Sounds good. And then I don't have to _____ [15] to the gym. How about meeting at your place at nine on Saturday? I usually _____ [16] up early anyway.

Maria   OK, let's do that.

2 Which is the odd-one-out?

1	rugby	basketball	gymnastics	cricket
2	bat	club	racket	ball
3	skiing	badminton	hiking	sailing
4	office	pitch	court	field

Work skills Emails 2: Problems and solutions

1 Put these sentences in the correct order to make two emails.

1   I apologise for any inconvenience caused.

2   I'm afraid I won't be able to pick you up at the airport as planned, as I have to attend a meeting.

3   I am writing regarding your order no. 339482.

4   I'm sorry about the change of plan.

5   The remainder of your order will be delivered within 10 working days.

6   I'll see you in the office on Wednesday. Have a good flight!

7   I'm writing about your visit next week.

8   We hope to receive them in four weeks' time and will deliver them then.

9   Fortunately, my colleague Liz Rowsen will be able to meet you instead.

10   Unfortunately, items 44 and 93 are currently out of stock.

Functions Making suggestions

We use the following phrases to make and respond to suggestions.

Making suggestions

How about -ing?	How about having a party?
What about -ing?	What about going out for dinner?
Let's + verb	Let's look for a new venue.
Why don't we + verb	Why don't we reduce our prices?
We could + verb	We could ask Max if he knows anyone.
I suggest we + verb	I suggest we phone the supplier and complain.

Responding to suggestions

Yes, that's a great idea.
That's a good idea.
OK, let's do that.
Yes, that's a possibility.
I'm sorry, but …
Absolutely not.

1 Match the suggestions and responses.

1 Let's email all staff and ask them for their ideas.
2 What about offering a free gift?
3 I suggest we find a new supplier.
4 We could advertise online.
5 Why don't we invite a different speaker?
6 How about introducing a bonus system?

a That's a good idea. But who can we ask?
b No way. Nobody else offers the same quality.
c Good idea. What websites are you thinking of?
d I'm sorry, but I don't think we have the budget for that.
e OK. Let's do that. I'll send a group mail now.
f Yes, that's a possibility, but we have to think about the cost of the gifts.

2 Complete the suggestions using an appropriate prompt from below.

get / flowers   go / sailing   move / cheaper office
phone / taxi   searching / hotel / online   try / new seafood place

Example   **A** I think we should buy a present for Ruth.
            B Why don't we get her some flowers.

1 **A** Oh no, the bus drivers are on strike!
   B Let's _____ .
2 **A** We need to save money.
   B We could _____ .
3 **A** The hotel has cancelled the booking.
   B How _____?
4 **A** I think we should take Mr Medwar somewhere special for dinner.
   B What _____?
5 **A** We need to plan the team-building weekend.
   B I suggest we _____ .

10 What next?

Grammar *will*; Zero and 1st Conditional

INTRODUCTION

1 **Look at the pictures. How do you prefer to do the following?**

pay for something   learn something   buy books

2 **Read the statements about future trends. Do you agree?**
1 Most people will do their shopping online and shops will disappear.
2 Direct payment by smartphone will replace cash and credit cards.
3 No one will go to classes at college or university.
4 People will stop buying paper books.

3 ◉)) **10.1** **Listen to the first part of the radio programme 'Your Future'. Complete the sentences.**
1 I _____ most shops _____ disappear.
2 _____ shops disappear, it _____ very sad.
3 _____ more people will use this sort of system?
4 _____ there's a better, safer system, people _____ stop using cash.

4 ◉)) **10.2** **Listen to the second part of the programme. According to the presenters, are these statements true or false?**
1 One advantage of online study is the low cost.
2 Maya thinks people will get a good education if they learn online.
3 A lot of listeners think people will stop buying books.
4 If you lose an e-reader, you can reload your books on another one.

Focus

Read the examples and complete the grammar rules with *will* or *won't*.

Some shops will disappear but not all of them.
In the future, there won't be any cash or credit cards.
I think in the future, people will stop buying paper books.
I don't think clothes shops will disappear.
Do you think more people will use this sort of system?

We use _____ and _____ + infinitive to predict future situations.
We use *don't think* + subject + _____ to predict something that will not happen.

Zero and 1st Conditional

We use the Zero Conditional to talk about things that are generally true.
If you lose an e-reader, you lose all your books.

We use the 1st Conditional to talk about a possible future condition and its result.
If they only learn online, they won't really get a good education.
If shops disappear, it will be very sad.

Complete the rules with *will*, *infinitive*, or *Present Simple*.

We form the Zero Conditional with *if* + Present Simple for the condition and _____
for the result.
We form the 1st Conditional with *if* + Present Simple for the condition and _____ +
_____ for the result.

▶ For more details and practice, go to the Review section on page 122.

PRACTICE

5 **Work in pairs. Make questions using the prompts. Take turns to ask and answer.**

Example   A In the future, do you think children will study only online?
            B Yes, they will. / No, they won't. They'll study …

1   in the future / children / study only online?
2   a lot of high street shops / disappear / next ten years?
3   you / be famous / ten years' time?
4   by 2050 / most people in the world / speak English?
5   one day / computers / be smarter than humans?
6   most cars / be electric / 20 years' time?
7   people / use drugs / improve their memory / this century?
8   by 2030 / scientists / find life / other planets?
9   in the future / the world / warm up by more than five degrees?
10 people's average age / increase / 120 years?

6 **Work in pairs. Use the prompts to ask your partner about going abroad on business trips.**

Example   A If you travel by plane, do you talk to the person next to you?
            B Yes, I usually try to start a conversation.

1   travel by plane   talk to the person next to you?
2   stay at a hotel   ask for a quiet room?
3   go to a restaurant   tip the waiter?
4   take a taxi   show the driver a map?
5   have a meeting   get there on time?
6   talk to someone   try to speak their language?
7   visit someone's house   take a present?

7 Choose the correct form of the verb.

1 If electric cars become more common, pollution levels *go / will go* down.
2 If I cycle to work, it *will always rain / always rains*.
3 I *miss / will miss* the meeting if the train is late.
4 If I take the bus to work, it generally *takes / will take* twice as long as the train.
5 If you order this product in the next two hours, you *get / will get* it by Nov 13.
6 This year, the company *pays / will pay* staff a bonus if it reaches its sales targets.
7 If you place an order on Amazon, you *have / will have* 30 minutes to cancel it.
8 If I wash a pair of socks, I *will always lose / always lose* one sock.
9 Delivery *is / will be* free if you spend more than £50.
10 My Internet connection *is usually / will usually be* slower if I use it in the evening.

8 Read about the Info Ladies. How do Info Ladies help local people?

Info Ladies

In Bangladesh, Info Ladies ride bicycles door-to-door to connect villages by Internet. They carry laptops with them and villagers can use the laptops for either personal or business use. Only 5 million of 152 million people have Internet access in Bangladesh.

In many places, there are no doctors for miles and deaths from easily curable diseases are very common. Info Ladies are also trained to test blood pressure and blood sugar levels and can save lives.

They help in other ways too. 'I use her laptop to chat with my Facebook friends,' says a local woman. They talk to farmers about the correct use of fertilizer and insecticides. For 10 takas (12 cents), they help students fill in college application forms online.

The Info Ladies project director intends to enlist thousands more workers in the next few years with start-up funds from the country's central bank.

9 Match the people in the story with the quotes below. Complete the quotes using information from the story.

1 'If I want to chat with my friends on Facebook, _____.'
2 'If I have a problem on my farm, _____.'
3 'If I need help filling out my college application form, _____.'
4 'If I am sick, _____.'
5 'If we get money from the central bank, _____.'

TASK 10 What do you think about the Info Ladies? What other projects do you know like this? Here are some examples. Talk about the projects in groups.

Malaria No More   Traidcraft   WaterAid

Watch the video for more practice.

Vocabulary Gerunds and infinitives; future phrases

1 ◀)) **10.3** **Read the quotes from workers about their jobs. Choose the correct verb forms to complete the sentences. Listen and check your answers.**

1 **CEO**
   I feel very positive about next year. We aim *to expand / expanding* our business by 20 per cent. And I hope *to increase / increasing* the workforce by another 50 people.

2 **IT engineer**
   I need *to concentrate / concentrating* when I'm programming so I enjoy *to have / having* my own space. But I like *working / to work* with people so I prefer *to work / working* in an open-plan office. I can't imagine *to work / working* from home.

3 **Older employee**
   I'm planning *to work / working* here for another two years and then retire. I'm looking forward to *have / having* more free time and travelling more.

4 **Entrepreneur**
   The number of permanent staff here is likely *falling / to fall*. So I've decided *to leave / leaving* the company and start my own business.

5 **HR manager**
   We expect *having / to have* more female staff in management positions. I would also like *to recruit / recruiting* more female graduates to work in the engineering department.

6 **Sales administrator**
   I don't mind *to work / working* in this department but I've been here for ten years. I really want *to have / having* a change so I've applied for a job in customer care.

2 **Work in pairs. How do you feel about your job? Take turns to ask and answer the questions. Use some of the phrases in 1.**

Example   I aim to finish my sales report by the end of the week.

1 What are your aims for this week / month / year?
2 What plans do you have for your career?
3 What do you hope to do this year at work / at home?
4 What recent decisions have you made?
5 What do you like / love / not mind doing at work?

3 Read the predictions and place them on the probability scale.

A The sun will rise tomorrow morning.

B I will finish work by six o'clock tomorrow evening.

C It will rain this weekend.

D I will change jobs this year.

E A cure for malaria will be found.

F The global population will reach seven billion by 2030.

G Almost all Brazil's rainforest will disappear by 2040.

0% ————————————————————————————————————→ 100%

definitely won't   probably won't   might / might not   probably will   definitely will

4 Work in pairs. Take turns to ask about the predictions in **3**.

Example Do you think the sun will rise tomorrow morning?
Yes, it definitely will.

5 Think of some more predictions using the prompts. Take turns to ask your partner questions using 'Do you think …?'

be promoted

get a pay rise

go abroad on holiday tomorrow / this week / month / year

buy a 3-D television

download some music

eat out

6 ◉)) 10.4 In which sentences do we use the short form of *will* and *will not*?

1 Do you think it will be sunny tomorrow?

2 I probably will not go to work tomorrow.

3 Will you change jobs this year? I probably will.

4 You will definitely get a promotion soon.

5 Do you think the company will survive?

6 He definitely will not be at the meeting.

Listen and check your answers.

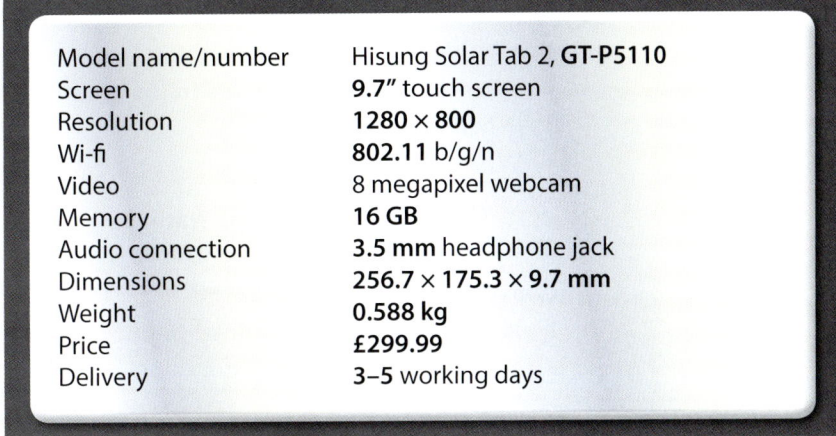

Work skills Telephoning 3: Checking details

1 Read the information about a tablet. How do you say the information in bold?

Model name/number	Hisung Solar Tab 2, **GT-P5110**
Screen	**9.7"** touch screen
Resolution	**1280 × 800**
Wi-fi	**802.11** b/g/n
Video	8 megapixel webcam
Memory	**16 GB**
Audio connection	**3.5 mm** headphone jack
Dimensions	**256.7 × 175.3 × 9.7 mm**
Weight	**0.588 kg**
Price	**£299.99**
Delivery	**3–5** working days

2 ●)) 10.5 Listen and check how the speakers say the information in **1**.

3 ●)) 10.5 Listen again and complete the information about the second tablet described in the conversation.

Model name/number	Hisung Solar Tab 3, _____
Screen	_____ touch screen
Resolution	_____
Wi-fi	_____ b/g/n
Video	8 megapixel webcam
Memory	_____ , _____
Audio connection	_____ headphone jack
Dimensions	_____ _____ _____
Weight	_____
Price	_____ , _____
Delivery	_____ working days

4 Complete the sentences from the conversation.

1 **A** It's got a 10.2 inch screen.
  B _____ , _____ ?
  A Correct.
2 **B** _____ ?
  A GT-P6110.
  B _____ ?
  A That's right.
3 **A** And it also has the same standard Wi-fi setting.
  B _____ a 1280 × 800 resolution and 802.11 Wi-fi.
  A Correct.
4 **A** The 32 GB model is £350.
  B _____ , _____ the second price.
  A £350.
  B £350, _____ £315.
  A That's right.

5 Work in pairs.

Student A Go to page 131.
Student B Go to page 133.

Functions Asking for information with indirect questions; farewells

INTRODUCTION

1 ◉)) **10.6 Paul Lee is talking to someone at reception in his hotel. Listen and answer the questions.**

1 Where does Paul want to go in the evening? Why?
2 Where is the restaurant?
3 What information does Paul need for the next day?

2 ◉)) **10.7 Paul, Emma, Ken, and Nathalie go to the farewell dinner with their friends. Listen to three conversations and answer the questions.**

Conversation 1

1 Will Paul come back to Brazil soon?
2 When might Fabio go to London?

Conversation 2

3 Where is Ken going to go?
4 Why does Ken have to leave?

Conversation 3

5 Where are Emma and Nathalie going to go?
6 What is Emma going to do?

3 ◉)) **10.7 Listen again and tick ✓ the phrases you hear.**

1 Thank you very much for your hospitality.
2 See you back in London.
3 Have a safe flight.
4 I'll be in touch.
5 Thanks for all your hard work.
6 I hope we can work together again sometime.
7 It was a lovely evening.
8 I really must be going.

PRACTICE   **4**   **Work in pairs. Read the situations. Have two conversations and practise the expressions in 3.**

1 You have just finished working on a project together. It was very successful. One of you is going back to Italy and the other is returning to the UK. One of you has to catch a plane.

2 You are business partners and have just finished lunch. One of you paid for the meal. One of you has to leave to get to a meeting. You hope to meet again in the near future.

5   **Change the direct questions into indirect questions.**

Example   Do you know what the capital of Brazil is?

1 What is the capital of Brazil?
2 When is Carnival in Brazil?
3 What is the largest city in Brazil?
4 Does the Brazilian football team wear a yellow jersey?
5 What is the name of Brazil's most famous waterfall?
6 Do Brazilians speak Spanish or Portuguese?
7 Who is the most famous Brazilian racing driver?
8 Does Brazil produce coffee?
9 Is the population of Brazil more than 200 million?
10 What is the most famous landmark in Rio de Janeiro?

6   **Work in pairs. Take turns to ask and answer the questions in 5. Use indirect questions.**

TASK   **7**   **Work in pairs. Ask for and give information about journeys. Use indirect questions where possible.**

Student A

You are at the airport, waiting for your flight from Rio de Janeiro to Hong Kong. The information board says your flight is delayed. Ask at the information desk for details.

- Reason for delay?
- Time of next flight?
- Gate?
- Direct flight?
- Upgrade?
- Your bags?

Student B

Go to page 131.

Review

Grammar *will*; Zero and 1st Conditional

will

Form

We use *will / will not (won't)* + the infinitive form of the verb.
Examples Prices will / won't rise next year.
Will prices rise next year?   Yes, they will. / No, they won't.

We put *think* before the subject and *will*.
Examples I think tablets will become cheaper.
Do you think fewer people will fly in the future?
Yes, I think so. / No, I don't think so.

We use *I don't think* to make a negative prediction (not *I think* + *won't*).
Example   I don't think clothes shops will disappear.

Use

We use *will* to talk about the future and make predictions. We add *I think* to show that we are talking about our personal opinion.

Zero Conditional

Form

The Zero Conditional form is *if* + Present Simple, Present Simple.
Examples If I'm too tired, I don't work effectively.
If a product is faulty, we replace it.
What do you do if a product is faulty?

Use

We use the Zero Conditional to talk about a condition and a usual result.
For example, when the condition is 'I am too tired' the result is 'I don't work effectively'. In this case, we are talking about something that is generally true (not a future condition).

1st Conditional

Form

The 1st Conditional form is *if* + Present Simple, *will* + infinitive.
Examples If he takes a taxi, he'll arrive on time.
If we win the contract, we'll go out and celebrate.
What will you do if you win the contract?

Note that we usually use the contracted forms of subject + *will*: *I'll, She'll, It'll*.

Use

We use the 1st Conditional to talk about what will happen if a certain action / state occurs in the future.

1 Insert *if* and a comma (if necessary) in the appropriate place in the sentences.

Example   If you buy one, you get one free.

1 You buy two you get one free.
2 I usually go for Chinese or Indian I eat out.
3 We have to work overtime we get paid for it.
4 House prices usually fall interest rates rise.
5 The company hires new staff they give them training.
6 My boss doesn't mind I'm a bit late for work.

2 Match the phrases below. Write complete conditional sentences.

Example   1c If sea levels rise, many islands will disappear.

1	sea levels rise	a	give you a discount
2	I find the file	b	have better job opportunities
3	you pay cash	c	many islands disappear
4	more people work at home	d	email it to you
5	the birth rate continues to fall	e	have to borrow money
6	he finishes university	f	not be enough workers
7	we want to expand	g	be less traffic on the roads

_____

_____

_____

_____

_____

_____

Vocabulary Gerunds and infinitives; future phrases

1 Put the words in the box in the correct group.

aim   decide   don't mind   enjoy   expect   hope   is likely
like   look forward to   need   plan   prefer   want   would like

followed by *-ing*	followed by *to* + verb	followed by *–ing* or *to* + verb
	aim	

2 Complete the sentences with the words below using *-ing* or *to* + verb.

get up   have   increase   look for   meet   move   send   speak   work

1 I have a lot of problems with my boss, so I've decided _____ a new job.
2 I'm looking forward to _____ you next week.
3 We hope _____ to a bigger office next year.
4 I can work the early shift if you like. I don't mind _____ early.
5 Alicia chose a career in teaching because she enjoys _____ with children.
6 I'd like _____ more responsibility, so I'm going to talk to my boss about promotion possibilities.
7 Production costs are likely _____ .
8 Our staff are expected _____ good English, so we plan _____ some of them on an intensive course.

3 Rewrite the sentences to give the opposite meaning.

Example   It'll probably rain tomorrow.
              It probably won't rain tomorrow.

1 I think I'll be able to retire when I'm 60.
2 We definitely won't use cash in the future.
3 They probably won't give us a bonus.
4 Sales of electric cars are likely to rise.
5 He might come to the workshop.
6 She doesn't think she'll be invited to the conference.
7 It'll probably snow at the weekend.
8 People will definitely work less in the future.

Work skills Telephoning 3: Checking details

1 Match the figures to how they are said.

1 3.5 kg   a three to five
2 3.5 days   b three point five
3 3–5 days   c three and a half
4 3.5" screen   d thirty-five fifty
5 $35.50   e three point five inch

2 Put the words in the correct order.

1 I / the dates / sorry / catch / didn't
2 in / I'm / conference facilities / your / interested
3 right / that's
4 can / how / you / help / I
5 113 / sorry / that / 130? / or / was
6 that / sorry / was / small meeting rooms? / four

3 Complete the conversation between a reservations manager (R) and a
customer (C). Use the phrases from **2**.

R Good morning, Corvinus Hotel.
C Hello, Sabrina Lee here, from ITNG. _____ [1].
R Yes, _____ [2]?
C The first question is, how many rooms do you have?
R We've got one large conference room, one workshop room, and four small
   meeting rooms.
C _____ [3]?
R _____ [4]. How many participants are you planning for?
C It's going to be quite big. About 130.
R _____ [5]?
C 130. One three oh. Is the conference room big enough?
R Yes, it seats 150, so that's no problem. And what dates were you thinking of?
C 13th to 15th February, from 9 a.m. to 6 p.m. Are those dates free?
R _____ [6].
C February 13th to 15th. Is that OK?
R Yes, those dates are fine at the moment.
C Great. Could you send me a quote? My email address is …

Functions Asking for information; farewells

Indirect questions

We form indirect questions with *Do you know / Could you tell me / I'd like to know* + question word + statement word order (subject +verb).

Examples Do you know where the station is?
Could you tell me why the plane is delayed?

For yes/no questions we use *if* in the place of a question word.

Examples Do you know if Mona is coming to the meeting?
I'd like to know if I can pay online.

Thanking

Thanks.

Thank you very much for your hospitality / all your hard work / the lovely dinner.

Farewells

I really must be going.

Have a safe flight.

Take care.

I'll be in touch.

I hope we can work together again sometime / meet again sometime.

1 **Change these indirect questions into direct questions.**

1 Could you tell me what time the bank opens, please?
2 Do you know if there's a cash point near here?
3 Could you tell me what your email address is?
4 Do you know how I can get to the airport?

2 **Complete the questions for the answers.**

Example Could you tell me … (post office)
Could you tell me where the post office is?
Yes, it's on the main square, next to the department store.

1 Do you know _____? (the meeting)
   Yes, it starts at 9.30 a.m.
2 Could you tell me _____? (Natasha's office)
   Yes, it's on the second floor, at the end of the corridor.
3 Could you tell me _____? (swimming pool)
   Yes, there's a nice one in the hotel spa.
4 Do you know _____? (Max / went home early)
   I think he had a headache.
5 Could you tell me _____? (a double room)
   Yes, it costs €200 a night, including breakfast.
6 Do you know _____? (Gloria / sent the price list)
   Yes, I think she emailed it last night.

3 **Match the phrases in the box with the sentence starters.**

a lovely evening	all your hard work	back at the office	be in touch
call you soon	good journey	have to go now	must be going
safe flight	soon	we can meet again soon	
we work together again sometime		your kind hospitality	

I really	Thanks for	I hope	Have a	I'll	See you

Task and activity notes

1 Grammar p.8

How hard does your partner work?
Add four questions to the list on the left. Then ask your partner the ten questions.
Make a note of the answers in the appropriate boxes on the right.

Do you ...	never	rarely	sometimes	often	usually	always
take work home?						
work more than 40 hours a week?						
work at weekends?						
take a lunch break?						
take all your annual holiday?						
spend evenings with friends or family?						

1 Vocabulary p.10

Student B

	Company name	Nationality	Headquarters	Type of company	Start	Revenue / Employees
1	Credit Suisse	Swiss	Zurich	financial services	1856	25.43 billion Swiss Francs / 49,700
2	EMI					
3	Amazon	USA	Seattle	online retailer	1994	US$ 48.07 billion / 69,000
4	Louis Vuitton					
5	Bayer	German	Leverkusen	pharmaceutical	1863	€36.53 billion / 111,800
6	K-Line					

2   Grammar p.20

Student B

Find and ask about these people in the picture: Paul, Lucy, Graham, Helen.

Examples   What does Paul do?
                 Is he sitting at his desk?
                 Is he wearing a grey suit?

Help Student A find these people:

Kenichi	General Manager
Mari	Customer Service Manager
Dave	Sales rep
Paula	Designer

2   Functions p.25

Student A

You are free on Tuesday morning, Thursday afternoon, and Friday morning.
You are busy the rest of the week.

3 Grammar p.32

Student B

Prepare questions for 1–3.

Example   What did he do in Las Vegas?

Read your notes 4–6 on three places Dan Seddiqui visited and prepare some sentences and include some details.

Example   He worked as a studio technician in Tennessee.

	Place	Job	Detail
1	Las Vegas, Nevada		
2	North Carolina		
3	Oregon		
4	Tennessee	Studio technician	He worked for a recording studio in Nashville that is famous for country music. Famous artists recorded there including Elvis Presley and Johnny Cash.
5	Orlando, Florida	Park entertainer	He worked for the film company Universal Studios in Orlando. He dressed up as an Egyptian king.
6	Chicago, Illinois	Ticket seller	He worked for Metra, the Northeast Illinois commuter rail system. He announced track numbers, directed lost customers, and sold train tickets.

4 Grammar p.43

Student A

Put the verbs in brackets into the appropriate form.

Tell Student B about the brand name below and ask them to guess what the current name is.

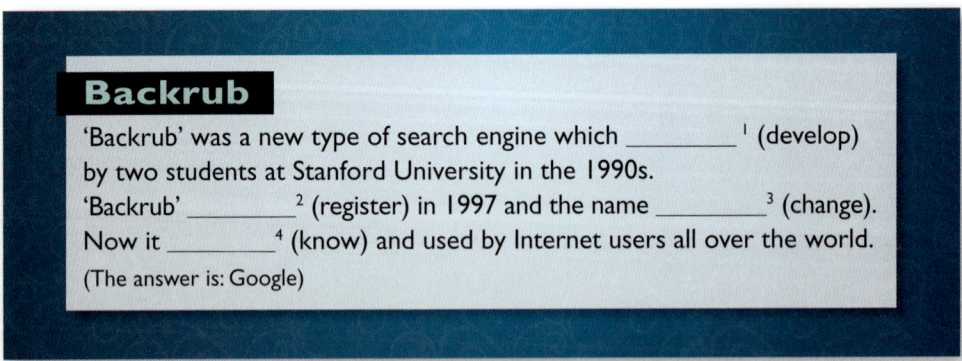

Backrub

'Backrub' was a new type of search engine which _____ [1] (develop) by two students at Stanford University in the 1990s.
'Backrub' _____ [2] (register) in 1997 and the name _____ [3] (change). Now it _____ [4] (know) and used by Internet users all over the world.
(The answer is: Google)

4 Grammar p.44

Student A

The answers to your quiz are: saxophone, denim, Nokia, Reebok.

6 Grammar p.68

Student B

		Zurich	Dubai	Shanghai
1	Distance from airport to city centre by taxi		12 kilometres	48 kilometres
2	A one-room apartment in city centre to rent	$1,900		$725
3	Pay (hourly rate)		$41	$17
4	Shopping mall	Einkaufszentrum Glatt 43,000 m²		Super Brand Mall 250,000 m²
5	Internet speed		4 mbps (normal)	Less than 1 mbps
6	Five-star hotels	10	74	

7 Grammar p.80

Student A

Sony Corporation

- Masaru Ibuka and Akio Morita started Tokyo Telecommunications Engineering Corporation in 1946.

- In 1958, the company was named Sony.

- Betamax video tape was released in 1975.

- In 1979, Sony introduced the Sony Walkman.

- PlayStation has been one of their most popular products since the early 1990s.

- Sony bought CBS Records in 1988 and Columbia Pictures in 1989.

- In 2005, Howard Stringer became CEO (Chief Executive Officer), the first foreigner to run a major Japanese electronics firm.

- Since 1976, Sony has held an annual Environmental Conference to discuss environmental issues.

Prepare questions to ask Student B about Philips using the prompts. Use the Past Simple or Present Perfect and the verbs in brackets.

1 Who _____ the Philips company? (start)
2 What _____ they _____ since the 1930s? (produce)
3 What _____ they _____ in 1972? (introduce)
4 _____ Philips ever _____ a non-Dutch CEO? (have)
5 What _____ Philips _____ since 2005? (do)
6 What improvements _____ Philips _____ recently? How? (make)

7 Vocabulary p.82

Student B
Describe the graph on the left below. Use the empty graph on the right to draw Student A's graph.

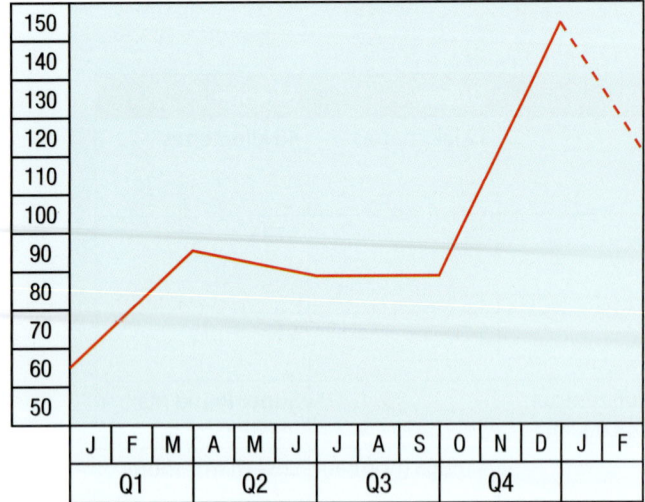

9 Grammar p.104

Student B
Answer your partner's questions about Flickr. Ask similar questions about your partner's company, Twitter.

FLICKR™

Flickr was launched in February 2004 by Ludicorp, a Vancouver-based company. Ludicorp was an online game company started by Stewart Butterfield and Caterina Fake. Stewart and Caterina met in California where Caterina was working for Netscape, another online company. They moved to Canada and started Ludicorp in 2002. They were developing a new game when they ran out of money. One of the team had the idea of sharing photos online. They gave up the game project and developed a website that allowed people to share photos instead. The website was called Flickr.

Stewart and Caterina sold Flickr to Yahoo for an estimated $35 million in 2005.

10 Work skills p.119

Student A

Exchange information with Student B about a new tablet. Use the checking phrases from **4** if necessary.

Model name/number	Asas, PT-G5110
Screen	8.6" touch screen
Resolution	1280 × 800
Wi-fi	802.11 b/g/n
Video	10 megapixel webcam
Memory	32 GB
Audio connection	_____
Dimensions	_____
Weight	_____
Price	_____
Delivery	_____

10 Functions p.121

Student B

You work at the information desk at an airport. Answer Student A's questions using the information.

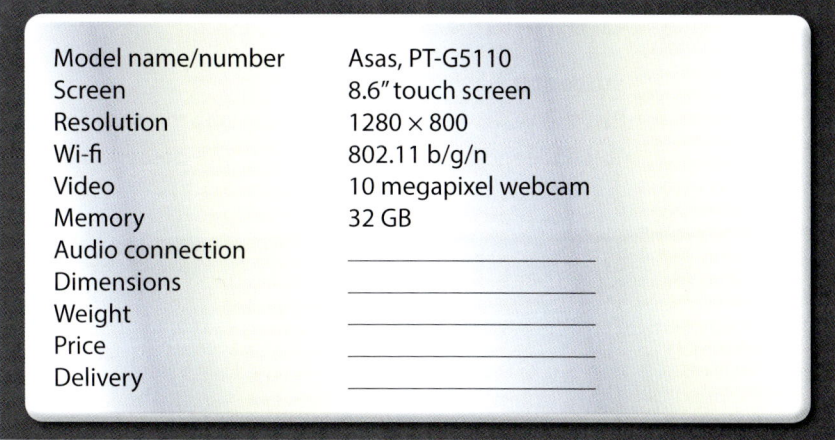

- flight delayed because of bad weather
- next flight 19.45
- gate 14
- fly to São Paolo, then Doha, Qatar and on to Hong Kong
- no upgrades
- automatic bag transfer

3 Grammar p.32

Student A

Read your notes 1–3 on three places Dan Seddiqui visited and prepare some sentences and include some details.

Example He worked as a wedding coordinator in Las Vegas.

Prepare questions for 4–6.

Example What did he do in Tennessee?

	Place	Job	Detail
1	Las Vegas, Nevada	Wedding coordinator	He married one couple. He was very nervous and nearly forgot their names.
2	North Carolina	Modelling	They took 3,000 photos of him. It took 7 ½ hours.
3	Oregon	Logging	Logging was a very dangerous job. Most loggers get up at 2.30 a.m.
4	Tennessee		
5	Orlando, Florida		
6	Chicago, Illinois		

2 Functions p.25

Student B

You are free all day Monday, Tuesday afternoon, all day Thursday, and Friday afternoon. You are busy the rest of the week.

4 Grammar p.43

Student B

Put the verbs in brackets into the appropriate form.

Tell Student A about the brand name below and ask them to guess what the current name is.

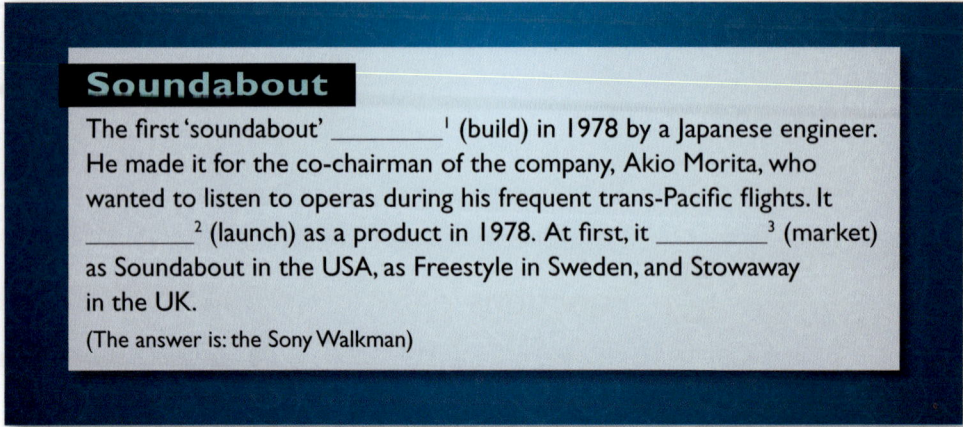

Soundabout

The first 'soundabout' _____ [1] (build) in 1978 by a Japanese engineer. He made it for the co-chairman of the company, Akio Morita, who wanted to listen to operas during his frequent trans-Pacific flights. It _____ [2] (launch) as a product in 1978. At first, it _____ [3] (market) as Soundabout in the USA, as Freestyle in Sweden, and Stowaway in the UK.

(The answer is: the Sony Walkman)

4 Grammar p.44

Student B

Here are the clues for your quiz. Read them to your partner and ask them to guess what the answer is.

1 It is the name of a tower. It was built in Paris. It was designed by Gustave Eiffel.
2 It is the name of a character in Moby Dick. It was used for the name of a coffee shop chain.
3 It is the name of a German car manufacturer. The initials stand for *Bavarian Motor Works*.
4 It is the name of a motorbike brand. The company is based in the USA. It was started by William Harley and Arthur Davidson.

The answers are: Eiffel Tower, Starbucks, BMW, Harley Davidson.

Student B

Philips

■ Gerard and Frederik Philips started the company in the Netherlands in 1891.

■ Philips have produced radios since the 1930s.

■ In the late 1950s, Philips started their own subsidiary record label, Fontana Records.

■ Philips introduced the Compact Audio Cassette tape in 1963.

■ Philips introduced the first combination portable radio and cassette recorder.

■ In 1972, Philips launched the world's first home video cassette recorder.

■ Philips have always had a Dutch CEO (Chief Executive Officer).

■ Since 2005 Philips have sold off or scaled down parts of the company.

■ Philips have recently made improvements in their impact on the environment by reducing the amount of waste they produce.

Prepare questions to ask Student A about Sony using these prompts. Use the Past Simple or Present Perfect and the verbs in brackets.

1   When _____ Sony _____? Who _____ the company? (start, start)
2   What _____ they _____ in 1975? (release)
3   What _____ _____ one of their most successful products? (be)
4   Which companies _____ Sony _____ in the 1980s? (buy)
5   In what way _____ Howard Stringer unusual? (be)
6   What sort of conference _____ Sony _____ every year since 1976? Why? (hold)

Student B

Exchange information with Student A about a new tablet. Use the checking phrases from 4 if necessary.

Model name/number	_____
Screen	_____
Resolution	_____
Wi-fi	_____
Video	_____
Memory	_____
Audio connection	3.5 mm headphone jack
Dimensions	246.7 × 165.3 × 8.7 mm
Weight	0.45 kg
Price	£349.99
Delivery	2–3 working days

Scripts

1

1.1 ◉))

L=Laura, K=Ken, P=Paul

L Hi, Ken.
K Hi, Laura. It's been ages.
L It must be six months.
K Yeah. How are you?
L I'm very well, thanks. Really busy. We're working on this new sports range.
K Yeah, it's looking great.
L Thanks.
K Do you still work in Rome?
L Yes, I do, but I'm in a new studio. It's in a good location so we're really pleased.
K Great.
L How about you? How are things?
K Good. I don't work for the sports magazine any more. I work freelance now, so I'm really enjoying my work.
L That's great. Do you live in the same place in New York?
K Yes, I do. I still live in Brooklyn.
L Nice area.
K Yeah. I really like it.

P Hi, sorry to keep you waiting.
L Not at all. It's nice to see you again.
P Nice to see you, too, Laura. And you must be Ken.
K That's right. Ken Martin. Nice to meet you.
P Nice to meet you, too, Ken. I'm Paul Lee. Do you two know each other?
L Yes, we are friends from way back.
P That's great. OK. Shall we get a coffee and then we can meet Emma?
L OK.
K OK.

1.2 ◉))

P=Paul, L=Laura, K=Ken, E=Emma

P OK, so I'd like to introduce Emma King. Emma, this is Ken Martin, our photographer for this project.
E Hi, Ken. Pleased to meet you.
K Very good to meet you, Emma.
P And Laura, the designer of our new sports range.
E Nice to meet you, Laura.
L Nice to meet you, too, Emma. I'm looking forward to working with you.
E Me, too.
P Emma is in the cycling team for the next Olympics, and she works part-time for a model agency.
K Really? That's amazing. Which event do you do?
E I'm in the road race team.
L Right. How often do you go training?
E I usually go cycling before breakfast every day.
K Wow, that's tough. Where do you cycle?
E I live near the river so I usually cycle there. Then I go to the sports centre. How about you?

K I've got a bike but I never ride it. I'm always too busy, I'm afraid. How about you, Laura?
L I've got a bike too, but it doesn't go very fast.
P And Rome isn't a safe place to ride a bike, I guess.
L You're right. I always take the bus to work.
P Me, too. Hong Kong is a really busy place. Well, if we're all ready, shall we get started?

1.3 ◉))

A Can you tell me a little bit about the company you work for?
B Sure. I work for Panasonic. Its full name is the Panasonic Corporation.
A OK. And is that a Japanese company?
B That's right. It started in Osaka. The founder was Konosuke Matsushita and Matsushita was the original name of the company. In fact, the company has used quite a few different brand names over the years.
A I see. Matsushita, Panasonic, …
B National and Technics are two others. But now they just use Panasonic.
A And is the company still based in Osaka?
B Yes, the headquarters are still based there and they also have a USA division which has headquarters in New Jersey.
A Right. And what type of company is Panasonic?
B Well, it produces a wide variety of products but its main area is electronic goods: televisions, cameras, mobile phones, and so on.
A And how old is the company?
B It's around 100 years old. It started in 1918 when it first made lamp sockets in a tiny two-room house. There were just three employees, Matsushita, his wife, and his brother-in-law.
A And now, how many are there?
B There are around 330,000 workers altogether.
A So it's a big company.
B Yes, it's one of the largest Japanese electronics producers.
A And what is the annual revenue?
B It's around 7.8 trillion yen. Or around 983 million dollars.
A And how about competitors? Are they mainly Japanese or are there foreign companies competing with Panasonic?
B Probably the biggest competitor is Samsung, the Korean electronics giant. They have grown considerably over the last few years and are taking some of Panasonic's market share.
A And what would you say is Panasonic's strongest area of business?
B Well, they are the fifth biggest producer of television sets and they have a very good record for reliability and quality.

1.4 ◉))

1 A What nationality is the company?
   B It's American.
   A Where are the headquarters?
   B They're in Detroit.
   A What type of company is it?
   B It's a car manufacturer.
   A What does it produce?
   B It produces a range of cars including Buicks and Cadillacs.
   A How old is it?
   B It's around 110 years old.
   A How many people does it employ?
   B It employs 202,000 people.
   A What's the annual revenue of the company?
   B Its annual revenue is 150.28 billion US dollars.
   A Who is the main competitor?
   B Their main competitor is probably Toyota.

2 A What nationality is the company?
   B It's a Spanish company.
   A Where are the headquarters?
   B They're in Madrid.
   A What type of company is it?
   B It's a department store chain.
   A How old is it?
   B It's over 70 years old.
   A How many people does it employ?
   B It employs around 90,000 people.
   A What's the annual revenue of the company?
   B Its annual revenue is 15.9 billion euros.
   A Who is the main competitor?
   B There are no serious competitors in the Spanish market.

3 A What nationality is the company?
   B It's a South Korean company.
   A Where are the headquarters?
   B They're in Seoul.
   A What type of company is it?
   B It's an electronic goods producer.
   A How old is it?
   B It's over 60 years old.
   A How many people does it employ?
   B It employs around 210,000 people. About 90,000 of these work overseas.
   A What's the annual revenue of the company?
   B Its annual revenue is 89.5 billion won.
   A Who is the main competitor?
   B In Korea, their main competitor is Samsung. Globally, probably Sony or Panasonic in Japan.

4 A What nationality is the company?
   B It's Italian.
   A Where are the headquarters?
   B They're in Turin.
   A What type of company is it?
   B It's a coffee producer.
   A How old is it?
   B It's around 120 years old.
   A How many people does it employ?

B It employs around 1,700 people.
A What's the annual revenue of the company?
B Its annual revenue is 930 million euros.
A Who is their main competitor?
B Their main competitors are probably Illy and Segafredo.

1.5 ●))
1 A What do you do, Junko?
   B I'm a sales assistant.
   A Who do you work for?
   B I work for a department store.
   A Which department are you in?
   B I work in the food department.
   A Can you tell me what you do in your job?
   B I'm responsible for the fresh food section. This involves making sure that all the fruit and vegetables look fresh and tasty.
   A Do you work full-time?
   B No, I don't. I work part-time, usually three days a week.
   A How many hours do you work a week?
   B I work about 20 hours.
   A Who do you work with?
   B I work with a team of about ten people.
   A Where do you usually work?
   B I usually work in the store serving customers.
   A Do you travel much for work?
   B No, I don't.
2 A What do you do, Linda?
   B I'm an editor.
   A Who do you work for?
   B I work for a publishing company.
   A Which department are you in?
   B I work in the fiction department.
   A Can you tell me what you do in your job?
   B I'm responsible for publishing novels. This involves working with authors and editing their work.
   A Do you work full-time?
   B Yes, I do.
   A How many hours do you work a week?
   B I work between 20 and 40 hours.
   A Who do you work with?
   B I work with my authors and two other editors.
   A Where do you usually work?
   B I usually work at home.
   A Do you travel much for work?
   B Sometimes I go to the company for meetings.
3 A What do you do, Karl?
   B I'm a systems engineer.
   A Who do you work for?
   B I work for a company called BEA Systems.
   A Which department are you in?
   B I work in the customer service department.
   A Can you tell me what you do in your job?
   B I'm responsible for our customers' computer systems.

A Do you work full-time?
B Yes, I do.
A How many hours do you work a week?
B I work about 45 hours a week.
A Who do you work with?
B I work with a small team of systems engineers.
A Where do you usually work?
B I usually work in the office.
A Do you travel much for work?
B Yes, I do. I visit customers pretty much every day.

1.6 ●))
1 K=Ken, N=Nathalie
   K Hi. Can I introduce myself? I'm Ken Martin.
   N Oh, hello Ken. I'm Nathalie Bourne, the art director for the new catalogue.
   K And I'm the photographer.
   N Nice to meet you.
   K Nice to meet you too, Nathalie.
2 P=Paul, C=Charles, L=Laura
   P Laura, let me introduce you to Charles Ward. Charles is our sales director. Charles, this is Laura Mancini. She is the designer for our new sports range.
   C Very pleased to meet you, Laura. I love the new sportswear design.
   L Thank you. It's very nice to meet you too, Charles.
3 K=Ken, J=Jason
   K Hey, Jason.
   J Oh, hi Ken. Great to see you.
   K Good to see you, too. How are things?
   J Pretty good. How are you?
   K Busy.
   J Me, too.
   K Did you get here OK?
   J Yes, thanks.
4 N=Nathalie, E=Emma, S=Scott
   N Oh, look. Here's Emma. Hi, Emma.
   E Hi, Nathalie. It's nice to see you again. How are you?
   N Very well, thanks. How are things?
   E Great. Sorry I'm late.
   N That's fine. You're just in time. Do you know Scott?
   E Yes, we've met before. It's good to meet you again.
   S Good to see you. How have you been?
   E Really good, thanks.
5 J=Jason, E=Emma
   J Hi, you must be Emma.
   E That's right.
   J I'm Jason. I'm an old friend of Ken's.
   E Oh, right. Pleased to meet you, Jason. How do you know Ken?
   J We're old school friends.
   E OK. Do you live in New York?
   J Yes, I do. How about you?
   E I live in London. Do you work for Unisports?
   J Yeah. I work in the marketing department.
   E Do you know Paul Lee?

J Yes, I do. We work in different branches, but we often meet here in London for meetings and projects like this one.
E Do you travel a lot?
J Yes, I travel from New York to London almost every month. And you?
E I sometimes travel for cycling events.
J So you're a cyclist?
E Yes, that's right.

2

2.1 ●))
C=Craig, P=Petra
C Hi, Petra. How's it going?
P I'm very busy at the moment. I've got a group coming for the festival in Siena next month and I'm trying to find them a hotel.
C Have you tried the Grand Hotel Continental?
P I'm just emailing them now. I hope they've got something.
C How many are there in the group?
P There are ten altogether, but I'm not sure about two guests. So I'm trying to contact them as well.
C Sounds like you've got a busy morning.
P How about you? What are you doing?
C I'm just booking a tour to St Petersburg for a group of students. It's a big group, about 50, so I'm looking for another tour guide.
P If you need any help, I know a contact who might be able to find you one.
C Really?
P Yeah, sure. I'll call him when I finish this email.
C I'd really appreciate that. Thanks.
P No problem.

2.2 ●))
1 Do you know when it starts?
   No, I'm afraid I don't.
2 Does the festival start soon?
   No, it doesn't. It starts next month.
3 Do you often go to Siena? Yes, I do.
4 What sports does he do?
   He does karate and judo.

2.3 ●))
architect
chef
electrician
hotel receptionist
journalist
optician
photographer
plumber
shop assistant
taxi driver

2.4 ●))
1 I help customers choose what they want. I help them with fittings and suggest the style and colour to suit them. I also make sure we have enough stock and make orders when stock is low.
2 I work in a restaurant. I do a variety of things. I prepare the dishes, I train the

junior staff, and I make sure the kitchen is clean and organized.

3 I'm self-employed. Everything I need is in my van and most of my customers are local. I fit bathrooms and kitchens, repair damaged pipes, and check heating systems.

4 I am a partner in a small business. I mainly design houses and apartments. This means talking to clients, drawing up plans, and managing the building of the house.

5 There are two parts to my job. Going out and getting information for a story, doing research. And then writing up the story for a newspaper or magazine article.

6 I work freelance and my main area of interest is travel. I travel around the world taking photos of interesting and unusual places and people. I sell my work online or directly to publishers.

7 I work in the centre of New York. Most of my customers are business people working on Wall Street or tourists who want to see the sights. Driving in New York is a dangerous business so I don't have much chance to talk to the passengers.

8 I work on the front desk mainly, so I help guests check in, tell them about the hotel and the services we provide. I also help guests check out, deal with payment, and help them with transport.

9 I am a lineman, which means I check and repair electricity cables. I also install and maintain telephone, telegraph, cable TV, and fibre optic lines.

10 I work for a local eye clinic. I look after patients who need to correct their vision. So I fit and provide glasses and contact lenses and, in some cases, refer patients to a doctor.

2.5 ●))

P=Paul, M=Maria

P Hello.

M Hi, Paul. It's Maria.

P Oh, hi.

M I'm just calling to give you a few more details about your trip.

P OK.

M I missed a few things on the schedule.

P Right.

M The first one is the meeting time at the check-in counter at Heathrow. You're all meeting at ten forty-five. That gives you plenty of time before the flight.

P Ten forty-five?

M That's right. The flight leaves at quarter past one. And then at the other end, you get in at about nine in the evening.

P OK, I've got that.

M The airport's about twenty kilometres from the centre of Rio, so it takes about thirty minutes depending on the traffic. Get a taxi, a blue one.

P Fine. So we should be at the hotel by about ten local time.

M That's right. It's pretty late so get some lunch at Heathrow airport.

P OK. Good point.

M And then on Thursday, everyone leaves the hotel at nine thirty. Emma and Nathalie are going to bring the clothes, and Ken's going to bring his camera equipment. Can you bring the bike? Emma's going to model some cycling clothes.

P Sure. Will it be at the hotel?

M Yes, the local bicycle shop are delivering it on Wednesday. Then the photo shoot starts at eleven, and there's a break at one o'clock for lunch. Are you meeting Fabio Pérez for lunch?

P Oh, yes. Thanks for reminding me. I'll give him a call and check.

M Right. Then everyone comes back to the hotel at five thirty and you're all having dinner at the hotel with the manager of a big sportswear chain.

P OK. Great.

M And that's about it. Have a great flight.

P Thanks, Maria.

2.6 ●))

P=Paul Lee, F=Fabio Pérez

F Fabio Pérez.

P Fabio, Hi. It's Paul Lee.

F Paul, hi. Good to hear from you. Are you in Brazil yet?

P No, I'm flying tomorrow.

F Good. Are you ready for a bit of Brazilian culture?

P Yes, I'm really looking forward to it.

F I'll make sure you get to see all the best places.

P Thanks. Actually, I'm just calling to check. Are you free for lunch on Thursday?

F I'm really sorry, but I can't make lunch on Thursday.

P Don't worry.

F Can we arrange another time?

P Yes, of course. Are you free at the weekend?

F Yes. How about Saturday?

P OK. When would be good for you?

F About 1.00?

P Yes, that's fine with me. Where shall we meet?

F How about that barbecue restaurant we went to last time?

P Good idea.

3

3.1 ●))

A So where did Dan Seddiqui travel to first?

B He started in Utah, in the mid-west of the USA. He worked there for a week and then he went to Colorado. After that, he went north to South Dakota. In each state, he found a job, stayed for a week and then moved on to the next state. He went to 48 states, including Alaska. From Alaska he went to Hawaii. He finished his journey in California 50 weeks later.

A Were all the jobs the same?

B No, they weren't. All the jobs were very different. For example, some jobs were really hard and not very pleasant, like packing meat in Kansas. Some jobs were easier, for example, he was a wedding coordinator in Nevada. He was also an engineer, a farmer, and a park ranger. He worked in a shop, he cut down trees, and he worked with the police. He made cheese, fixed cars, and worked in a recording studio. He did one job in every state.

A Were they well-paid jobs?

B Yes, some of them were very well-paid. He was paid for 40 of them. But he did 10 of them for free.

A Did he enjoy it?

B Yes, I think he did. Every week he learnt something new and met different people. He found most people were really kind and helpful. He ate great food. He saw beautiful places and things like the sunsets in New Mexico. After his journey he wrote a book and became a popular public speaker.

3.2 ●))

A Can you tell me some more about the types of jobs he did?

B Well, he started his journey in September and the first state he visited was Utah. He got a job there in a church. Then, after Utah, he went to Colorado, the state next to Utah. In Colorado, he worked with a team of scientists.

A What did he do?

B He did research into fresh water.

A What did he do next?

B He continued his journey around the northern states – South Dakota, North Dakota, Minnesota, Iowa, and Nebraska. In Nebraska, he worked as a corn farmer. Nebraska is one of America's biggest corn producers. Then he worked his way down the west side of the USA.

A Did he do any dangerous jobs?

B Well, he worked in some dangerous places. For example, as he travelled south, he worked in Arizona with the border police. It's one of the most dangerous places in America.

A Where did he go next?

B He went east to Texas. When he arrived in Texas, he got a job working in the oil business. Texas is a big producer of oil in America. Next he went up the east coast. In Maryland, he was a cook in a seafood restaurant. Crab is a famous dish in this part of the USA.

A Was he a good cook?

B He was OK, I think. But he said it was really hard work. The restaurant was busy and orders were coming in all the time.

A Did he do any office jobs?

B He did a lot of outdoor jobs. But in New York, he worked in a marketing department.

A Which month was that?

B That was July. So he was nearly finished. He had eight more states to visit.

A What did he do next?

B He got a job catching lobster in Maine in the north-east.

A Was he good at catching lobster?

B No, he wasn't. He got seasick and the lobster tried to bite him. So that didn't go so well.

A What was his last job?

B The last state he went to was California, which is famous for wine making. So Dan got a job working in a wine cellar.

A So was he successful?

B Yes, he was. He did 50 jobs in 50 states in 50 weeks. An amazing achievement.

3.3 ●))

liked, stayed, started, developed, lived, wanted, asked, decided, arrived

3.4 ●))

F=Fiona, H=Hana

F Where did you go on your last holiday, Hana?

H Last year, I went to Japan. It was mainly a sightseeing holiday. I wanted to see the temples in Kyoto and I really wanted to see Mount Fuji.

F Oh, really! How did you travel?

H Well, I flew from London to Tokyo. It was a direct flight which wasn't too bad. It took about eleven hours.

F And how about in Japan?

H I took the Shinkansen, the super express train, from Tokyo to Kyoto. It was brilliant. It's a 513 kilometre journey but it only took just over two hours.

F I heard Kyoto's really nice. How long did you stay there?

H I stayed in Kyoto for three days. I wanted to stay in traditional accommodation so I booked a kind of Japanese bed and breakfast called a ryokan. They serve traditional Japanese food and you sleep on a mattress rather than a bed. It's a great experience.

F And did you stay in Tokyo?

H Yes, I stayed there for two days. It was completely different from Kyoto. It's so big.

F Mmm. Where did you stay in Tokyo?

H I stayed in a very modern hotel on the top floor. I could see Mount Fuji from my room. It was really exciting. It's pretty scary trying to get around, though – there are so many different trains. I took the subway most of the time. People were so kind and showed me which train to get and everything. The whole trip was fantastic.

F Yeah. It sounds great. I'll have to go there myself some day.

3.5 ●))

Call 1

C=Cathy, R=Ralf Manners, A=Alex Borini

C Good morning. DD Designs. Cathy speaking. How can I help you?

R Hello, could I speak to Alex Borini, please?

C Certainly. May I ask who's calling?

R It's Ralf Manners.

C OK. Could you hold the line? I'll put you through.

A Hello, Alex Borini speaking.

R Hello, Alex. This is Ralf Manners. I'm just returning your call. You wanted to talk about a new IT project?

A Oh yes, thanks for getting back to me. I wanted to tell you about this project to link all our offices with a new file sharing system.

R OK.

Call 2

L=Lara, R=Ralf, N=Naomi

L Hello.

R Hi, is that Naomi?

L No, this is Lara. Naomi's on another line.

R OK. Could you ask her to call me back?

L Sure. Who's calling?

R It's Ralf.

L Oh, hi Ralf. Sorry I didn't recognize your voice.

R No problem. Could you tell Naomi …

L Oh, actually she's just finished. Hold on a second.

R OK.

N Hi, Ralf.

R Hi.

N How are you?

R Fine thanks. Listen, this is just a quick call. I'm coming to Berlin next week.

N That's great!

R What are you doing on Friday week?

N Nothing at the moment.

R Great. How about …

3.6 ●))

G=Geoff, K=Ken, E=Emma

E Thanks for helping us out, Geoff.

G No, problem.

K OK, for starters, it's a long way from England to Brazil. What should we do about jet lag?

G Good question. So you're leaving London at one fifteen and get to Rio at about nine in the evening. And there's a change at Madrid airport. So, if I were you, I'd try to sleep for an hour or two between Madrid and Rio.

K Right. What's the best way to get travel information?

G Someone told me about a really good app. You should have a look at Tripit, that's T-R-I-P-I-T. It tells you the arrival time, the gate and terminal for each side of the trip, a map of the destination airport, and lots of other useful stuff. And the best website is the CIA site.

E You mean the Central Intelligence Agency CIA? Isn't that for spies?

G No, it's for anyone. Their website is called the CIA World Factbook and it tells you about the country, the economy, the geography, any security issues, and so on.

E Is Rio a safe sort of place? Is there anything we need to be careful about?

G No, not really. Rio's pretty safe. The best thing to do is check where you are going and be sensible.

E Right. And about money. Should we change some money at the airport?

G Yes, that's a good idea. You need to pay for a taxi from the airport. It's a good idea to have cash for shopping and tipping and so on.

K That sounds like good advice. Do we need to get insurance?

G Yes, I think you should get travel and medical insurance.

K OK. And when we get to Rio, what's the best way to get around?

G Taxis are probably the best way. So you need to know the different types of taxi. So, for example, Radio Taxi is very reliable but it's also expensive. So when you have to be somewhere on time, it's a good idea to use this company. Ordinary taxis are pretty good and the drivers usually know the way. But it's a good idea to write the address down and show it to the driver. Not many taxi drivers speak English.

E And the last thing. Do you think we should learn some Portuguese?

G Yes, that's a great idea. Why don't you try something like googletranslate? You just type in what you need to say and it translates it for you. You can translate things you need to read, like menus, and signs as well.

K Amazing.

3.7 ●))

1 I'm in Caracas Airport in Venezuela. My flight back to the UK was due to leave an hour ago. I just heard that my flight has been cancelled because of a hurricane.

2 I'm in a taxi and I asked the taxi driver to take me to the Sheraton Hotel in the city centre. I'm looking out of the window and I can see fields and trees. I'm pretty sure we're going the wrong way. I can't speak the language.

3 I'm on my way to a meeting with a really big client. I took the wrong train on the subway and I'm going to be late. I don't have the client's phone number with me.

4 I'm in Tokyo. I'm shopping in Ginza and I just checked my wallet. I can't find my credit card.

4

4.1 ●))

I=Interviewer, F=Fiona

I So, Fiona, can you tell me something about these two items?

F Certainly. The first one is a guitar. It was played by Jimi Hendrix at the Woodstock music festival in 1969, one of the most famous festivals in the 60s.

I Could you tell us a bit about Jimi Hendrix?

F Jimi Hendrix is one of the great guitar players. His performance at the music festival was a really important stage of his career.

I And how about his guitar?

F Well, it was made by the Fender guitar company and is called the Fender Stratocaster. It's an electric guitar that is still played by a lot of guitarists. In the sixties it was used by the Beatles' George Harrison and Eric Clapton.

I Is it an expensive guitar?

F Not really. A new one today costs about 700 dollars. Back in the sixties, Jimi Hendrix's guitar was bought originally in New York for around 200 dollars.

I And what happened to it after the Woodstock festival?

F Unfortunately, Jimi Hendrix died the next year. It had several owners after his death and was finally sold in 1993.

I How much for?

F For 1,390,000 dollars.

I That's a lot of money.

F It is. But the guitar is now estimated to be worth nearer 5 million dollars.

I And how about the second item?

F It's called *Action Comic*. It's a comic that was published in the 1930s. This comic is special because it's the first time that Superman appears. The story was written by Jerry Siegel and Joe Shuster, and much later the same story was used in the Superman films.

I So this comic was the start of a very successful and profitable brand.

F Indeed, and it cost just ten cents when it was first published.

I I guess it's worth a bit more than that now.

F A lot more. 200,000 copies of the comic were sold when it was first published. But now only a few copies remain so they are very rare and very valuable. In 2011, a copy of the first *Action Comic* was sold at auction for 2.16 million dollars.

4.2 ◆))
I=Interviewer, P=Pete Fox

I So, Pete, you are a product designer.

P That's right.

I Can you talk us through what a logo does?

P Sure. A logo is based on an idea or concept. It tells people something about a product and the company that made it.

I Can you give us an example?

P Well, a really famous example is the Amazon logo. The A and Z letters in Amazon are linked by an arrow. This suggests that Amazon covers the whole range of products starting with A all the way through to Z, from alarm clocks to zippo lighters. The other image is the arrow itself, which can be seen as a smile. The colour yellow also presents a positive image.

I A pretty simple idea.

P Yes, absolutely. A great logo is always simple. Take the Nike swoosh or tick symbol. The shape actually comes from the wing of the Greek goddess Nike. The designers very cleverly made the shape of the wing into the simple curve of the Nike symbol.

I What other features does a good logo have?

P Well, logos are used in lots of different ways – on the product itself, and on various types of advertising such as TV ads, magazine ads, online catalogues, and so on. So a good logo is flexible and it works when it's very small or very big. An example of this would be the Apple logo. There is a huge Apple logo on the front of their main store in Manhattan.

The same logo works as a very small image on an iPhone.

I So how is a logo made or designed?

P Well, first of all, the company has to decide what they want. This is usually the marketing department's job. So they discuss the image of the company, what the values of the company are, and how the logo will work with their products.

I So it's a big first step.

P Yes, it is. It's also very expensive. For a big company, it costs millions of dollars. All their product design, their advertising, their signs, even their stationery changes. It is reported that the British oil company BP spent over 200 million dollars on their logo.

I Is it worth that much?

P Well, to a global company, their image, especially for an oil company, is very important. They want to have an image that says they care about the environment.

I So what's the next stage in the process?

P The designer is given a brief telling them what the company wants and they then produce a variety of logos with different designs. The designer then gives a presentation to the client and the various designs are discussed and assessed. The designer may be asked to do a second set of designs if the company is not satisfied. Finally, a logo is chosen and then is transferred to all products, advertising, and so on.

I How long does this take?

P It can take several years for an international company. For a small company it can take just a few weeks, or for a start-up company you can design your own logo online which could take just a few days.

4.3 ◆))
1 A Who are you working with at the moment, Cathy?
   B I'm working with Lena on the new digital project.
   A I don't think I know Lena. What's she like?
   B Well, she's very friendly. She always smiles and says 'Hello' and asks you how you are.
   A Does she wear a sort of light grey suit with a white blouse?
   B Yes, that's her. And she dresses very nicely, you know, she always looks smart.
   A Oh, I know.
2 A Which one's Bill?
   B He's the serious looking guy.
   A I don't think I know him.
   B He's got dark hair, very ambitious. He's always in his office looking at sales figures – very hard-working.
   A Is he quite tall?
   B Yes, about six foot.
   A Is he quiet?
   B Yes, he is pretty quiet, I think.
   A Is he married?
   B No. He's going out with someone in Marketing.

3 A Who's coming to the meeting?
   B The IT team and a new person, Michelle Bouchard.
   A I don't think I've met her.
   B She's about thirty, very nice. A bit shy.
   A Has she got black hair, sort of medium height?
   B Yes, that's her. Apparently, she's very good at languages.
   A Really?
   B Yes, she can speak English, French, and fluent Chinese. She's got a very interesting background. Her father was a diplomat in Shanghai.

4.4 ◆))
1 He's got dark hair.
2 Which one's Bill?
3 Yes, that's her.
4 She's very friendly.
5 Who's coming to the meeting?

4.5 ◆))
Object 1
It's very light. It weighs 66 grams. It tells you how fast you're running. It's mainly black with a silver strip for the logo. It's got a square face and the time is shown in digital numbers. The strap is black and green and made of plastic.

Object 2
It's square. It's got a grey strap about 120 centimetres long. It's got a handle at the top to make it easy for carrying. It's useful for people who need to carry books and papers. It's made of strong, waterproof material.

4.6 ◆))
Good morning, everyone. First of all, let's introduce ourselves. As you know, my name's Rene Cassells. I'm the deputy manager.

Shall we make a start? The main aim today is to review our recent sales performance. The first item on the agenda is 'Sales trends in Europe'. Gina, would you like to talk about Italy?

Thanks very much, Gina. Some very good results there. So let's move to the next item on the agenda.

The last item for today is our overseas strategy for the second quarter.

Has anyone got any questions?

Could everyone check their sales figures after the meeting and get back to me?

Thank you very much for your ideas and suggestions. That's all for today, I think. We meet again at the same time next week.

4.7 ◆))
C=Charles Ward, L=Laura Mancini, P=Pietro, T=Tiffany, G=George

C OK. Morning, everyone. Thanks for coming today. First of all, let's introduce ourselves. As most of you know, my name is Charles Ward and I'm the sales director for Unisports. Laura.

L Good morning, everyone. I'm Laura Mancini. I am a sportswear designer and I'm currently working on the new outdoor range for Unisports. Pietro is my senior designer.

P Thank you, Laura. Yes, my name is Pietro Capello. Very pleased to meet you all.

T And I'm Tiffany. I work with Laura, too, as assistant designer.

G George. Good morning. I work with Charles in the sales department.

C Great. Thanks everyone. Shall we make a start, then? The first item on the agenda is the new outdoor range Laura mentioned. The design details are on the handout and we have some samples on the table. We have five designs to look at. Laura, would you like to take us through these?

L Yes, of course. These are the new designs for the UK and Brazilian markets. We would like to get some comments on the designs and some help positioning them in the market. George, would you like to start?

G Thanks, Laura.

L What do you think about the first design, number one?

G I really like it. The colour is great and the check design is really strong. I think it would be great for beachwear.

T I think you're right. It's a classic design. The short sleeves are great for the summer. How do you feel about age group? Do you think it's a bit old?

G It could be, I guess. Probably not for the 16 to 18 market.

C I agree with George. It's mainly for the twenty five plus market.

L OK. So let's move on to the next item. Number two.

T I love this one! It's very pretty but practical. It's perfect for casual evening wear.

G I'm not sure, but I was thinking more for the hiking and walking market.

T No, I don't think so. The material isn't that hard-wearing.

G I see.

L Charles?

C I think I agree with Tiffany. It's more of a casual look.

L OK. Good. Shall we move on to number three?

G I really like number three. I think this will be really popular for all sorts of sports.

T Really? Don't you think it's mainly for beachwear?

G I see your point, but it could work for hiking or maybe cycling.

T OK.

L Good. That's a very positive start. And how about number four?

P The colour works well for men and women but the design is definitely for men.

C I see. And number five. Would that be for the women's range?

P That's right. It would do very well in the UK market, I think.

G I'm sure it would. Great for the UK market, but too heavy for Brazil.

T I totally agree. This is for winter hiking in the UK. It's really warm. I love the orange colour too.

C I'm happy with that. So I think we are all agreed on the designs so far. Could everyone take these handouts back with them and send me written confirmation of the designs they like and which markets they work in?

All Sure. OK.

C And thank you everyone for your ideas and suggestions. I think it's been a very useful meeting. We'll meet again at the end of the month. A reminder will go out a little nearer the time.

All Thank you.

5

5.1

G=George Allen, C=Claudio Fernández

G Hello. This is George Allen in Chile. I'm joined by one of the people who followed the rescue, Claudio Fernández. Welcome, Claudio.

C Thank you, George.

G So Claudio, could you give us some background to the miners' story? For example, how much food did they have?

C Actually, they didn't have much food at the beginning. Each day, they had some biscuits, some milk, some tinned fish, and some peaches. They also had a little water.

G Did their families know what the situation was?

C No. Their families didn't have any information at first. But when a hole was made, they received the famous message, 'We are well in the shelter, the 33'.

G And what did the miners eat after their discovery?

C At first, the doctors gave them a few vitamins. Their first real food was some cereal and some pears.

G How many calories a day did they have?

C They had about 2,300 calories a day. They didn't eat much because they needed to be thin to fit in the escape tube.

G Did they have much fresh air?

C There wasn't much fresh air after the accident happened. Things got a lot better on day seventeen when they finished the hole from the surface and pumped fresh air down to the miners.

G I see. And how about space? Could they move around?

C Yes, they had lots of space. The space they lived in was about fifty square metres, and there were about two kilometres of tunnels.

G Did they have any treats?

C Yes, they did. Their families sent down music, and lots of cigarettes.

G And did they take any exercise?

C Yes, they did. They did up to an hour a day. Some, like Edison Peña, did much more. He ran the New York marathon a few weeks after his rescue.

G Amazing. And finally, how did they get back to the surface?

C Well, there weren't any ladders in the mine or any way of making a hole in the tunnel. So the rescuers made a new hole and sent down a metal tube. The miners got in the tube one-by-one until all the miners reached the surface.

G It's great to hear a story with a happy ending.

C It is. And it's a story we will remember for a long time.

5.2

H=High Flyer, J=Josh Kantner

H Do you have a work phone, Josh?

J Yes, I take it everywhere with me.

H Do you ever switch it off?

J No, I get a lot of calls during the week and at the weekend. I always check my messages before I go to bed.

H Is that stressful?

J In some ways. It means I never switch off from work. But at the same time, I don't miss any important calls or emails and I get the job done.

H How about computers? How often do you use them?

J Well, I take an iPad on business trips. I can check spreadsheets, watch the news, follow the stock markets, and so on. I've got a Twitter account which has about 1,000 followers, so that keeps me busy. And I've got a laptop at work which I can unplug and take home if I need to.

H So how often do you access the Internet?

J All the time, I guess.

H And how many hours a day do you think you work?

J I probably work about ten hours a day but I spend a lot of time travelling, and work on planes, in hotels, so it's probably more than that.

H How many hours do you usually sleep?

J I usually sleep about six hours a night, maybe a bit more at the weekend.

H Do you get any exercise?

J Yes, I cycle to work and I always take my running shoes with me on trips. I'm doing a marathon next month.

H And how about food? What do you normally eat?

J I eat a lot of fast food when I'm busy – burgers, sandwiches, pizzas, and so on. And I eat ready-cooked meals in the evening – curries, pasta, that sort of thing.

H How about fruit and vegetables?

J I don't eat many vegetables and I generally drink fruit juice.

H Do you drink much?

J I drink a lot of coffee during the day. And in the evening, I do spend a lot of time with clients and some of them like to go out for a meal and a drink, so I do drink alcohol but I try to limit the amount I drink.

H Do you drink water during the day?

J Not really. I have a mineral water with lunch but that's about all.

H   And lastly, about how many days' holiday do you get a year?

J   I don't get much holiday. About a week in the summer, and then maybe a week in the winter. I love skiing so I sometimes take a long weekend, leave on Friday and come back on Monday.

H   Well, thank you, Josh. It sounds like you're a very busy man.

J   I guess I am.

5.3 🔊

Good morning. First of all, thank you all for coming. Today I'm going to talk about ways in which we can keep healthy. And as we all know, if we're healthy, we're happier, and we work better.

I've divided my presentation into three areas. Firstly, diet – what we eat and drink. Secondly, exercise. And finally, some tips to encourage you to continue a healthy lifestyle, even when you're working hard or under stress. I'm happy to take questions at the end of the presentation.

OK, so that's diet. Now I'd like to move on to exercise. I think we all know how important exercise is, but do we do it? At this point, I'd like to hand over to my colleague, Rachel, who is going to look at the type of exercise we need to do …

So that brings us on to the final part of this presentation: some practical advice on what we can do. I've got a handout here, which I'll pass around.

I suggest I finish my presentation here and we can all work in groups to look at some of the ideas and discuss how we can bring them into our lives. But before I do that, I'd like to make some general conclusions.

To sum up, a good diet and plenty of exercise is essential for good health. That is obvious. But it also makes us happier people. You don't need to make major changes to your life. It's often the little things that make all the difference, as we shall see when we look at the advice on the handout. Thank you for listening.

5.4 🔊

P=Paul, K=Ken, E=Emma, N=Nathalie

P   OK. Where would everyone like to eat?

E   There's a nice Italian place.

K   I went there last month. It's OK, but the service wasn't great.

N   Do you know the restaurant that does sushi?

P   I do. To be honest, it isn't very good. It isn't like the sushi you get in Japan.

E   That's true.

K   Are we going to have lunch or just a snack?

P   Well, we'll probably just get a snack on the plane, so I'm going to have a full meal now.

E   Anyone have any ideas?

N   A friend said there's a place that does sandwiches and salads that's quite good. And they do proper lunches as well.

P   Sounds good. What are the prices like?

N   Pretty reasonable.

P   OK. Is everyone happy with that?

E   I can't eat things like bread or pasta, I'm afraid.

N   That's OK. This place has got really nice salads and soups and things. We can ask about gluten-free food, just in case.

E   Thanks, Nathalie. That's very kind.

P   So, are we ready?

All Yes.

P   Great. Ah … Does anyone know where it is?

5.5 🔊

P=Paul, K=Ken, E=Emma, N=Nathalie, W=Waiter

P   Is this it?

N   Yes, I think so.

P   OK.

W   Good afternoon. Shall I show you to a table?

P   Yes, please. Could we have a table by the window?

W   Certainly. For four people?

P   Yes.

W   OK. This way, please.

P   Thanks.

W   Here are your menus.

All Thank you.

W   Are you ready to order?

N   Yes, I'll have a caffè latte, please.

E   Same for me.

K   I'd like a cranberry juice.

P   Some mineral water, please. Sparkling.

W   And for food?

N   Could I have the grilled chicken salad?

E   Can I just ask? Does the soup have any gluten in it?

W   Today's potato soup is actually gluten free.

E   OK, I'll have that.

W   Certainly.

E   Thanks.

K   A classic burger for me, please. With barbecue sauce topping.

W   Certainly.

P   And I'll have the fish and chips. We're in a bit of a hurry so could you bring the bill now?

W   Of course.

P   Have you got any bread?

W   Yes. I'll bring some right over.

P   Thanks.

5.6 🔊

1   Could we have a table by the window?
2   I'll have a caffè latte, please.
3   I'd like a cranberry juice.
4   Some mineral water, please. Sparkling.
5   Could I have the grilled chicken salad?
6   Can I just ask? Does the soup have any gluten in it?
7   We're in a bit of a hurry so could you bring the bill now?
8   Have you got any bread?

6

6.1 🔊

Here we are in Zurich, the largest city in Switzerland. So, what is living and working in Zurich like? And how does it compare with two other very popular cities, Shanghai and Dubai?

With a population of about 370,000, Zurich is smaller than Shanghai and Dubai. Shanghai has a population of over 23 million, which is a lot more than the whole population of Switzerland. Dubai is in the middle with about 1.8 million.

In terms of transport, Shanghai has a good metro system and it has the fastest train service in the world, the Maglev, which goes from the city centre to the airport. It can travel at 500 kilometres an hour. Dubai has a new metro, lots of buses, and hundreds of taxis, but the population is growing fast and there are lots of traffic jams. Overall, Zurich probably has the best transport system. It has the most efficient bus and tram system, not too much traffic, and is easy to get around.

Zurich has a pretty good climate too. The summers are warm, around twenty three degrees in July, and winters are cold, with temperatures going down to minus four or colder. So Zurich is the coldest city, but for some people that's a good thing. It means great skiing. In Dubai, in the summer, temperatures go up to 40 degrees or higher, making it the hottest of the three cities.

For shopping, Zurich has a very pleasant shopping district but overall Zurich has fewer shops than the other two cities. Shanghai has the famous Number 1 department store. It opened in 1934, and is one of the oldest department stores in the world. Shanghai also has lots of expensive brand stores as well as lots of more traditional shops and stores. But the best shopping city has to be Dubai, which is the most famous place for duty-free shopping and also has one of the largest shopping malls in the world.

So all three cities are great places to live and work. Dubai is the most modern and developing the quickest. It also has the tallest building, the Burj Khalifa. Shanghai is probably the most interesting city with both an amazing history and some exciting modern architecture. Zurich is an older, more traditional city, which some people, especially the locals, love. It is also a city that many professionals think is the best place to live and work.

6.2 🔊

A=Adam, F=Fiona

A   So, Fiona, you live in Zurich, but you've spent time in both Shanghai and Dubai.

F   Yes, that's right.

A   Tell me, what did you like about Shanghai?

F   Well, Shanghai was a very exciting place to live. The nightlife was fantastic, you can buy anything, and the food is really international. I miss that here!

A   But Zurich is quite international, isn't it?

F   Yeah, yeah! I just think I felt more relaxed in Shanghai. Here, in Zurich, it's really clean, and it's easier to get around than Shanghai, but there are a lot of rules! I think I'm getting used to them – slowly!

A You mentioned shopping. How do Shanghai and Dubai compare?

F Well, I think Shanghai was the cheapest place I've worked in. Clothes are cheap, unless you want something special. You can get all the latest fashions, but they are much more expensive, of course!

A And compared to Dubai?

F Well, Dubai is shopping heaven, but in a very different way, you know, with shopping malls and lots of western outlets. I actually preferred the souks, you know, the traditional markets in Dubai. They were a lot of fun!

A So do you feel your money goes further here?

F Well, I obviously earn more now in Zurich. In fact, I earn a lot, but it isn't cheap living here. Just everyday things, like transport and concert tickets; they cost a fortune! Of course in Shanghai, these sorts of things are much cheaper.

6.3 ●))
A=Alex, L=Lisa, P=Peter

A Lisa, you're here for four months, is that right?

L Yes. I'm so excited! I've never been to Kraków before.

A Well, it is a lovely city.

L It does look beautiful. How do people get around?

A Well, the best way to get around the Old Town is on foot.

P Actually, we've rented a flat in the suburbs so it's a bit further out.

A OK, then it's probably better to get a one-month travel card. It's valid on both buses and trams.

L OK. And what about intercity trains? Next week, I'm travelling to Warsaw. I was wondering how long it takes?

A It's about two and a half hours by train to Warsaw. It's a good service, and as you know, the train station is just outside the Old Town.

P OK. That sounds good. And what about prices in general? Is it expensive to live in Kraków?

A Well, transport isn't expensive. As for food, if you eat out all the time, then yes! But actually, it's very reasonable, and these days, you should be able to get everything you need in the shops. Imported things, like peanut butter, are more expensive of course!

P Yeah. Sure. And if we need to change money?

A Well, there are cash points all over the city. Don't change money in the hotels, because the rate isn't very good.

L Right. We're here for a few months, but can you recommend anything in particular we should do?

A Well, obviously you must visit the Castle, and now that summer is coming, it gets very crowded in the city centre, so do your sightseeing early! And then further out you can go to Kazimierz. It's the old Jewish quarter, and it's really interesting.

L Oh, right! And shopping? It mentions Florian Street in the brochure.

A Yes, that's a great place for shopping, but also for sightseeing too. It's a very attractive street. The buildings are beautiful, and it has a great atmosphere.

P Isn't there a famous restaurant near there?

A Well, there are lots, but maybe you're thinking of the Jama Michalika café? It's not far away. It's popular with locals and tourists too, and the cakes are especially good!

P Yes, I think that was it! We must take you there.

A That's very kind.

L Not at all. You've really helped us settle in.

A My pleasure.

6.4 ●))
Call 1

A Good morning.

B Good morning.

A Great. Now Brian's here, I think we can start. [phone noise] Oh, I'm sorry. I thought I'd turned it off. Do you mind if I take this?

B No, go ahead.

A Hello, Tom. I can't speak right now. I'm in a meeting. Can I phone you later? Sorry about that everyone.

Call 2

A Thank you for calling Avalon. The office is closed at the moment. Please leave a message after the tone. [beep]

B Hi, this is Jeff from the San Francisco branch. What time is it over there? Can you call me back urgently? Thank you.

Call 3

A Avalon Dreams. Justine speaking. How can I help you?

B I'd like to speak to Mr Myers, please.

A Can I ask who's calling?

B It's James Albrecht.

A Thank you, Mr Albrecht. Please hold, I'll see if he's there … I'm sorry, he's on another call at the moment. Do you want to hold or shall I ask him to call you back?

B Could you tell him it's James Albrecht and I've got his email, and everything's fine? Nothing to worry about.

A OK. Would you mind spelling your name?

B It's A-L-B-R-E-C-H-T.

A Thank you. And can I ask what your number is?

B He's got it, but it's 07794 16283.

A 07794 16283. Thank you, Mr Albrecht. I'll see he gets your message.

B Thank you.

A You're welcome.

6.5 ●))
R=Reception, P=Paul Lee

R Good evening.

P Good evening.

R Welcome to Rio.

P Thank you. We'd like to check in.

R How many of you are there?

P There are four of us.

R Four people. OK. Could I have your passports, please?

P Yes, of course. Here they are.

R So you are staying for five nights?

P Yes, that's right.

R And you are in four single rooms.

P Yes.

R Could you fill out these forms, please?

P Sure.

R Breakfast is included in the room rate. Breakfast is served from six till eleven in the morning. It's in the Mirador Restaurant on the fifth floor. There's a very nice view of the sea.

P That sounds great. Do you have a business centre?

R Yes, we do. We have work stations that have high-speed Internet access and other facilities. Please ask at the business centre for more details.

P Thank you. That's very useful.

R For payment, are you all on one credit card?

P Yes, here's my card.

R Thank you. Here are your key cards. You're all on the same floor.

P Good. Is there Internet access in the rooms?

R Yes, there is. There's a small charge per day.

P Fine.

R If you have any questions, please call reception. I'll get someone to help with your bags.

P Ah, can I just check one thing? Did a bicycle arrive for us today?

R A bicycle? Let me just check. Ah, yes. There is a bicycle waiting for you. Please ask the concierge and he'll show you where it is.

P Thank you.

R Is there anything else I can help you with?

P Yes, we're going to Corcovado tomorrow morning. Could you order a large taxi for us at 9.30?

R Yes, of course.

P That's great. Thank you.

R My pleasure. I hope you enjoy your stay.

6.6 ●))
1 R=Reception, E=Emma King

R Reception, how can I help you?

E This is Emma King, in room 412. I'm calling about the air conditioning. It's very cold in the room, but I can't change the temperature on the air conditioner.

R I see. Are you using the remote control or the control on the wall?

E I'm using the remote control.

R In that case, the batteries may be low. Could you try turning the dial on the wall?

E OK. Just a moment … yes, that seems to be better.

R Oh, good. Please let me know if you have any more trouble.

E I will. And thanks for your help.

R My pleasure.

2 R=Reception, K=Ken Martin

R Good evening.

K Hi. I need to get up early tomorrow and I can't seem to set the alarm in my room.

R I see, sir. I can arrange for you to receive a wake-up call.
K Oh, great. I'd like a call at 5.50.
R So that's a call at 5.50. Is there anything else?
K No, thanks. That's all.
R Have a good evening, sir.
K You, too. Thank you.

3 R=Reception, N=Nathalie Bourne
R Good afternoon. Room service.
N Oh, hi. I'd like to order some food.
R Certainly, madam.
N Could I just have an order of fries and a salad?
R No problem. Would you like some dressing with your salad?
N No, but could I have some ketchup with my fries?
R Yes, of course. I'll have it sent up straight away.
N Thanks very much.

4 R=Reception, P=Paul Lee
R Reception.
P Hi. It's Paul Lee in room 414. I arrived this evening and the sheets and pillows are dirty.
R I'm very sorry to hear that, sir. I'll get someone to change them immediately.
P Thank you.

6.7 •))
R=Reception, P=Paul Lee
P I'd like to check out, please.
R Certainly, sir. Do you have your key card?
P Yes, here it is.
R OK. Could you just check your room charge?
P That looks fine.
R Did you have anything from the mini-bar last night?
P No.
R OK. If I could just have your credit card, please.
P OK.
R Could you enter your PIN number?
P Yes, sure.
R I'm sorry, your payment hasn't been accepted.
P Maybe I mixed up my PIN numbers. I'll try again.
R OK, that's fine. Here's your receipt.
P Great. Thanks.

7

7.1 •))
S=Susie, J=Jon
J When did you last buy a CD, Susie?
S Oh, I can't remember. I haven't bought a CD for ages!
J Really?
S No. There's no point if you don't like all the tracks.
J So you just buy single tracks?
S Yes!
J But that's so expensive.
S No, it's not. I bought two tracks off one album yesterday and they cost about two dollars. The whole album costs seven.

J But you've only got two tracks.
S OK. Sometimes I buy a whole album. What about you? What have you downloaded recently?
J Nothing.
S Have you ever downloaded anything?
J No, I haven't. I've bought lots of albums online but I buy the real thing. With LPs and CDs, you get the whole atmosphere, the sleeve, the artwork, the lyrics … Have you ever listened to an LP?
S No, I don't think so.
J They sound really different. It's like being in the studio with the band.
S Cool. My dad's got some in the loft, but he's never played them.
J Bring them round to mine and we'll see if they still work.
S OK.

7.2 •))
I=Interviewer, A=Alex Garner
I Hi, Alex. Thanks for coming in.
A Thanks for having me.
I Could you tell us a little bit about the band?
A Sure.
I So, when did you start the band?
A Last year, when we were all living in Manchester.
I Have any band members changed since you started?
A No, we've had the same line-up for 18 months now.
I How many live gigs have you played?
A So far, we've played five gigs in London and we did a mini tour of the USA, which was six gigs.
I How did you promote the band at first?
A We started a blog which we've updated quite a lot since.
I And have you recorded an album yet?
A No, not an album. But we recently recorded an EP, which came out last month.
I When did you start using social media sites?
A We went on Myspace at the same time as the EP came out. You can hear and buy the tracks online.
I Have many people listened to your EP online?
A Yes, our best track has had over 30,000 plays, which is really great.
I What have your reviews been like so far?
A We've had a really good response from most people.
I That's great. Well, thanks for coming in and good luck with the EP.
A Thanks.

7.3 •))
P=Presenter, M=Mitch Alek
P Welcome to this week's podcast. We have in our studio today Mitch Alek. Mitch is interested in music streaming and how it has changed our listening habits. Tell us, Mitch, what is 'music streaming'?
M Well, it's similar to Internet radio. People can go to a website and listen to music for free. But with music

streaming, listeners have more choice about what they listen to.
P Are there limits to how much customers can listen to?
M It depends on the service. Some services offer a free trial, or a free subscription, but there are limitations. For example, with a free account there may be advertisements between songs. You also have less control over what you listen to.
P Are there other services?
M Yes. You can pay and get better sound quality and personalize your playlists more.
P And what do the musicians and artists think about this service?
M Well, it's quite difficult. Some musicians don't like streaming services because people buy less music.
P Yes, of course. And what about digital downloads?
M Well, generally the number of digital downloads has risen over the last few years. At the same time, a lot of people have stopped buying CDs.
P How about the number of people using streaming services?
M That's interesting. Last year, over a twelve-month period in the USA, online music listening hours increased by 50 per cent.
P That's a big increase.
M It is. So it means that people now listen in a wide variety of ways. Some still listen to CDs or LPs. Some listen to the radio. More of these people are listening to online radio. And a growing number of people are using streaming services.
P It must be very difficult for the record companies.
M Yes, their revenues have fallen. But the good news is more people are using Twitter and Facebook to tell friends about music they've heard on music streaming sites. That didn't happen before, and it must be good for the industry overall.

7.4 •))
I=Interviewer, J=János Bogrács
I Thanks for coming along, János.
J Thanks for inviting me.
I So János, can you tell me first about your qualifications?
J Yes, sure. I've got a Degree in Business Studies from the London School of Commerce. I graduated in 2004.
I Have you taken any other courses since you graduated?
J Yes, I did management training at Kappa. And I did a course when I was promoted in 2011 to Assistant Product Manager at Adidas.
I And was that useful?
J Yes, it really helped me manage larger teams and improved my communication with team members.
I And how about project management tools? Have you done any training in that?

J Yes, I had training in Microsoft Project, which has really helped me keep track of schedules and make sure I keep to deadlines.

I Right, good. Another important part of the job will be to give presentations to people here at the headquarters and to other departments. Can you tell me about any presentation experience you've had?

J Well, as a product designer, I had to give presentations to my team, and sometimes to the marketing team. So I'm used to presenting to large groups and handling a bit of pressure.

I Good. Well, you'd certainly need that in this job. You'd also need to do quite a bit of travelling. How do feel about that?

J I haven't done much travelling recently. I've been pretty busy with my job and looking after my family. But I'm looking forward to travelling more in the future.

I How many countries have you been to so far?

J So far, I've lived in four countries: Hungary, England, Italy, and Germany. And I've been to most of Europe, either on holiday or for business.

I I see. How about outside Europe?

J Not really, no.

I The reason I ask is we're developing a new product line in South America and some of the travel will include Brazil and perhaps Chile.

J That sounds great. I'm a big football fan.

I That always helps in Brazil. You didn't put any languages on your CV. I was wondering if you've studied Portuguese at all?

J No, I haven't. I studied English at school and Italian while I was at college.

I And German?

J Yes, I've learnt some German but I'm only about intermediate level.

I OK. You've been in Germany since 2009. How do you feel about moving again?

J Well, I'm really excited about working for Unisports so moving isn't really a problem.

8

S=Sreenath Aravind, R=Rosa Kent, J=Jay Desai

S So, Rosa, you're new to Mumbai?

R Yes, I am. I'm very excited. Jay's told me so much about it!

J Only the good things, of course!

S Did you live here, then, Jay?

J Yes, I was born here. I'm British-Indian and I grew up in Manchester.

S Oh, right.

J And now we're both just starting jobs here.

S So you want to know a bit about what we do here, in India.

J&R Yes, please.

S OK. Let's start with the basics. Generally, you don't have to wear formal clothes to work. Shirts and trousers for men and Western or Indian clothes for women. So no ties or suits. It's too hot, especially in April and May.

J That suits me.

R Are people pretty strict about time?

S Not really. You don't have to get to meetings exactly on time. Just don't be really late, like over half an hour.

J I was in a meeting last week and most of the junior staff were quite quiet.

S Yes, generally, it's better to listen, especially when someone senior is speaking. You mustn't interrupt someone when they're talking.

J But I noticed in my company that some people call their boss by their first name.

S Well, generally there are two types of company, the traditional and the modern. In a traditional company, you must address your boss as 'Sir' or 'Madam'. But in a modern company you can call your boss by their first name.

R How about speaking Hindi?

S Again, it depends on the type of company. A lot of people speak English in the workplace, so no, you don't have to learn the language. But it's probably a good idea to learn a few phrases.

J My boss took me out the other night and a lot of people left food on their plate. Is that a custom?

S Actually, yes. You should leave a little food on your plate at the end of a meal. Eating everything means you're still hungry and your boss would have to keep ordering more food.

J OK. That explains it.

R And how about meeting someone? Should I hug or shake hands or what?

S You shouldn't hug or shake hands with a person of the opposite sex. Just say 'Hello'.

R OK. Anything else we should know?

S It may sound rude, but we don't say 'Thank you' so much. So, for example, don't say 'Thank you' after a clerk hands you your grocery bag. And tipping is quite tricky. You don't have to tip taxi drivers, but you should tip hotel and train station porters. About 20 rupees for a bag.

R Sounds like there's a lot to learn.

S Yes, this is just the beginning.

1 OK. My name's Ben and I'm one of the ground staff working here at Heathrow Airport. I'd like to tell you a bit about some of the rules about security. Right, first of all, you must have your passport ready for airport security. You should buy any bottled water or other drinks after you've gone through security. So don't buy water just before you go through departures. Before you get to the security search, don't forget to take your laptop out of your bag. And remember you mustn't take any carry-on items containing blades over six centimetres on board. Check all your bottles and creams and take out any bottles bigger than 100 millilitres. You can take bottles under 100 millilitres.

2 G=Greg, M=Makiko

G So Makiko, this is my first time in Japan and I'm going to be taking a lot of taxis around Tokyo, visiting customers. Could you give me a few tips so I don't get things wrong?

M Sure. Well, the first thing is you should have some cash ready in case the taxi driver doesn't take credit cards.

G OK.

M In Japan, people generally don't tip, so you don't have to tip the driver.

G Right. Not even for bags?

M No, that's all part of the job.

G OK.

M Roads in Tokyo are pretty busy, especially in a business area like Marunouchi. So you should get out on the left side of the taxi.

G Right.

M And taxi doors are automatic so you shouldn't try to close the taxi door yourself.

G Oh, really? That's completely different from New York.

M You're right. I got really confused when I was in Manhattan.

G I bet.

M OK, back to Tokyo. Taxi drivers know most of the big places, but you should have a map and the address of where you are going in Japanese. Just in case.

G Right.

M And the last thing, taxi fares are fixed in Japan so don't try to negotiate a cheaper fare.

G Is there a meter?

M Yes, you pay a minimum fare and then more depending on how far you go.

G OK.

I=Interviewer, H=Hazel Masterson

I Hazel, what are the main problems that people face when they move abroad for work?

H Well, first of all there are practical problems.

I OK. What sort of things do people have problems with?

H The obvious one is finding accommodation. Most people start off in a hotel. But this is expensive so we find them an apartment as soon as possible. This can be difficult if the person wants to live in a very popular part of town. These are usually the most expensive places and there is a lot of competition for the best apartments.

I How about workers with a family?

H Good question. Being near a good school is really important to families with children, and most of our clients want their children to go to an international school. So either they pay more for a place near a good school or they have a long journey to take their children to school.

I And international schools aren't cheap, are they?

H No, absolutely.

I So how about money? It must be difficult at first.

H Employees need some money to get started, so we help them set up a bank account and transfer money from their home country. Or we can arrange a loan so they can buy furniture or rent a car and so on.

I Do companies usually help?

H Yes, they can pay the first month's salary in advance and then the employee pays it back.

I Are there any other things that people find difficult?

H Everyone is different. One person may love living in a country but another person may not like it at all.

I Is that because of the difference in culture?

H Yes, that is an important factor.

I What sort of things do they have problems with?

H Everything from food to making friends. The weather can be a problem, especially in extreme climates like the Gulf States or places like Finland or Alaska.

I So how do you help people?

H We usually put all people who are relocating on an intensive 'cultural awareness' course, which includes things like business customs, social customs, and so on in the host culture.

I And do these courses work?

H Yes, but you can't prepare for everything. I had one Italian man who was going to the north of Finland. He knew about the local culture there, he knew about the climate and the weather, he knew that for much of the year the days are very short, he knew that the food would be different. He was as prepared as he could be.

I But …?

H But it didn't work out. He got very homesick. He missed his family, he missed his favourite meals, he missed his social life. He tried his best, but in the end, he came home after only three months of a one-year contract.

I You can't win them all!

H Indeed.

8.4 ●))

1 You must let people finish speaking.
   You mustn't interrupt someone senior talking in a meeting.

2 People do arrive late for meetings.
   You don't have to get to meetings exactly on time.

3 You should let the taxi driver close the door.
   You shouldn't try to close the taxi door yourself.

4 You can wear casual clothes at home.
   You can't wear casual clothes in the office at the weekend.

8.5 ●))

When I graduated from design school, I wanted to get a job in product design, so I looked online at lots of different design companies and finally found Go Media, a company based in the US. They do designs for a whole range of websites, company logos, album covers, and so on. I applied online and they offered me an interview. They wanted to see all the designs I did in college, which was really embarrassing.

I was lucky because I have dual nationality so my visa wasn't a problem.

Anyway, they offered me the job and of course I accepted. They didn't give me any formal training but the design team I worked with were really supportive. I didn't have a contract, they just said stay as long as you like, just keep doing great designs. I stayed there for two years and had a really good time.

Then I decided to go freelance. I had lots of contacts from my work with Go Media so I had enough projects to get started. After six months, there was too much work so I found a partner and we started up our own business. Being self-employed is great but it's really hard work. We worked 20 hours a day and slowly built up our customer base. We hired three more designers and got a contract with a big corporation in New York, so we're thinking of moving office there this year.

8.6 ●))

P=Peter, H=Harriet, C=Charles

P I think we should have more training for our staff before we send them overseas. It doesn't make sense to let them …

H Sorry to interrupt, but have you thought about the budget for this?

P We could put in a proposal for next year but I think …

C Could I just say, I think it's a really good idea, but people often have to leave very quickly and there just isn't time.

P That's true, but we could do something online.

H But that's also going to cost money.

P OK. But maybe less than running actual courses.

8.7 ●))

J=John, P=Paula, C=Charles, K=Karl

J So Peter and Charles agree that training is a good idea. Harriet is worried about the budget. Paula, what do you think?

P I like the idea, too, but who will do the training? I can't …

C Surely we can do it ourselves.

J Sorry, Charles, could you let Paula just finish?

C Yes, of course.

P I just wanted to say that we are all very busy doing other things. I think an outside company is a better solution.

J Any comments, Karl? You've used outside training companies before.

K Yes, and they've been pretty good. But we still need …

8.8 ●))

A=Alberto, S=Shelley, E=Emma King

A So, it's good to see you again, Emma. How are you?

E Well, a little tired, but fine, thanks.

A Would you like a coffee?

E Yes, I'd love one. Thanks.

S Well, we have lots of ideas for you.

A Yes, first of all, some friends are coming round later. Would you like to stay for dinner?

E I'd love to.

S Good. I think you'll like them. They're local artists. One of them is a photographer and he's done some amazing photos of Rio.

E Fantastic.

S And I guess you'd like to have a look round the city centre?

E Yes, I haven't seen much yet.

S OK. Well, I think you might like the area in the city centre called Lapa. There's a great place called Rio Scenarium, which is a bar with samba and bossa nova music. Would you like us to show you around tomorrow?

E Yes, please. It sounds great.

A OK. How about the afternoon? You probably need to sleep in the morning.

E You're right. I could sleep for ever.

A OK. I'll pick you up at your hotel at about 2.00.

E Thanks. That's perfect.

S And we thought you might like to see a bit of Brazil outside Rio.

E That sounds good.

S We're planning to go away on Sunday.

E OK.

S Would you like to visit our beach house? It's in a place called Paraty, a few hours' drive down the coast.

E I'd love to, but I've promised to meet Ken on Sunday.

S Oh, really. That sounds much more interesting …

E It's not really. He just asked if I'd like to go the beach.

8.9 ●))

A=Alberto, E=Emma, S=Shelley

1 A Would you like a coffee?
   E Yes, I'd love one. Thanks.

2 A Would you like to stay for dinner this evening?
   E I'd love to.

3 S Would you like us to show you around tomorrow?
   E Yes, please. It sounds great.

4 A I'll pick you up at your hotel at about 2.00.
   E Thanks. That's perfect.

5 S Would you like to visit our beach house?
   E I'd love to, but I've promised to meet Ken on Sunday.

9.1 ●))

1 He was living in Hong Kong.
2 Was he living in Hong Kong?
3 They were working together.
4 Were they working together?
5 The company was making a lot of money.
6 Was the company making a lot of money?

9.2 ●))

HF=High Flyer, Z=Zita Flores

HF Which industry do you work in?
Z I work in language training.
HF And what were you doing when you started using Twitter?
Z Well, we were organizing a conference, and obviously we were trying to reach a wide audience.
HF So how did you do that?
Z Well, we usually just send out mailshots on email and by post to regular participants, but it didn't seem to be enough. People weren't responding, so we got a bit worried.
HF So what did you do?
Z Well, I had a Twitter account. I was only using it for fun with friends really, but I thought it might be useful. So then I tweeted about the conference, you know, with links to our website, and some information, and I started following a few work-related people, and you know, suddenly people were retweeting my messages.
HF That's exciting!
Z Yes, that was such a good feeling – it made me feel that others thought this conference was important too, which of course it was!
HF Of course!
Z Anyhow, this retweeting increased the number of followers I had. Then I noticed that, at the same time, people on Twitter were transferring the information to Facebook too, so that their friends could read about it there. So in the end we built up a huge following.
HF That sounds excellent!
Z Yes, and, you know, with Twitter, people follow events when they can't be there.
HF Really? What do you mean?
Z Well, some participants at the conference were tweeting during the talks, and meanwhile, the people who were reading the tweets were retweeting them: the messages spread really fast! We had this hashtag, #English4All, so that people who weren't there could focus in on the conference events. All in all, it was a huge success.
HF Well done!
Z Afterwards, we put some photos up on Flickr, and we've now got these linked onto our training pages. You know, I don't know how we ran conferences before, without these sites!

9.3 ●))

K=Kara, J=Jack

K I really have to get fit.
J Why?
K I just sit at my desk at work or sit watching television at home.
J That's true.
K I'm going to get up earlier and go for a run before breakfast.
J But it's dark at that time.
K Is it? Oh. OK. I know. At the moment, I get home late and just have dinner and watch TV.
J True.
K So, I'm going to get home earlier and have a run before dinner.
J Brilliant. But how can you get home earlier?
K I don't know.
J I know. You could get a bike.
K And …?
J And cycle to work.
K You're joking. It's ten kilometres.
J Oh. That's quite far, isn't it?
K But you're right. I should try. I couldn't get into my jeans this morning. They were too tight.
J Oh. I'm sure it'll get better. You just need to eat a bit less.
K What do you mean?!
J OK. OK. Don't get angry.

9.4 ●))

M=Mike Webber, T=Tamara Wilcox, E=Ed Hudson

M Well, thank you for coming along. Ed, Tamara. I know you're both very busy at the moment.
T You're welcome.
E No problem. So what's up, Mike?
M Well, a couple of things, actually. Firstly, one of the ships arriving from Indonesia is going be delayed by about three days.
T Again? They're always late!
M Yes, but the most important issue is a different one. It's about the new collection of shirts and jackets for the summer collection. If you remember, these are part of our new line in adult clothing.
E Is that the design with the new high-tech material?
M Yes, that's right. They offer special protection from the sun. They're made with UPF material.
T So what's happened?
M Well, the firm that makes this special material has gone bust …
E Oh dear.
M So the factory in Manila can't make the clothes.
T But these clothes are a key part of our marketing strategy. We've spent a fortune advertising this new line.
M I know, I know. So we need to come up with a solution.

9.5 ●))

M=Mike Webber, T=Tamara Wilcox, E=Ed Hudson

M So, I'd like to hear if you have any suggestions. Ed?
E Well, let's see …
T Well, what about getting the material from another supplier?
M Yes, that's a possibility. Do you have any suggestions, Ed?
E Well, we used to have a partner in Taiwan. They make the same material. Why don't we contact them?
M That's a good idea. Except I think they are about 20 per cent more expensive.
E Yes, I think you're right.
M How about using a cheaper alternative?
T I'm sorry, but I don't think that will work. If the quality isn't as good, then no. The material we chose has a Sun Protection Factor of 50, but if it's cheaper, it will probably be lower. I don't think it's good enough. We must make sure the clothes are top quality. This is what our customers expect.
M Well, we could postpone introducing these new items until next year …
T Postpone this new line? Absolutely not. They're part of the plan, and they will give us the competitive edge over other brands. I'm sorry.
M Well then, I don't think we have a choice. Let's contact the suppliers in Taiwan.
E OK. Let's do that. I can do that now.
M Thanks, Ed.
T Great. Thanks, Mike. I'm sure this is the right thing to do. Now what about the other problem?
M Well, we have a shipment coming from Jakarta with camping goods – tents, backpacks, and so on. But they've had really bad weather, so they will be at least two days late, perhaps three.
T Right. So this is camping equipment. And which outlets are they for?
M Well, most of these goods are for shops in Spain and Italy, and also some in central Europe, including Slovenia and Croatia.
E OK. Let's get in touch with the transport people. They're usually quite flexible. They have lots of drivers.
M I agree. Thanks, Ed.
T Wait a minute. I'm not sure. Why don't we contact the outlets first? We need to tell them about the delay first. Then later I can tell them when the goods will arrive.
E Yes, but if we can give them the delivery date at the same time, perhaps it's more useful?
T Maybe you're right.
M Well, look, as it's Thursday now, I suggest we send an email to both the shops and the transport company today, to warn them. And then I hope by Monday we'll have more information about the shipment. I don't think two or three days is a major

problem. As long as we can get the
drivers.

T   Good idea, Mike. OK.

E   Yes, agreed.

9.6 •))

M=Mike Webber, T=Tamara Wilcox,
E=Ed Hudson

1   T   What about getting the material
        from another supplier?
    M   Yes, that's a possibility.
2   E   Why don't we contact them?
    M   That's a good idea.
3   M   How about using a cheaper
        alternative?
    T   I'm sorry, but I don't think that will
        work.
4   M   We could postpone introducing
        these new items until next year.
    T   Absolutely not.
5   M   Let's contact the suppliers in Taiwan.
    E   OK. Let's do that. I can do that now.
6   M   I suggest we send an email to both
        the shops and the transport company
        today.
    T   Good idea, Mike.

10

10.1 •))

M=Maya, R=Ron

M   So, continuing our series on predictions
    about the future, today's edition of
    'Your Future' looks at things we will do
    online.

R   Yes, that's right, Maya. And we've had a
    lot of texts this morning. Our listeners
    really want to know what their future
    will be like! So, let's start with shopping.

M   OK.

R   Well, Juan from Bilbao, says 'I think
    most shops will disappear because
    people will do their shopping online'.
    Well, the fact is, about half of all
    European adults already shop online.

M   Yes, one example is in Britain. About
    70 per cent of British adults shop
    online, mostly for clothes and food.
    In Italy though, the number is very
    low, only 15 per cent.

R   And in Britain, an estimated 20 shops
    close every day across the country. One
    expert says that shops will disappear
    forever if they don't change and
    improve.

M   That's a lot of shops. But I hope clothes
    shops won't disappear. I love a day
    out with a friend shopping, you know,
    trying on and buying clothes. If shops
    disappear, it will be very sad.

R   Yes, I think so too. But some shops
    should try harder. Queues are too
    long and the prices are higher than
    online. So the not-so-good shops will
    disappear but the better ones will
    probably survive.

M   Exactly.

R   OK, well tell us about our next topic,
    Maya!

M   OK, right. I've got one here from Jawal
    in Manchester. He says, 'In the future,
    there won't be any cash or credit cards.'

R   No cash, even! What do you think,
    Maya?

M   Well, I agree with Jawal. People want
    a safe way to pay for things. Cash and
    credit cards aren't very safe. People
    can lose or forget their cards, cash gets
    stolen, and so on.

R   That's true.

M   So there are other ways like Google
    Wallet.

R   Google Wallet? What's that?

M   Well, it's basically a mobile payment
    system, and it means no cash or cards,
    and no paper. At the moment, there are
    over 150,000 places in the USA where
    you can pay with Google Wallet. That
    includes New York taxis.

R   Do you think more people will use this
    sort of system?

M   Yes, I think so. If there's a better, safer
    system, people will stop using cash.

R   I think you're right. It sounds like a
    great idea.

10.2 •))

M=Maya, R=Ron

R   OK. Let's move on. I have a text here
    from Seb in Brussels. He doesn't think
    anyone will go to classes at college or
    university. He also says he's doing an
    online course at the moment, and can't
    imagine attending classes again.

M   Sorry, Seb, but I don't agree. I think
    people like going to college. They make
    friends, have fun, learn social skills,
    and do lots of things you can't do
    online.

R   But more and more people are
    studying online these days. In the US,
    three quarters of institutions say that
    students want more online courses
    because of the economic situation.

M   OK. It's a cheaper way to study – there
    are no accommodation costs, and you
    can study where and when you like.
    But if you only learn online, you won't
    really get a good education.

R   OK. Moving on, we have a text from
    Iain in Glasgow. This is about digital
    books. Iain says 'I think in the future,
    people will stop buying paper books'.

M   Well, a lot of listeners don't think they
    will. And I agree with them. After
    all, books don't need batteries, and
    they look nice. You can share them
    with your friends, and they're always
    around. I like that.

R   Yes, but why carry a lot of books
    around, when you can have everything
    on just one e-reader? It's much more
    convenient.

M   Yes, I'm sure it is, but it's expensive too.
    And if you lose an e-reader, you lose all
    your books, maybe hundreds.

R   OK. But you can reload the books on
    another e-reader.

M   Yes, but it's still more expensive than
    losing one paperback.

R   True. Well, on that note, we have to
    finish there. Join us next week for more
    hot topics on 'Your Future'.

10.3 •))

1   CEO

I feel very positive about next year. We aim
to expand our business by 20 per cent. And
I hope to increase the workforce by another
50 people.

2   IT engineer

I need to concentrate when I'm
programming so I enjoy having my own
space. But I like working with people so
I prefer working in an open-plan office.
I can't imagine working from home.

3   Older employee

I'm planning to work here for another two
years and then retire. I'm looking forward
to having more free time and travelling
more.

4   Entrepreneur

The number of permanent staff here is
likely to fall. So I've decided to leave the
company and start my own business.

5   HR manager

We expect to have more female staff in
management positions. I would also like to
recruit more female graduates to work in
the engineering department.

6   Sales administrator

I don't mind working in this department
but I've been here for ten years. I really
want to have a change so I've applied for a
job in customer care.

10.4 •))

1   Do you think it'll be sunny tomorrow?
2   I probably won't go to work tomorrow.
3   Will you change jobs this year?
    I probably will.
4   You'll definitely get a promotion soon.
5   Do you think the company'll survive?
6   He definitely won't be at the meeting.

10.5 •))

S=Sales advisor, G=Gavin Strong

S   You're through to the Sales Team. Simon
    speaking. How can I help you?

G   I'm interested in buying one of the new
    Hisung tablets.

S   OK.

G   I'm looking at your website and I
    wanted to ask a few questions.

S   Sure. Go ahead.

G   I'm looking at the current model, the
    GT-P5110 with the nine point seven
    inch touch screen.

S   Right.

G   And I wanted to know if there is a
    model with a slightly larger screen?

S   No problem. A new model has just
    come out, the Hisung Solar Tab 3.
    It's got a ten point two inch screen.

G   Sorry, was that ten point two?

S   Correct.

G   And the model number?

S   GT-P6110.

G   GT-P6110?

S   That's right.

G And has it got the same resolution as the GT-P5110?
S Yes, it has.
G Fine.
S And it also has the same standard Wi-fi setting.
G So that's a 1280 by 800 resolution and 802.11 Wi-fi.
S Correct.
G How about memory?
S There are two memory sizes. Sixteen gigabytes, the same as the current model, and thirty-two gigabytes.
G How about the other features?
S They are the same, so there's a 3.5 mm headphone jack. And the dimensions are the same – 256.7 by 175.3 by 9.7 mm. The current model is 0.588 kg, but the new model is a little lighter at 0.5 kg.
G OK. That sounds fine. Is it the same price?
S The sixteen gigabyte model is the same at £299.99. The thirty-two gigabyte model is £350.
G Sorry, I didn't catch the second price.
S £350.
G £350, not £315.
S That's right.
G And the delivery dates are the same?
S Yes. Standard delivery is three to five working days. Would you like to go ahead and order?
G Yes, please.

10.6 ◀))
P=Paul Lee, R=Reception
P Hi. Our friends have arranged a farewell party at the Cipriani Restaurant. Do you know where that is?
R The Cipriani Restaurant?
P Yeah.
R Just a moment, please. I'll just check for you.
P Thanks.
R OK. It's on the Avenida Atlântica.
P Could you tell me where that is?
R It's in Copacabana.
P I see. So do you know where the Cipriani Restaurant is on the Avenida Atlântica?
R Sure. It's actually in the hotel called Copacabana Palace.
P The Copacabana Palace?
R Yes, it's on the seafront, overlooking the beach in Copacabana. You can't miss it.
P Great. Do you know if they have a dress code?
R I'm afraid I'm not sure. But it is a five-star hotel so people probably dress smartly.
P OK, thanks. Just one more thing. I'd like some information about the airport.
R OK.
P Could you check the terminal for our flight back to London? I need to tell the taxi driver.
R Certainly, do you have your flight details?
P Yes, the flight number is BA 0248.
R BA 0284.
P Sorry, BA 0248.

R BA 0248. OK. Let's see. Your flight leaves from terminal 1B.
P 1B. Excellent. Thanks very much.
R My pleasure.

10.7 ◀))
Conversation 1
P=Paul Lee, F=Fabio Pérez
P Fabio, thank you very much for your hospitality.
F It's my pleasure. I'm glad you could make it. Will you be back in Brazil again soon?
P I'm afraid not. We've got lots to do with this promotion campaign back in the UK.
F Of course.
P Next time, you must come to London.
F I would love to. Maybe in the spring, when it's a little warmer.
P Good point. It's probably snowing there now.
F Well goodbye, Paul, and have a safe flight.
P Thanks, Fabio. And good luck with your business. I'll be in touch.
F Me, too. All the best.
P Bye.

Conversation 2
P=Paul Lee, K=Ken Martin
P Emma tells me you've changed your plans.
K Yes, I'm afraid something came up back home in New York.
P I'm sorry to hear that.
K Thanks.
P Well, thanks for all your hard work.
K No problem. It's been a pleasure working with you.
P Yes, I think it's been a very successful trip.
K I hope we can work together again sometime.
P I'm sure we will.
K Right. I really must be going or I'll miss my flight.
P Bye, Ken. Take care.

Conversation 3
N=Nathalie, E=Emma
N So Ken's not coming back to London with us?
E No, he's got to go back to New York.
N That's a shame. What are you going to do?
E Save up for a trip to New York, of course.

Answer key

1

Grammar pp.6–8

1
1 Emma King
2 Paul Lee
3 Laura Mancini
4 Ken Martin

2
1 Hong Kong
2 sportswoman / London
3 New York / photographer
4 sportswear
5 King
6 marketing manager / Unisports

3
1 True
2 True
3 False
4 False
5 True

4
1 cycling
2 model
3 morning
4 bikes
5 bus

Focus
We add **-s** / **-es** to the verb for *he, she,* and *it.*
We use the verbs *do* and **be** to make questions.
We use **not** to make negative statements.
We use the Present Simple to talk about **facts** and regular activities.
Wh- and *How* question words come at the **beginning** of a sentence.
We usually put frequency adverbs **before** all verbs except *be.*

5
1 takes
2 doesn't design
3 are
4 doesn't live
5 speaks / doesn't speak
6 doesn't work
7 don't cycle
8 isn't

6
1 Does Ken take photographs? Yes, he does.
2 Does Laura design men's suits? No, she doesn't.
3 Are Ken and Laura friends? Yes, they are.
4 Does Emma live in Scotland? No, she doesn't.
5 Does Paul speak Cantonese / Japanese? Yes, he does. / No, he doesn't.
6 Does Ken work for a sports magazine? No, he doesn't.
7 Do Paul and Laura cycle to work? No, they don't.
8 Is Paul a sales manager? No, he isn't.

8
1 what
2 who
3 where
4 which
5 when
6 what time
7 how much
8 how far
9 how often
10 how many
11 how long

9
1 What (job) does Laura do?
2 Who does Ken know?
3 Where does Laura live?
4 How often does Emma train?
5 How long does Emma cycle for?
6 Which company does Paul work for?
7 What time does Emma get up?
8 When does Emma go to the sports centre?
9 How far does Ken run?

Vocabulary pp.9–10

1
1 television company
2 car manufacturer
3 oil company
4 department store
5 airline
6 coffee producer
7 bank
8 e-commerce company
9 electronic goods producer

2
1 bank
2 electronic goods producer
3 department store
4 coffee producer
5 oil company
6 television company
7 car manufacturer
8 airline
9 e-commerce company

3
1 Panasonic (Corporation)
2 Japanese
3 Osaka, Japan
4 Electronic goods producer
5 100 years old (1918)
6 330,000
7 7.8 trillion yen / 983 million dollars
8 Samsung

4
1 Panasonic (Corporation)
2 Japanese
3 Osaka, Japan
4 electronic goods / televisions, mobile phones, cameras
5 1918
6 330,000
7 7.8 trillion yen / 983 million dollars
8 Samsung

5 1 c   2 a   3 b   4 d

6
1 What nationality is the company?
2 How old is it?
3 Where are its headquarters?
4 How many people does it employ?
5 What type of company is it?
6 What's its annual revenue?
7 What does it produce?
8 Who is its main competitor?

Work skills p.11

1

	Jan	Linda	Karl
1	Sales assistant	Editor	Systems engineer
2	Department store	Publishing company	BEA Systems
3	Food	Fiction	Customer service
4	Fresh food section	Publishing novels	Customers' computer systems
5	Part-time (3 days)	Full-time	Full-time
6	20	20–40	45
7	Team of 10	Authors and two editors	Small team
8	In the store	At home	In the office
9	No	Sometimes	Every day

2
1 What
2 Who
3 What type
4 Which
5 Do
6 How many
7 Who
8 Where
9 Do
10 Can

Functions pp.12–13

1 1 g   2 d   3 f   4 a   5 h   6 c   7 e   8 b

3
1 Bourne
2 sales
3 old friends
4 knows
5 Emma and Nathalie
6 travels to

Focus
1 to introduce yourself:
Can I introduce myself? I'm Ken Martin.

2 to greet someone you know:
Oh, hi Ken. Great to see you.
It's nice to see you again.
How are things? / How are you?

3 to introduce or greet someone for the first time:
How are you?
Very pleased to meet you, Emma.
Nice to meet you too, Nathalie.
You must be Emma.

4
1 a right
b I'm
c Nice / Pleased / Good
d Nathalie
2 a know
b this
c Emma
d Charles
3 a Good
b you / things
c And
d Same / Busy
4 a live
b work
c don't
d you
e in

Review

Grammar p.14

1
2 works
3 is
4 have
5 loves / doesn't like
6 loves / doesn't like
7 go
8 cycles
9 doesn't have
10 takes

2 1 c   2 d   3 e   4 b   5 a

3 1 Where does she live?
2 What time does she get up?
3 Who / What company does she work for?
4 What does she do?
5 How many computers does she have?
6 What languages does she speak?
7 How often does she go to the cinema?

4 1 **Do** you like playing football?
2 They **don't** have a car.
3 He **rarely goes** swimming.
4 What **do** you do?
5 How **long** is the lesson?

Vocabulary p.15

1 1 True 2 True 3 False 4 True 5 False 6 True
2 1 Where are its/the headquarters?
2 What type of company is it?
3 What does it produce?
4 How old is it?
5 How many people does it employ?
6 Who are its main competitors?

3 1 manufactures 4 competitors 7 manufacturer
2 competition 5 employ 8 employer
3 producer 6 products

Work skills p.16

1 1 How many hours do you work a week?
2 Who do you work with?
3 Where do you work?
4 Do you travel (much) (in your job)?
5 What are your responsibilities?
6 Do you like your job?
Eva: make-up artist; Jakob: farmer

Functions p.17

1 1 d, b, a, e, c   3 c, b, a, e, d
2 b, d, c, a, e   4 b, e, d, a, c

2

Grammar pp.18–20

3 1 Twice a year on July 2 and August 16.
2 Three times.
3 Ice sculptures and statues of famous people and places.
4 On stages made of ice.
5 St Petersburg, Russia.
6 Around one million.

4 1 a hotel
2 the Grand Hotel Continental
3 a tour to St Petersburg
4 another tour guide

Focus

Present Simple:
The Palio di Siena horse takes place twice a year.
The race usually takes less than two minutes.
Do you need any help?

Present Continuous:
I'm trying to find them a hotel.
What are you doing?

Rules:
We use the **Present Simple** to talk about facts and regular events.
We use the **Present Continuous** to talk about events happening now or around the present time.
We don't usually use the **Present Continuous** with verbs like *be*, *want*, *need*, *like* and *understand*.
We use phrases like *now*, *currently*, *at the moment*, *still*, and *this (week)* with the **Present Continuous**.
We use phrases like *every (week)*, *usually*, and *on (Sundays)* with the **Present Simple**.

5 1 are you doing / I'm planning
2 Do you know / it's
3 I'm still staying
4 is / He's / is he staying / He's staying
5 do you get

6 is your project going / It's going
7 he's photocopying
8 I'm writing

6 Student A:
1 What does Craig do?
2 What is he working on at the moment?
3 Who is Craig living with at the moment?
4 What does he want to do?
5 What does he love doing?
6 Which language is he currently studying?

Student B:
1 Where does Petra live?
2 Which languages does Petra speak?
3 What is she trying to develop at the moment?
4 What is she doing this week?
5 What is she currently studying?
6 How often does she study?

8 1 /du/, /dəʊnt/   3 /du/, /duː/
2 /dʌz/, /ˈdʌznt/   4 /dʌz/, /duː/, /dʌz/

Vocabulary pp.21–22

1–2 1 elec<u>tri</u>cian   6 pho<u>tog</u>rapher
2 ho<u>tel</u> re<u>cep</u>tionist   7 <u>op</u>tician
3 <u>tax</u>i <u>dri</u>ver   8 <u>ar</u>chitect
4 <u>plum</u>ber   9 <u>shop</u> as<u>sis</u>tant
5 <u>jour</u>nalist   10 <u>chef</u>

3 a shop assistant   f plumber
b chef   g journalist
c photographer   h electrician
d architect   i optician
e taxi driver   j hotel receptionist

4 1 shop assistant   6 photographer
2 chef   7 taxi driver
3 plumber   8 hotel receptionist
4 architect   9 electrician
5 journalist   10 optician

5 See Script 2.4, pp.135–136

8 1 plumber (not medical)
2 designer (not financial)
3 engineer (not publishing)
4 travel agent (inside) / taxi driver (not tourism)
5 builder (not customer service)
6 teacher (not IT)

9 2 make money   6 have fun
3 do well   7 do research
4 do someone a favour   8 have a bath
5 make a decision   9 have a look

10 make: a complaint / a phone call / a profit / an appointment / an arrangement / (trouble)
do: a good job / some exercise
have: a break/rest / a chance / a good time / an idea / trouble

11 1 has 4 do 7 do 10 have
2 make 5 make 8 makes 11 making
3 have 6 have 9 make 12 having

Work skills p.23

1 1 Meeting to discuss Brazil strategy
2 Dear Kay
3 It was very good to meet you last week.
4 Would it be possible to have another meeting to discuss the next stage?
5 Could you let me know which dates are good for you next week? / Please let me know if you have any questions.
6 I've attached a copy of our latest catalogue …
7 With best regards
8 Paul Lee, Marketing Manager, Unisports, Hong Kong

2 1 j 2 e 3 a, d 4 b, f 5 g 6 c 7 i, k, l 8 h

Functions pp.24–25

1 1 Brazil   4 Sheraton Rio
2 Four   5 11.00 (Thursday 16th)
3 20.55 (Wednesday 15th)

2 1 10.45   4 Paul – bike
2 30   5 Fabio Pérez
3 9.30   6 manager of a big sportswear chain

3 1 free   2 but   3 arrange   4 about   5 good   6 fine

Focus

We use **going to** to talk about plans and intentions.
We use the **Present Simple** to talk about fixed times, days, and dates.
We use the **Present Continuous** to talk about arrangements with other people.
Change arrangement: Can we arrange another time?
Suggest a time: How about Saturday?
Ask when someone is free: When would be good for you?
Give a positive response: Yes, that's fine with me.
Give a negative response: I'm really sorry, but I can't make lunch on Friday.

4 Are you going to buy something expensive …?
Are you going to meet someone for dinner …?
Are you going to watch television …?
Are you going to go on a business trip …?
Are you going to move house …?
Are you going to study another language …?
Are you going to fly abroad …?

6 1 I can't make   4 When would be good
2 Can we arrange   5 Are you free
3 How about   6 that's fine

Review

Grammar p.26

1 1 c, 2 d, 3 e, 4 a, 5 f, 6 b

2 2 is   5 are staying   8 visiting
3 is raining   6 not getting up   9 eat
4 are enjoying   7 drinking   10 love

3 1 does the race take place   4 you live in Siena
2 are you riding   5 do you ride / do you go riding
3 are you representing   6 you nervous

Vocabulary p.27

1 1 executive assistant   6 travel agent
2 HR manager   7 vet
3 sales representative   8 chef
4 hairdresser   9 plumber
5 architect   10 accountant

2 ~~make an idea~~ / have an idea
~~do a complaint~~ / make a complaint
~~have research~~ / do research

3 1 complaint   4 appointment
2 exercise   5 deal / research
3 well / money   6 favour / trouble

Work skills p.28

1 1 I look forward to meeting you.
2 Please find our brochure attached. / Please find attached our brochure.
3 I'm writing about the sales conference.
4 Could you send me the presentation slides, please?
5 Please contact me if you have any questions.
6 Thanks for calling this morning.

2 1 It was nice to meet you   5 Please
2 I'm writing to say   6 Please let me know if
3 Could you please tell me   7 We look forward to
4 I'm attaching (I've attached)   8 Best regards

Functions p.29

1 1 leaves   4 have   7 are
2 are meeting   5 Is   8 going to bring
3 are staying   6 meeting

2 1 I'm calling about …   5 Is 12 o'clock fine/OK for you?
2 What's the problem?   6 Can we do 12.30?
3 I'm going to be …   7 In the canteen?
4 Can we arrange another time?   8 Yes, that's fine for me.

3

Grammar pp.30–32

3 1 He wanted to get a job.
2 He had 40 interviews.
3 Because all his interviews were unsuccessful.
4 He travelled by car.

4 1 Utah   2 One week   3 Fifty   4 No   5 Fifty   6 Yes

5 Utah: in a church
Colorado: scientist; fresh water research
Nebraska: corn farmer
Arizona: border police
Texas: oil business
Maryland: seafood cook
New York: marketing department
Maine: lobster fisherman
California: in a wine cellar

Focus

We add **–ed** to the verb to make the Past Simple of regular verbs.
Some verb endings in the Past Simple are **irregular**, for example go/ went, buy/bought.
We use **was** with I, he, she, and it, and **were** with you, we, and they to form the Past Simple of be.
We use did, was, or were to make **questions**.
We use didn't, wasn't, and weren't to make the **negative**.
We use the Past Simple for **finished** actions and situations in the past.

6

Infinitive	start	visit	get	go	work	do
Past Simple	started	visited	got	went	worked	did

Infinitive	continue	stop	marry	be	forget
Past Simple	continued	stopped	married	was/were	forgot

7 1 What was your first job? h
2 How did you find it? j
3 Did you move to get the job? f
4 What qualifications did you need? a
5 Did you enjoy the job? d
6 What did you like about the job? b
7 Was it well paid? e
8 How long did you stay? c
9 What job did you do after that? g
10 What was your favourite job? i

9

	liked	stayed	started	developed	lived
/d/		✓			✓
/t/	✓			✓	
/id/			✓		

	wanted	asked	decided	arrived
/d/				✓
/t/		✓		
/id/	✓		✓	

10 1 In the USA.
2 At least once every three years.
3 That cultures are different, not better or worse.
4 Four.
5 To say where she was from and make friends.
6 Say 'goodbye'.

Vocabulary pp.33–34

1 Types of holiday: cycling; beach; hiking; wildlife; package
Accommodation: rented flat or villa; resort; campsite; bed and breakfast
Transport: taxi; coach, bus; hire car; ship, ferry; metro, underground, subway; train, TGV, Shinkansen

2 1 Types of holiday
2 Transport
3 Accommodation

3 Type of holiday: sightseeing
Transport: (plane), train (Shinkansen), subway
Accommodation: bed and breakfast, hotel

6
1	overhead locker (air)	8	ticket office (train)
2	flight attendant (air)	9	departure lounge (air)
3	ticket inspector (train)	10	train ticket (train)
4	window seat (both)	11	passport control (air)
5	hand luggage (air)	12	excess baggage (air)
6	check-in desk (air)	13	in-flight entertainment (air)
7	security announcement (both)	14	boarding card (air)

7
1 At an airport departure lounge, when boarding a plane.
2 In a plane, after landing while taxiing to a gate.
3 In a train, just before arriving at a station.
4 At an airport check-in desk, when checking in.
5 In a train station, just before a train arrives.
6 In an airport or train station, at any time.
7 In an airport, just before a flight departs.
8 At an airport check-in desk, when checking in.
9 In a train, at any time.
10 At an airport check-in desk, when checking in.

Work skills p.35

2 Call 1:
1 Cathy
2 Ralf Manners
3 Alex Borini
4 A new IT project

Call 2:
1 Lara
2 Ralf Manners
3 Naomi
4 Coming to Berlin next week

3 Call 1:
1 d, 2 f, 3 c, 4 a, 5 e, 6 b

Call 2:
1 c, 2 d, 3 f, 4 g, 5 b, 6 e, 7 a

5 Call 1: b (A = Naomi, B = Ralf)   Call 2: a (A = Alex, B = Ralf)

Functions pp.36–37

2 1 f, 2 e, 3 g, 4 a, 5 d, 6 b, 7 c

Focus

Asking for advice	Giving advice
Is there anything we need to …?	The best thing to do is …
Do we need to …?	I think you should …
What's the best way to …?	… are probably the best (way)
Do you think we should …?	Why don't you (try) …
	It's a good idea to …

3
1 Caracas Airport, Venezuela; flight cancelled because of hurricane
2 In a taxi; going the wrong way and can't speak the language
3 In a subway; took the wrong train, going to be late and don't have client's phone number
4 Ginza, Tokyo; can't find credit card

4 1 C   2 B   3 D   4 A

Review

Grammar p.38

1 Across:
2 said
3 went
5 gave
7 thought
8 made
10 took
12 felt
13 saw

Down:
1 came
3 wrote
4 left
5 got
6 bought
9 drove
11 knew

2
1 The meeting started at 11 a.m. and lasted for an hour and a half.
2 Sorry, I didn't have time to write the invoice because I had so much to do.
3 Sales of cinema tickets went up in winter and fell in summer.
4 Did you know what their best-selling products were?
5 Magda thought she knew the answer, but she didn't.
6 Terence felt very tired when he got home.

Vocabulary p.40

1
1 False   3 True   5 True   7 True
2 True   4 False   6 False   8 False

2
1 Flight attendants
2 boarding card
3 departure lounge
4 Hand luggage
5 overhead locker
6 board

3
1 We went **on** a great camping holiday last summer.
2 Are you going to **stay** in a hotel or an apartment on your trip to Prague?
3 Did you travel to London **in** a taxi?
4 We enjoyed **hiking** in the mountains.
5 We travelled **by** TGV and it was really fast.

Work skills p.40

1
1 Could you hold the line?
2 May I ask who's calling?
3 Thanks for getting back to me.
4 Could I speak to Yan, please?
5 Marie speaking. How can I help you?
6 Could you ask him to call me back?

2 b, f, c, e, a, i, h, g, j, d

Functions p.41

1 1 c, f, i   2 a, e, h   3 b, d, g

4

Grammar pp.42–44

3 Order of value:
1 *The Scream*   2 The *Codex*   3 *The Wittelsbach-Graff Diamond*

4 1 False   2 True   3 False   4 True   5 False   6 False

5
1 Jimi Hendrix's guitar; the first edition of *Action Comic*.
2 $1.39 million; $2.16 million.
3 Jimi Hendrix was one of the great guitar players in history; it was the first comic with Superman in it.

Focus

We form the Passive with **be** + part participle.
We use the Passive to focus on the **object**.
We use the active form to focus on the **doer (agent)**.
We use **by** before the agent.

7 See Script 4.1, p.137–138 (16 examples)

8
1 was started   5 was given   9 was/is played
2 was sold   6 was introduced 10 is watched
3 was created   7 is sold   11 played
4 was/is made   8 was invented   12 is held
eBay, Pepsi, Tennis

9 Student A:
1 was developed
2 was registered
3 was changed
4 is known

Student B:
1 was built
2 was launched
3 was marketed

11
1 FedEx (between 'E' and 'x')
2 BR (31)
3 NBC (multi-coloured feathers)
4 amazon (between 'a' and 'z')
5 Sun (4 times in logo)

12
1 It tells people something about a product and the company that made it.
2 It shows that the company covers a large range of products by linking the letters 'a' and 'z' with an arrow; the arrow also looks like a smile which suggests a positive shopping experience.
3 It should be simple.
4 On products and in various types of advertising.
5 A company's marketing department decides the image and values of the company they want to represent; a designer is briefed on the type of logo the company wants; the designer presents their sample logos to the company and may be asked to provide more samples before the company chooses which one to use.

Vocabulary pp.45–46

2–3

	Facts	Personality	Appearance
Lena	wears a suit	friendly	smart
Bill	hard-working	ambitious	tall
Michelle	good at languages	shy	about 30, medium-height

4

Facts	Personality	Appearance
good at problem solving married hard-working likes sports	easy-going quiet	about five foot four long black hair brown eyes dresses casually dresses smartly short brown hair

5 See Script 4.4, p.138.

8 Object 1: e   Object 2: d

9
1 weighs
2 tells you
3 square
4 made of
5 centimetres long
6 handle at the top
7 useful for
8 strong, waterproof material

11 1 d, 2 f, 3 g, 4 h, 5 j, 6 i, 7 a, 8 b, 9 c, 10 e

12 extremely; very; pretty; quite; a bit; not very

Work skills p.47

1 2 k, 3 f, 4 c, 5 b, 6 e, 7 l, 8 i, 9 d, 10 a, 11 h, 12 j, 13 g

Functions pp.48–49

2 1 e, 2 b, 3 a, 4 c, 5 d

3 1 True 2 False 3 True 4 True 5 False 6 True

4
1 do you think
2 do you feel
3 Do you think
4 you think
5 your point

Focus

Asking for opinions: Don't you think …?
Replying: I think …
Agreeing: Absolutely!
Disagreeing: I see your point, but …

5
1 Do you think / Don't you think
2 How do you feel / What do you think
3 How do you feel / What do you think
4 Do you think / Don't you think

Review

Grammar p.50

1
1 A new security system was introduced last month.
2 The office is cleaned every day.
3 My new motorbike was stolen.
4 Tickets are always checked on the train.
5 When was the microscope invented?
6 A new edition of the book was published last year.

2
1 My sister bought a new car.
3 We buy fresh fruit and vegetables for our lunch menu every day.
4 They found a great new restaurant for dinner.

3
1 When was the new shopping centre opened?
2 Where are the empty bottles taken?
3 Where was it made?
4 Why is the road closed?
5 How much was spent on the new headquarters?

Vocabulary p.51

1 1 b, 2 d, 3 a, 4 c

2 Facts: ~~dresses smartly, in her forties~~
Personality: ~~fair-haired~~, easy-going
Appearance: ~~easy-going~~, fair-haired, dresses smartly, in her forties

3
1 tough
2 leather
3 big
4 comfortable
5 reasonably-priced
6 delicious
7 small
8 easy to use
9 convenient
10 expensive

Work skills p.52

1–2
1 d Good afternoon. Let's introduce **ourselves**.
2 b Shall we **make** a start?
3 f Olga, **would** you like to start?
4 a Now, let's move on to the next **point** on the agenda.
5 e Could everyone look **at** their figures after the meeting and get back to me?
6 c Thank you very much **for** your ideas and suggestions.

Functions p.53

1 1 False 2 False 3 True 4 False 5 False 6 True

2
1 how do you feel about
2 Absolutely
3 Do you think so
4 don't think so
5 That's right
6 Don't you think so
7 see your point
8 not sure

Grammar pp.54–56

2
1 Copper
2 Computer circuit boards, wiring, and other electrical devices
3 Deep in the Atacama Desert, in northern Chile
4 33
5 69 days

3 Not mentioned: oranges, apples, magazines

4
1 much
2 some / some / some / some
3 a little
4 any
5 a few
6 many
7 much
8 lots of
9 any
10 any

Focus

Countable: biscuits, peaches, vitamins, pears, calories, treats, cigarettes, ladders
Uncountable: food, milk, tinned fish, water, information, cereal, fresh air, space, music, exercise
Countable nouns have a singular and a plural form.
Uncountable nouns do not have a plural form.
We use *the* with countable and uncountable nouns.
We only use *a* or *an* with **countable** nouns.

		some	any	a lot of / lots of	(how) much	(how) many	a few	a lit
Countable	*positive*	✓		✓		✓	✓	
	negative		✓	✓		✓		
	question		✓	✓		✓		
Uncountable	*positive*	✓		✓	(✓)			✓
	negative		✓	✓	✓			
	question		✓	✓	✓			

5
1 much
2 a little
3 a lot of
4 a few
5 many
6 information
7 any
8 some / some
9 lots of
10 any

6
2 How much water did the miners drink every day?
3 How much space was there in the mine?
4 How many vitamins did the miners take every day to keep healthy?
6 How did the miners send information to the surface?
7 How much music did they have (at first)?
8 How much cereal and how many pears did they eat?
9 How many cigarettes did the rescuers send down?
10 How many ladders were there in the mine?

7
1 businesses
2 exercise
3 room (space)
4 times
5 coffee
6 paper
7 rooms (times)
8 sports

8
1 paper(s)
2 spaces
3 Sport
4 time
5 business
6 exercises
7 space (room)
8 coffees

9
1 False
2 True
3 True
4 False
5 True
6 False
7 True
8 False

10
3 How many emails do you send a day?
4 How much exercise do you do/get a week?
5 How much time do you spend on the Internet or social network sites?
6 How many days holiday do you get/have/take a year?
7 How much sleep do you have a night?
8 How many people do you talk to in a day?
9 How much coffee do you drink every day?
10 How many hours do you spend travelling to work?

Vocabulary pp.57–58

1
2 fuel
3 fruit
4 material
5 information
6 sport
7 mail
8 drink
9 transport
10 cereal
11 print media
12 entertainment

2 Countable (and uncountable) group names: fuel(s), fruit(s), material(s), sport(s), drink(s), cereal(s)

3
1 note
2 Oil
3 bananas (pineapples / grapes)
4 wood / plastic
5 Statistics
6 sports
7 letter
8 juice
9 transport
10 Rice (maize/corn / wheat)
11 books (magazines)
12 films

4 1 h, 2 i, 3 j, 4 c, 5 g (a), 6 b, 7 d, 8 a (g), 9 e, 10 f

5 1 c, 2 c, 3 a, 4 b, 5 (1 c, 2 a, 3 b), 6 b, 7 c, 8 (1 b, 2 a, 3 c)

Work skills p.59

1 1 Diet, exercise, and tips to stay healthy when you're working hard or under stress.
2 Ask questions

2–3 1 M 2 I 3 F 4 I 5 F 6 M 7 I
8 I 9 F 10 I 11 F

Functions pp.60–61

2 1 The service isn't good
2 A full meal
3 No
4 Bread or pasta
5 No

3 1 c, 2 d, 3 b, 4 a

4 1 Could we
2 I'll have
3 I'd like
4 please
5 Could I have
6 Can I
7 could you
8 Have you got

Focus

1 c, d, f, g   2 h   3 b, e   4 a

5 1 the
2 some
3 a
4 any
5 the (a)
6 (blank)
7 any
8 a
9 a
10 the (a)

Review

Grammar p.62

1

countable	uncountable	both
printer	advice	business(es)
suitcase	information	room(s)
table	luggage	coffee(s)
song	money	space(s)
motorbike	traffic	sport(s)
suggestion	equipment	ice cream(s)
	weather	
	furniture	
	music	
	news	

2 1 much (a lot of)   3 a lot of (many)   5 some
2 many   4 any

3 1 My boss gave me some great **advice**.
2 Sorry, we don't have **any** tea.
3 Do you usually do **much** exercise?
4 I read **some** interesting news this morning.
5 How **many** employees are there in your company?
6 My **luggage hasn't** arrived.

Vocabulary p.63

1 1 ~~iron~~ / sport
2 ~~DVD~~ / print media
3 ~~coal~~ / material
4 ~~photo~~ / mail
5 ~~tea~~ / fuel
6 ~~coffee~~ / cereal

2 2 a cup of coffee
3 a bottle of water
4 a carton of milk
5 (a) slice(s) of bread
6 a bag of flour
7 a piece/slice of cake
8 a jar of coffee

3 1 True
2 False
3 False
4 False
5 True
6 False
7 False
8 True

Work skills p.64

1 1 Thank you for listening.
2 I've divided my presentation into three areas.
3 Now I'd like to move on to …
4 Today I'm going to talk about …
5 Does anyone have any questions?
6 Moving on to my final point
7 I'd like to make some general conclusions.
8 First of all, thank you all for coming.

2 1 First of all, thank you all for coming.
2 Today I'm going to talk about
3 I've divided my presentation into three areas
4 Now I'd like to move on to
5 Moving on to my final point
6 I'd like to make some general conclusions.
7 Thank you for listening.
8 Does anyone have any questions?

Functions p.65

1

Things in a restaurant	Main courses	Desserts	Snacks	Drinks
cloth	fish and chips	apple pie	crisp	lemonade
bill	seafood pizza	cheesecake	croissant	fruit tea
menu	spaghetti bolognese	ice cream	muffin	sparkling water
knife and fork	chicken noodles		sandwich	espresso
	steak and salad			

2 1 e, 2 a, 3 b, 4 c, 5 d

3 1 ready to order
2 I'll have the / please
3 Is there any
4 it's vegetarian (vegan)
5 I'd like
6 can I have some
7 course
8 What would you like to drink
9 An orange juice
10 for me

6

Grammar pp.66–68

2 1 Zurich
2 Dubai
3 Shanghai

3 1 smaller
2 best
3 hottest
4 wider
5 biggest
6 most
7 interesting
8 an older / traditional

Focus

1 one syllable
2 one syllable ending in consonant + vowel + consonant
3 two syllables ending in -y
4 two syllables not ending in -y
5 three or more syllables
6 irregular adjectives

4 1 small, wide, fast, quick, cold
2 hot
4 modern, famous
5 efficient, exciting, traditional

5 1 bigger / smaller
2 fastest
3 worse
4 coldest
5 best
6 less modern
7 tallest
8 oldest

7 1 It was an exciting place to live with good nightlife, shopping, and food.
2 There are a lot of rules.
3 Clothes are cheap, but brands are expensive.
4 Shopping malls, western outlets, souks (traditional markets).
5 Zurich is much more expensive than Shanghai.

9 1 largest
2 more expensive
3 most complicated
4 hotter
5 most famous
6 better
7 biggest
8 best
9 more popular
10 most crowded

Vocabulary pp.69–70

4 1 The Old Town (Rynek Główny)
2 No
3 Outside the city wall, to the south, by the river
4 Trams, buses and trains
5 From newspaper kiosks, ticket machines, or from the driver
6 11 km
7 From a cash point or currency exchange office
8 The Cloth Hall (Sukiennice)

5 2 train line
3 cash point (machine)
4 city centre
5 currency exchange
6 direct train
7 newspaper kiosk
8 pedestrian zone
9 public transport
10 shopping mall
11 ticket machine

6 1 currency exchange
2 art gallery
3 pedestrian zone
4 newspaper kiosk
5 cash point
6 train lines
7 shopping malls
8 ticket machine (newspaper kiosk)
9 public transport
10 Direct trains

7 1 False
2 True
3 False
4 True
5 False
6 True
7 False

Work skills p.71

2 1 Do you mind if I take this?
2 I can't speak right now.
3 Can I phone you later?
4 Can you call me back urgently?
5 I'd like to speak to Mr Myers, please.
6 Can I ask who's calling?
7 Please hold.
8 He's on another call at the moment.
9 Do you want to hold or shall I ask him to call you back?
10 I'll see he gets your message.

Functions pp.72–73

2 1 Five
2 Four (single rooms)
3 Between 6 a.m. and 11 a.m.
4 Yes
5 A bicycle
6 9.30 a.m.

3 1 check in
2 your passports
3 these forms
4 room rate
5 credit card
6 your stay

4 1 b, 2 c, 3 a, 4 d

5 1 False
2 True
3 False (but Paul uses the wrong PIN number at first)

Focus

Arriving at reception	We'd like to check in.
Asking for identification	Could I have your passports, please?
Giving information	Breakfast is included in the room rate.
Asking about facilities	Do you have a business centre?
Asking about payment	Are you all on one credit card?
Complaining about something	I'm calling about the air conditioning.

6 1 c, 2 a, 3 b, 4 f, 5 d, 6 e

Review

Grammar p.74

1 1 Our profits were lower this year than last year.
2 I think traditional art is less interesting than modern art.
3 Travelling by train is slower than travelling by plane.
4 Charles de Gaulle airport is further (away) from Paris than Orly airport.
5 Beijing has a smaller population than Shanghai.
6 In the past, fewer people worked at home.

2 1 more traditional
2 the cheapest
3 quieter
4 more expensive
5 further (away)
6 wider

Vocabulary p.75

1 Across:
2 souvenir
7 cash point
8, 10 shopping mall
12 sightseeing
16, 3 currency exchange

Down:
4, 2 train station
5, 13 art gallery
6, 1 newspaper kiosk
9, 11 pedestrian zone
15, 14 public transport

2 1 d, 2 e, 3 g, 4 a, 5 c, 6 h, 7 b, 8 f

Work skills p.76

1 1 b, a, c
2 c, b, a
3 b, a, d, c, e

2 1 I ask who's
2 I speak to
3 you want to leave a
4 you mind if I
5 I ask him to call

Functions p.77

1 1 c, f, d, a, e, b
2 b, d, f, c, a, e
3 d, b, e, a, f, c

7

Grammar pp.78 80

4 1 In 1860
2 'Rock Around the Clock'
3 Since 1982
4 You could record and store music on it
5 £1 billion
6 Some high street music stores have closed

5 1 No
2 No
3 They're going to (try to) listen to Susie's dad's old LPs

Focus

Present Perfect: a, c
Past Simple: b, d
Past Simple: 1, 2
Present Perfect: 3, 4
We form the Present Perfect with **have + past participle.**
We form questions in the Present Perfect with **have** + subject + **past participle.**
We form negatives in the Present Perfect by putting not/n't after **have.**
Present Perfect: just, since, so far, yet
Past Simple: in 1963, last week, a year ago, when?

6 1 have
2 have closed
3 had
4 joined
5 didn't
6 've had
7 Did you download
8 Have you seen them

7 1 When did you buy your first single?
2 How long have you had your CD player?
3 Has the number of downloads increased?
4 Did the record company make a profit last year?
5 Have you ever been to a music festival?
6 When were 45s popular?

9 1 did / start
2 Have / changed
3 have / played
4 did / promote
5 Have / recorded
6 did / start
7 Have / listened
8 have / been

10 1 ~~Liverpool~~ Manchester
2 ~~16~~ 18
3 ~~three~~ five
4 ~~website~~ blog
5 ~~two months ago~~ last month
6 ~~Facebook~~ Myspace
7 ~~10,000~~ 30,000
8 ~~poor~~ good

13 Student A
1 started
2 have / produced
3 did / introduce
4 Have / had
5 have / done
6 have / made

Student B
1 did / start / started
2 did / release
3 has been
4 did / buy
5 was
6 has / held

Vocabulary pp.81–82

1 1 e, 2 d, 3 c, 4 f, 5 a, 6 b

2 1 by / to
2 at
3 in
4 from / to
5 at
6 of / in

3
1 The number of tourist fell sharply in November.
2 There has been a slight increase in inflation so far this year.
3 There was a decrease in the value of the dollar from 0.67 to 0.62 pounds sterling.
4 There has been a sharp rise in the number of hours I work each week.
5 The number of unemployed has dropped slightly.
6 There was a rise in the EBC share value to 235.09.
7 Company profits have increased steadily in the first quarter.
8 There was a steady fall in the number of new recruits last month.

4
1 fell steadily	4 peaked
2 remained	5 decreased
3 rose dramatically	

6
1 True	3 False	5 False
2 False	4 True	6 True

Work skills p.83

2 Before: 1, 2, 5, 6, 8, 9, 10, 11
During: 3, 7, 12, 13
After: 4, 14

Functions pp.84–85

2
1 Since 2004 (for more than 5 years)
2 In 2009
3 Business Studies
4 Yes
5 2004

3
1 Have you taken	4 didn't put
2 helped / improved	5 studied
3 've been	

Focus

1 b, 2 c, 3 a
We use **for** with a period of time and **since** with a point in time.

4
1 have	8 have you been
2 got	9 have been
3 did you work	10 Have you ever worked
4 worked	11 haven't worked
5 for	12 's been
6 did you learn	13 have really enjoyed
7 learnt	

Review

Grammar p.86

1
1 just	4 so far
2 yet	5 last week
3 six months ago	

2
1 Have you ever learnt / wasn't
2 Have you downloaded / I downloaded
3 Did you buy / I bought
4 Have you ever been / I've never been
5 Did you sing / I sang
6 Have you ever met / I chatted

3
1 was born
2 started learning the recorder
3 started learning the piano and cello
4 has been in (a member of) the Royal College of Music
5 has learned (to play)
6 has won

Vocabulary p.87

1
Verb	Past Simple	Present Perfect	Noun
increase	increased	have increased	increase
decrease	decreased	have decreased	decrease
rise	rose	have risen	rise
fall	fell	have fallen	fall
grow	grew	have grown	growth
drop	dropped	have dropped	drop
level off	levelled off	have levelled off	–
peak	peaked	have peaked	peak
remain stable	remained stable	have remained stable	–

2
1 True
2 False (it was lower in June)
3 False (it has increased since September)
4 False (it fell sharply/dramatically/significantly)
5 True
6 False (it has grown sharply/dramatically/significantly)

3
1 in	3 slightly	5 by
2 remained stable	4 sharply	6 of

Work skills p.88

1
1 Keep	4 Prepare	7 Practise	10 read
2 Check	5 Keep	8 Give	11 Keep
3 Use	6 Find out	9 Decide	12 breathe

Functions p.89

1
1 started	5 have just got back
2 have had	6 had
3 have made	7 did
4 taken part	8 Have / found

2
1 How long have you worked for Seymourpowell?
2 What have you learned there?
3 Where did you work before?
4 Have you ever managed a team?
5 What did you know about our company before coming to this interview?

 8

Grammar pp.90–92

2
1 True	4 False	7 True	9 True
2 False	5 True	8 True	10 True
3 True	6 False		

Focus

Meaning	Example
It's necessary / important to	must / have to
It's important not to	mustn't / Don't
It's a good idea to	should
It's not a good idea to	shouldn't
It's not necessary to	don't have to
It's OK / possible to	can
It's not OK / possible to	can't

3
1 Japan	5 Japan
2 UK	6 Spain, Japan
3 India	7 Spain, Japan
4 India	8 India

4
2 You can keep business cards in your pocket.
3 You mustn't use your left hand to give and receive business cards.
4 You don't have to translate your business cards into Hindi.
5 You should place the business cards on the table in front of you in the order people are seated.
6 You must treat someone's card with respect and take time to read the information.
7 You mustn't put a card straight into your card case.
8 You should include your degree or important qualifications on your card.

5 Heathrow airport:
You must have your passport ready for security.
You should buy any bottled water after you've gone through security.
Before you get to the security search, don't forget to take your laptop out of your check-in bag.
You mustn't take any blades over 6 cm on board.
You can take bottles under 100 millilitres.
Tokyo taxi:
You should have some cash ready in case the taxi driver doesn't take credit cards.
You don't have to tip the taxi driver.
You should get out on the left side of the taxi.
You shouldn't try to close the taxi door yourself.
You should have a map and the address of where you are going in Japanese.
Don't try to negotiate a cheaper fare.

6 Saudi Arabia

8

accommodation	education	money	culture
People often start in hotels but they are expensive	Important for families with children	Help them set up a bank account and transfer money from home	Affects people in different ways
Apartments in popular parts of town are expensive and difficult to get	International schools are popular	Can arrange a loan to help people buy furniture or rent a car	Food, making friends, and weather can all cause problems
	Families either pay more to live next to a good school or pay less and travel longer distances	Companies might pay first month's salary in advance	Put people on an intensive 'cultural awareness' course

9 1 No difference   **3** No difference
    2 Change from /uː/ to /əʊ/   4 Change from /ə/ to /ɑː/

Vocabulary pp.93–94

1 1 A product design company
    2 She had dual nationality
    3 No formal training ('on-the-job' training)
    4 Two years
    5 She went freelance
    6 It's very successful (works with four other designers; thinking of moving to New York)

2 1 j, 2 e, 3 i, 4 b, 5 a, 6 c, 7 k, 8 g, 9 h, 10 f, 11 d

Work skills p.95

2 Sorry to interrupt, but … / Could I just say …

4 Paula, what do you think? / Any comments, Karl? / Sorry, Charles, could you let …

Functions pp.96–97

1 1 a coffee   4 I'll
    2 stay for dinner   5 visit our beach house
    3 to show you around tomorrow

2 1 one   3 please   5 but (negative response)
    2 to   4 Thanks

Focus

Invitation:
Would you like + **to** + **verb**
Offer:
Would you like + **me/us** + **to** + **verb**
Would you like a/some + **noun**
I'll + **verb**
Responses to invitations:
I'd love to.
I'd love to, but … (negative)
Yes, please.

Responses to offers:
I'd love some/one.
Thank you very much. / Thank you. / Thanks.
Thanks for the offer, but … (negative)
Yes, please.

3 1 b, 2 a, 3 f, 4 d, 5 c, 6 e

Review

Grammar p.98

1 1 must   3 don't have to   5 can
    2 should   4 shouldn't

2 1 He should check what time his visitors' plane arrives.
    2 You can borrow mine (my pen).
    3 You must arrive on time for meetings.
    4 She has to register before 20th February.
    5 Employees don't have to go to the workshop.
    6 You can't sit here (at this table).

3 1 Do I have to wear a uniform?
    2 Do I need to take my driving licence with me?
    3 Can I eat in the office?
    4 Who should I ask for?
    5 When can I go home?
    6 Can I take any company files out of the building?

Vocabulary p.100

1 1 c, 2 f, 3 e, 4 b, 5 g, 6 h, 7 a, 8 d

Work skills p.100

1 1 what do you   6 just wanted to say
    2 Sorry to interrupt   7 How about you
    3 Can I just say that   8 May
    4 Sorry   9 Any comments
    5 can you let / finish

Functions p.101

1 1 c, e, g, b, a, h, f, d   2 e, a, g, c, h, d, b, f

2 1 Would you like to go shopping? (Yes), I'd love to.
    2 Would you like me to call a taxi? Thanks for the offer, but I'd prefer to walk.
    3 Would you like some cake? Thanks, but I'm full.
    4 I'll give you a lift to the airport. Thanks. That's perfect.
    5 Would you like us to translate for you? Yes, please.

9

Grammar pp.102–104

2 1 Mark Zuckerberg
    2 A website similar to Facebook (Facemash) / Cameron and Tyler Winklevoss and Divya Narendra
    3 They thought he used some of their ideas to build Facebook (Thefacebook)
    4 Yes
    5 900 million

Focus

a was studying / were working on / was working on (Past Continuous)
b asked / had (Past Simple)
The Past Continuous is formed with the past tense of the verb *be* and the present participle (*was/were* + *-ing*).
We often use the Past Continuous with *while* and *meanwhile*.
We often use the Past Simple with *when* and *then*.

4 1 False (He was studying at Harvard University)
    2 True
    3 True
    4 False (Zuckerberg was helping the Winklevosses)
    5 True
    6 False (They weren't happy when Thefacebook was launched)
    7 True

6 1 was watching / came   7 were you working / got
    2 wasn't going / got   8 arrived / was uploading / was cooking
    3 started / were trying
    4 met / was working   9 won / was looking
    5 was trying / walked   10 started / was living
    6 discovered / didn't have

7 1 /wəz/   3 /wɜː(r)/   5 /wəz/
    2 /wɒz/   4 /wə(r)/   6 /wɒz/

8 1 Twitter, Flickr
    2 They increased the number of people interested in her conference.

Vocabulary p.105

2

do	get	go	have
(my/your) homework	ready/up/ dressed	for a run/walk/ bike ride/drive	a drink/ takeaway/ break
some exercise	a drink/ takeaway/ break	out for a meal	lunch
the washing/ washing-up	lunch	shopping	
	some exercise	to a concert/ friend's house	
		to bed	
		to the cinema/gym	

5

	Kara	Jack
get fit	✓	
get up earlier	✓	
get home late	✓	
get a bike		✓
get into my jeans	✓	
get better		✓
get angry		✓

6
1 basketball
2 pool
3 rugby
4 tennis
5 soccer / football
6 golf
7 baseball
8 table tennis
9 American football
10 cricket

7 bat: baseball, cricket (table tennis)
club: golf
cue: pool
racket: tennis, table tennis

8 Play

9

Do	Go	Play
aerobics	running	badminton
judo	cycling	squash
gymnastics	sailing	hockey
	skiing	
	hiking	
	swimming	

Work skills p.107

1 Email 1 is a reply to Email 3
Email 4 is a reply to Email 2

2
1 Email 3: a speaker can't attend a conference / Email 2: a printing error
2 Email 1: another speaker was asked to attend the conference / Email 4: the printing error was corrected
3 Give good news: Fortunately, …
Give bad news: Unfortunately, … / (However,) I'm afraid …
Apologize: I (do) apologize for …

Functions pp.108–109

1 The ship arriving from Indonesia is going to be delayed by about three days.
The company (firm) that makes the special material for the new clothing design has gone bust (bankrupt).

4 1, 4, 5, 6

5
1 getting the material from another supplier
2 contact them
3 using a cheaper alternative
4 postpone introducing these new items until next year
5 contact the suppliers in Taiwan
6 send an email to both the shops and the transport company today

6
✓ Yes, that's a possibility.
✓ That's a good idea.
✗ I'm sorry, but I don't think that will work.
✗ Absolutely not.
✓ OK. Let's do that. I can do that now.
✓ Good idea, Mike.

Focus

Infinitive verb without *to*: 2, 4, 5, 6
-ing form: 1, 3

7
1 go
2 go
3 cancel
4 watching
5 having
6 finish

Review

Grammar p.110

1 1 c, 2 a, 3 d, 4 e, 5 b

2
1 while (when)
2 then
3 at the same time
4 Meanwhile (at the same time)
5 When
6 while

3
1 met
2 was living
3 were / doing
4 was studying
5 was going
6 was walking
7 saw
8 were shouting
9 could
10 got
11 couldn't
12 was
13 was / doing
14 was / looking
15 dancing
16 waited
17 were waiting
18 came out
19 disappeared
20 didn't / meet
21 was standing
22 came
23 did / look
24 was wearing

Vocabulary p.112

1
1 doing
2 going
3 do
4 go
5 go
6 do
7 going
8 do
9 get
10 going
11 get
12 going
13 get (do)
14 get
15 go
16 get

2
1 gymnastics (*do*, not *play*)
2 ball
3 badminton (*play*, not *go*)
4 office

Work skills p.112

1 Email 1 (order): 3, 10, 8, 5, 1
Email 2 (meeting): 7, 2, 9, 4, 6

Functions p.113

1 1 e, 2 f, 3 b, 4 c, 5 a, 6 d

2
1 phone a taxi
2 move to a cheaper office
3 about searching for a hotel online
4 about trying the new seafood place
5 go sailing

10

Grammar pp.114–116

3
1 think / will
2 If / will be
3 Do you think
4 If / will

4 1 True   2 False   3 False   4 True

Focus

We use **will** and **won't** + infinitive to predict future situations.
We use *don't think* + subject + **will** to predict something that will not happen.
We form the Zero Conditional with *if* + Present Simple for the condition and **Present Simple** for the result.
We form the 1st Conditional with *if* + Present Simple for the condition and **will** + **infinitive** for the result.

5
2 Do you think a lot of high street shops will disappear in the next ten years?
3 Do you think you will be famous in ten years' time?
4 By 2050, do you think most people in the world will speak English?
5 One day, do you think computers will be smarter than humans?
6 Do you think most cars will be electric in 20 years' time?
7 Do you think people will use drugs to improve their memory in this century?
8 By 2030, do you think scientists will find life on other planets?
9 In the future, do you think the world will warm up by more than five degrees?
10 Do you think people's average age will increase to (in) 120 years?

7
1 will go
2 always rains
3 will miss
4 takes
5 will get
6 will pay
7 have
8 always lose
9 is
10 is usually

8 They connect people by giving them Internet access and can also help them look after their health.

9
1 I (can) use the Info Ladies' laptop (Local woman)
2 I (can) talk to the Info Ladies about the correct use of fertilizer and insecticides (Local farmer)
3 I (can) pay 10 takas to the Info Ladies (Local student)
4 I (can) ask the Info Ladies for help (Local woman or man)
5 we will enlist thousands more workers in the next few years (Info Ladies project director)

Vocabulary pp.117–118

1 1 to expand / to increase
2 to concentrate / having / working (to work) / working (to work) / working
3 to work / having
4 to fall / to leave
5 to have / to recruit
6 working / to have

6 All except number 3 (Question and answer)

Work skills p.119

3

Model name/number	Hisung Solar Tab 3, **GT-P6110**
Screen	**10.2"** touch screen
Resolution	**1280 x 800**
Wi-fi	**802.11** b/g/n
Memory	**16 GB, 32 GB**
Audio connection	**3.5 mm** headphone jack
Dimensions	**256.7 x 175.3 x 9.7 mm**
Weight	**0.5 kg**
Price	**£299.99, £350**
Delivery	**3–5 working days**

4 1 Sorry, was that 10.2?
2 And the model number? / GT-P6110?
3 So that's
4 Sorry, I didn't catch / not

Functions pp.120–121

1 1 The Cipriani Restaurant for a farewell party
2 It's in the Copacabana Palace Hotel
3 Which terminal his flight leaves from

2 1 No
2 In the spring
3 New York (the airport)
4 He has to catch his flight (to New York)
5 London
6 Save up money for a trip to New York

3 Conversation 1: 1, 3, 4
Conversation 2: 5, 6, 8
Conversation 3: –

Focus

We put the question word **after** the phrases *Do you know* and *Could you tell me*.
We use *if* when there **isn't** a question word.
The word order of an indirect question is the same as a **statement**.
Thanking: 1, 5
Farewell phrases: 2, 3, 4, 6, 7, 8

5 2 Could you tell me when Carnival is in Brazil?
3 Do you know what the largest city in Brazil is?
4 Do you know if the Brazilian football team wears a yellow jersey?
5 Could you tell me what the name of Brazil's most famous waterfall is?
6 Do you know if Brazilians speak Spanish or Portuguese?
7 Can you tell me who the most famous Brazilian racing driver is?
8 Could you tell me if Brazil produces coffee?
9 Do you know if the population of Brazil is more than 200 million?
10 Do you know what the most famous landmark in Rio de Janeiro is?

Review

Grammar p.122

1 2 I usually go for Chinese or India if I eat out.
3 If we have to work overtime, we get paid for it.
4 House prices usually fall, if interest rates rise.
5 If the company hires new staff, they give them training.
6 My boss doesn't mind if I'm a bit late for work.

2 2d If I find the file, I'll email it to you.
3a If you pay cash, I'll give you a discount.
4g If more people work at home, there will be less traffic on the roads.
5f If the birth rate continues to fall, there won't be enough workers.
6b If he finishes university, he'll have better job opportunities.
7e If we want to expand, we'll have to borrow money.

Vocabulary p.123

1

followed by *–ing*	followed by *to* + verb	followed by *–ing* or *to* + verb
look forward to don't mind enjoy	aim decide need plan expect hope want is likely would like	like prefer

2 1 to look for
2 meeting
3 to move
4 getting up
5 working
6 to have
7 to increase
8 to speak / to send

3 1 I don't think I'll be able to retire when I'm 60.
2 We'll definitely use cash in the future.
3 They'll probably give us a bonus.
4 Sales of electric cars are unlikely to rise.
5 He might not come to the workshop.
6 She thinks she'll be invited to the conference.
7 It probably won't snow at the weekend.
8 People definitely won't work less in the future.

Work skills p.124

1 1 b (c), 2 c (b), 3 a, 4 e, 5 d

2 1 Sorry, I didn't catch the dates.
2 I'm interested in your conference facilities.
3 That's right.
4 How can I help you?
5 Sorry, was that 113 or 130?
6 Sorry, was that four small meeting rooms?

3 1 I'm interested in your conference facilities.
2 how can I help you?
3 Sorry, was that four small meeting rooms?
4 That's right.
5 Sorry, was that 113 or 130?
6 Sorry, I didn't catch the dates.

Functions p.125

1 1 What time does the bank open, please?
2 Is there a cash point near here?
3 What is your email address?
4 How can I get to the airport?

2 1 when the meeting starts
2 where Natasha's office is
3 if there's a swimming pool (in the hotel / near here)
4 why Max went home early
5 how much a double room costs
6 when Gloria sent the price list

3

I really	Thanks for	I hope
have to go now	a lovely evening	we can meet again soon
must be going	all your hard work	we work together again sometime
	your kind hospitality	

Have a	I'll	See you
safe flight	call you soon	soon
good journey	be in touch	back at the office
	(have to go now)	

Alastair Lane

INTERNATIONAL EXPRESS

PRE-INTERMEDIATE

Pocket Book

Contents

Pocket Book Guide

Here is some information about the Pocket Book.

1 There are short examples of conversations for each section of the Student's Book. You can listen to these conversations using the audio files on the website. Here are some suggestions.

  1 You can practise your listening. Just play the audio and listen. Listen a little bit every day to improve your listening skills.

  2 You can practise your speaking. You can take the **B** part and answer **A** in each conversation.

  3 You can practise your pronunciation. Listen carefully to how the people speak. Copy their pronunciation.

  4 You can improve your memory. Cover the **B** line. Then read the **A** line. Repeat until you can remember the **B** line.

2 You can check the notes in the Student's Book for each language point. The reference page is at the end of each section.

3 You can use the *Classroom language* section in class. Keep your Pocket Book on your desk and check the right phrase to use to ask questions, check meaning, and so on.

4 The *Grammar terms* section gives you some more study words to help you understand grammar.

5 The *Irregular verbs* section gives you a reference for common irregular verbs from the Student's Book.

6 Take the Pocket Book with you to work. Keep it on your desk. Practise when you have spare time. Use it when you make a phone call or before you meet someone.

7 Take the Pocket Book on business trips or on holiday.

Grammar

UNIT 1 Present Simple

1 **A** *How are* you?
  B *I'm* fine thanks, and you?

2 **A** *Do* you *know* Brian Moore?
  B Yes, I *do*.

3 **A** *Does* Rick *speak* Russian?
  B No, he *doesn't*.

4 **A** *Where does* Kai *live*?
  B He *lives* in Stuttgart.

5 **A** *When does* your English class *start*?
  B It *starts* tomorrow.

6 **A** *What do* you *do*?
  B *I'm* a doctor.

7 **A** *Which* company *does* Tina *work* for?
  B She *works* for Google.

8 **A** *What time do* you *get up*?
  B I *usually get up* at 6.30.

9 **A** *How often does* Andrew *go* running?
  B He *goes* running every day.

10 **A** I *always work* from home on Fridays.
  B Really? I *never work* from home.

11 **A** I *travel* a lot for work. I *sometimes fly* abroad three times a month.
  B Do you? We *rarely travel* for work.

12 **A** *Why does* the shop *close* on Mondays?
  B It *closes* on Mondays because it *opens* on Saturdays and Sundays.

Reference: Student's Book **p. 14**

UNIT 2 Present Continuous; Present Simple

1 A *Is* Karen *having* a coffee break?
  B Yes, she *is*.

2 A *Is* Ricardo *staying* here *all week*?
  B Yes, he *is*.

3 A Why *are* you *working* in the conference room?
  B Because they*'re painting* my office *at the moment*.

4 A *Do* you *need* any help, Mike?
  B No, it's OK, thanks. Susan*'s helping* me today.

5 A Who *is* Ian *speaking* to on the phone?
  B He*'s speaking* to the Sales Director in Helsinki.

6 A How many languages *do* you *speak*?
  B Two. I *speak* Chinese and English.

7 A When *does* the city marathon *take place*?
  B It *usually takes place* in June.

8 A There are lots of people in the city centre today.
  B Yes, they*'re taking part* in the city marathon.

9 A *Do* you *like* opera?
  B No, I don't. I *don't understand* it.

10 A *Are* you *enjoying* your meal?
  B Yes, we are. It's delicious, thanks.

11 A *Are* you *leaving now*?
  B No, I'm not. I*'m still working*.

12 A Is Sharon here today?
  B No, she*'s currently working* in our Paris office.

Reference: Student's Book **p. 26**

UNIT 3 Past Simple

1 A *Was* the conference in Belgrade last year?
B Yes, it *was*.

2 A *Were* you busy last week?
B No, we *weren't*.

3 A *Did* you *enjoy* your visit to our offices?
B Yes, I *did*.

4 A *Did* Masako *finish* the report yesterday?
B No, she *didn't*.

5 A When *did* they *do* their homework?
B They *did* it this morning.

6 A How much money *did* the project *make*?
B It *didn't make* any money. We *lost* $1,000!

7 A Why *did* the customers *make* a complaint?
B Their order *didn't arrive* on time yesterday.

8 A *Were* you on time for the meeting?
B Yes, I *was*. I *wasn't* late.

9 A *Did* Tamsin *book* our flights yesterday?
B No, she *didn't*. She *forgot*.

10 A Where *did* you *take* the customers for dinner?
B We *took* them to a Japanese restaurant. We *ate* sushi.
Delicious!

Reference: Student's Book **p. 38**

UNIT 4 Passives: Present Simple, Past Simple

1 A *Is* your English class *taught* by Martin?
B Yes, it *is*.

2 A *Are* your products *made* in the UK?
B No, they *aren't*. They're *made* in China.

3 A *Were* the computers *transported* by ship?

   B Yes, they *were*.

4 A *Was* the report *written* by Stefania?

   B No, it *wasn't*. It *was written* by Eva.

Reference: Student's Book **p. 50**

UNIT 5 Countable and uncountable nouns

1 A Do you have *any advice* for me?

   B Yes, I have *some suggestions* for you.

2 A Do you have *lots of luggage*?

   B No, I just have *a suitcase* and *a rucksack*.

3 A *How many visitors* did the company have yesterday?

   B We didn't have *any visitors*.

4 A I have *a few* problems with my *homework*. I don't understand it.

   B It is difficult, isn't it? There's *a lot of information* to read.

5 A *How much sugar* do we need in the cake?

   B About 10 grams, and you need *a little salt* too.

Reference: Student's Book **p. 62**

UNIT 6 Comparisons

1 A The bus is *cheaper than* the train.

   B Yes, but the bus is *more crowded than* the train.

2 A Can you tell me about the new company cars? Is the BMW *more expensive than* the Mercedes?

   B Yes, and it's *bigger than* the Mercedes too.

3 A Is London's Heathrow Airport *busier than* Amsterdam's Schiphol Airport?

   B Yes, it is. Heathrow is *the busiest* airport in Europe.

4 A The Bristol Hotel *is further* from the city centre *than* the Crown Hotel.

B Yes, but I prefer the Bristol. It's *more modern than* the Crown.

5 A This year's advert is *less successful than* last year's.

B I agree. Last year's advert was *much funnier than* this year's.

6 A Victor's blog is *the least popular* blog on the website.

B Yeah, nobody reads it. Annabelle's blog is *the best* one. Her blog is *much better than* Victor's.

7 A Fiona is *the worst* salesperson in the company. Her results are terrible.

B That's not true. Hakan is *worse than* Fiona. His sales in January were 15% *lower than* Fiona's.

Reference: Student's Book **p. 74**

UNIT 7 Present Perfect; Past Simple

1 A How long *have* you *had* your smartphone?
B I*'ve had* it for about twelve months. I *bought* it last year.

2 A How long *have* you *lived* in Seoul?
B We*'ve lived* here *since* 2009.

3 A *Has* Gary *ever worked* with you?
B Yes, he *has*. We*'ve worked* together lots of times.

4 A *Have* you *ever been* to Tokyo?
B No, I *haven't*. I*'ve never been* to Japan.

5 A *Have* you *ever been* to Brazil?
B Yes, I *have*.
A When *did* you *go* there?
B I *went* to Rio in 2011.

6 A *Have* you *told* everyone about the new management team?

B I've spoken to almost everyone in Europe *so far*.

A OK. *Have* you *told* the Italy office *yet*?

B No, but Carol *has already told* them the news. She *emailed* them *yesterday*.

A What about the team in Germany? *Have* they *heard*?

B Yes, *they have*. Helmut *has just sent* them an email.

Reference: Student's Book **p. 86**

UNIT 8 Modals and related verbs

1 A *Do* I *have to get* a visa before I travel to Turkey?

B No. Most people *can get* a visa at the airport when they arrive.

2 A How *can* we *find* new staff?

B We *should put* an advert online.

3 A *Can* I *buy* entrance tickets for the museum here?

B Yes, but *you don't have to pay* today. It's free on Mondays.

A That's great! Thanks.

4 A Sorry, you *can't take* your bags into the museum. You *must leave* them in the cloakroom.

B OK. No problem.

5 A I *mustn't forget* to send flowers on Mother's Day. I found this company online. Is it OK?

B Oh, no. You *shouldn't use* that company. You *should try* Interflora.

Reference: Student's Book **p. 98**

1 A *Did* you *speak* to Martina yesterday?

B Yes, I *saw* her while I *was waiting* for my train.

2 A This time last year *we were designing* our new website.

B I remember. *I was writing* the software while *you were talking* to journalists.

3 A How *was* the interview?

B Not good. I *felt* stupid because I *wasn't wearing* a suit. Everyone in the company *was wearing* very formal clothes.

4 A Carl's in hospital.

B Why?

A He *broke* his arm while he *was playing* football.

5 A Last year, Niko *was doing* a Master's course. At the same time, he *was working* in a fast food restaurant.

B Yeah, it was a difficult year. He *was working* all the time.

6 A Last year, sales *were falling* in Europe. Meanwhile, they *were increasing* in Asia.

B I see. *Were* sales *falling* in North America?

A Yes, they *were*.

B *Were* they *falling* in South America, too?

A No, they *weren't*.

7 A Last night, I *needed* some milk, so I *went* to the supermarket. But when I *got* there, it was closed.

B Why?

A They *were filming* an advert there.

B Really? In our supermarket? That's amazing!

Reference: Student's Book **p. 110**

1 A *Will* we *get* a pay rise next month?
  B Yes, we *will.*

2 A *Will* the company *open* any new branches next year?
  B No, it *won't.*

3 A *Will* a lot of people *come* to the meeting tomorrow?
  B Yes, I *think so.*

4 A I have a work trip to Moscow in May. Do you think it *will be* cold?
  B No, I *don't think so.*

5 A Do I have to buy a train ticket for my daughter? She's three.
  B No. If you *travel* with young children, they *travel* for free.

6 A *Will* the swimming pool *be open* today?
  B No. If it *rains,* they *close* the pool.

7 A I can't understand this email. It's in Portuguese.
  B If you *show* it to me, *I'll translate* it for you.

8 A I saw this job advert online. Do you think I should apply for it?
  B Of course! If you *don't apply* for the job, you *won't get* an interview.

Reference: Student's Book **p. 122**

Vocabulary

UNIT **1** Talking about companies

1 A What's the *name* of your company?
  B It's called McCabe Ltd.

2 A What *nationality* is Aer Lingus?
  B It's Irish.

3 A Where does Coca-Cola have its *headquarters?*
  B In Atlanta, Georgia in the USA.

4 A I work for Lagostina in Italy.
  B What *type of company* is that?
  A We make cutlery: knives and forks, and other things for cooking.

5 A How old is Marks and Spencer?
  B It's over a hundred years old. It *started* in 1884.

6 A How many people work at your factory?
  B A lot. I think the *number of employees* is about 600.

7 A How much money does your company make?
  B Its *annual revenue* is about €150,000.

8 A What's the main *competitor* of KFC?
  B Other fast food companies like McDonald's or Burger King.

UNIT **2** Jobs

1 A Did Norman Foster design this airport?
  B No, it was a different *architect*.

2 A Do you know a good restaurant?
  B Oh, yes. Go to Dino's. Their *chef* is amazing.

3 A The air conditioning doesn't work.
  B Let's call an *electrician* to fix it.

4 **A** How was your hotel?
   B Perfect. The *hotel receptionist* was very friendly and helpful.

5 **A** I saw your company in the newspaper.
   B Yes, a *journalist* interviewed me last week. She wanted to write about our business.

6 **A** Is Mehmet at work today?
   B No, he went to see the *optician*. He needs new glasses.

7 **A** Tomorrow, a *photographer* is visiting our sports centre to take pictures for the website.
   B OK. Thanks for telling me.

8 **A** There's no hot water in the bathroom.
   B Right. I'll call a *plumber*.

9 **A** Can you see a *shop assistant*? I want to try on these shoes.
   B Yes, there's one over there.

10 **A** Phew! We got to the airport in time.
   B Yes, that *taxi driver* was great.

make, do, have

1 **A** I have $600 in the bank, but I don't know why.
   B Oh no! I *made a mistake*. I thought I sent $60.

2 **A** Do you know the location for next year's conference?
   B Yes, it's Rio. Laurence *made the decision* yesterday.

3 **A** How much *money do you make* on eBay?
   B About $50 a month.

4 **A** I passed my final Law exams!
   B Congratulations. You *did really well*.

5 **A** What bands are popular with today's teenagers?
   B I don't know. We need to *do some research* to find out.

6 **A** Neil, can you *do me a favour*? I need some help with my report.
   B No problem. Let's look at it together.

7 A The office summer party is a great event.
  B Yeah, everyone *has fun*.

8 A Does this shop sell birthday cards?
  B I don't know. Let's *have a look* inside.

9 A We did a lot of sightseeing today. My feet hurt now.
  B Mine too. I want to go back to the hotel and *have a bath*.

10 A I'm really tired.
  B *Have a break.* You'll feel better.

11 A Excuse me. I need to *make a phone call*.
  B No problem. We'll wait for you.

12 A Do you *do a lot of exercise*?
  B Yes, I go to the gym three times a week.

13 A Do you think I'll get the job?
  B Your interview went well so you *have a chance*.

14 A Is your company successful?
  B Yes, it is. We *make a profit* every year.

15 A Are you the manager? I want to *make a complaint*.
  B Yes, I am, madam. What's the problem?

16 A I'd like to see the director, please.
  B Do you *have an appointment*?

17 A Everyone was pleased with my presentation.
  B Yeah, you *did a good job*.

18 A Ana, can you book my flight to Moscow, please?
  B Yes, sure. I'll *make all the arrangements*.

19 A Did you *have a good time* in Marrakesh?
  B Yes, we did. We loved it.

20 A I *have an idea* for a new advert.
  B Really? Tell me about it.

UNIT 3 Talking about travel

1 A Where are you staying on your *hiking* holiday?
   B We're staying on a *campsite*.

2 A We're going *cycling* in Patagonia in the summer.
   B Great! You'll see lots of *wildlife* there.

3 A I think we'll go to Rome by *coach*.
   B Really? I prefer the *train*.

4 A Let's get a *taxi* to the airport.
   B No, let's use the *underground*. It's only €1.50.

5 A What was the *resort* like?
   B Lovely. It was next to the *beach*.

6 A I want to stay in a *bed and breakfast* but they're all booked up.
   B Why not get a *rented flat* or a *villa*? They're great for families.

7 A What do you think of this *package holiday*?
   B Excellent. It includes a *hire car*, too. That's perfect for us.

8 A Would you like to do some *sightseeing* this afternoon?
   B I can't, I'm sorry. I'm catching my *plane* in an hour.

9 A I have two suitcases and one piece of *hand luggage*.
   B I'm sorry, sir. You can only have one suitcase. There is a charge for *excess baggage*.

10 A I can't get my bag in the *overhead locker*. There's no space.
   B Ask the *flight attendant* to help you.

11 A We need to go through *passport control*.
   B OK. Do we need to show our *boarding passes*?

12 A The train's leaving in two minutes. Let's sit down here. Do you want the *window seat*?
   B Yes, please. Oh, the *ticket inspector*'s coming.

13 A What did they say? Was that a *security announcement*?
   B No, they said there will be a delay.

UNIT 4 Describing people and objects

1 **A** You said that Stefania has an *interesting background*.
   B Yes, she's *about 40* but she's had 25 different jobs!

2 **A** Is Frank very *ambitious*?
   B Yes, he's very *hard-working*. He wants to be the boss one day.

3 **A** Ishmael is *good at languages*, isn't he? He speaks French, English, and Arabic.
   B And he *has a great sense of humour* too. He's funny in all three languages.

4 **A** Everyone at the company in Vienna was very *friendly*, weren't they?
   B Yes, but I felt *shy* because I don't usually speak German.

5 **A** Becky, do people wear *smart* clothes in your office?
   B Yes, all the men *wear suits*.

6 **A** What does Orlando look like?
   B He's about *medium height* with *long dark hair*.

7 **A** Tell me about the new programmer, Vladimir.
   B He *dresses casually* – T-shirts and jeans. He's quiet and he's very *good at problem-solving*.

8 **A** Who is Suzanne? Is she the one who *likes sports* and adventure holidays?
   B That's right. She's *about five-foot four with short brown hair* and *brown eyes*.
   A Right. I know her!

9 **A** Do you have a *large* office?
   B No, it's very *small* and I share it with two other people.

10 **A** Are people dressing *casually* for the wedding?
   B No, it's very *formal*.

11 **A** People say the new website is *difficult to use*.
   B That's because it's new. After a couple of weeks, it gets easier.

12 A Most of the restaurants in the centre of town are *expensive*. Do you know a *cheap* one?

B The Gold Dragon is *reasonably priced* and their food is delicious.

13 A Did you have a *comfortable seat* on the flight?

B No, it was really *uncomfortable*. I was in economy.

14 A Our new call centre is very *efficient*. Our customers are very satisfied.

B Good, because the old call centre was very *inefficient*. They never answered the phone quickly.

15 A Are your bags *heavy*?

B Only the blue one. The yellow one is very *light* because it only has a few papers in it.

UNIT 5 Quantity

1 A Did you know that we're opening a new office in Malaysia?

B That's an interesting *piece of information*. Thanks!

2 A In Brazil, they have *kilo* restaurants. You get *a plate of food* and you pay by weight.

B That's a good idea.

3 A Do you have any tea?

B No, sorry. But there is a *jar of coffee* in the kitchen.

4 A I'll write a note for Bruno. Do you have a *piece of paper*?

B Sure. Here you are.

5 A Are you bringing anything for the coach trip?

B Yes, I have some sandwiches and *a bottle of water*.

6 A I bought *a litre of olive oil* in the duty free shop. It was only five euros.

B That's cheap.

7 A Do you need anything from the supermarket?

B Yes, can you buy me a *packet of sugar*, please?

8 A On the news, they said *a gallon of oil* is now $3.70.

B That's expensive.

9 A Did you fix your suitcase?
  B Yes, but it was difficult. I put a *metre of tape* around it.

10 A What do you want for breakfast?
  B Just some toast. Can you pass me *a slice of bread*, please?

UNIT 6 Talking about cities

1 A What's the best *art gallery* in New York?
  B The Metropolitan Museum of Art is fantastic. You should go there.

2 A Which *train line* do I need to go from the centre of Cologne to the University?
  B You need line 8.

3 A Is there a *cash machine* near here?
  B Yes, there's one in the bank on the next street.

4 A Where's your hotel?
  B It's in the *city centre*.

5 A Can I get Russian roubles at the post office?
  B No, but you can get some in the *currency exchange* at the airport.

6 A Can I take a *direct train* from Pamplona to Barcelona?
  B Yes, you can.

7 A Where do you buy tickets for the metro in Naples?
  B Most people buy them at a *newspaper kiosk*.

8 A The city centre is now a *pedestrian zone*.
  B Yes, it's better for shopping now without the cars.

9 A Do you have any advice for using *public transport* in London?
  B Yes, get an Oyster Card. You can use it to pay for buses and the underground.

10 A I want to buy some presents for my children.
  B I'll take you to the city *shopping mall*. You'll find something there.

11 A This *ticket machine* doesn't accept credit cards!
  B Try the one next to it.

UNIT 7 Talking about changes and trends

1 **A** Did sales *rise* last year?
  B Yes, they went up *by* 2% *to* £625,000.

2 **A** There was *a decrease in* our transport costs in the last quarter of the year.
  B They *fell by* $1,000 in the third quarter, too.

3 **A** Our sales *remained stable* last year.
  B Yes, they *peaked at* €45,000 in January and *stayed the same* every month after that.

4 **A** Why was there *an increase* in our production costs last month?
  B The electricity bill went up *by* 1%.

5 **A** There was *a decrease* in sales in almost all our stores over the holidays.
  B Don't worry. There was *a drop* in sales at the same time last year, too.

6 **A** The number of visitors to our website rose *dramatically* last year.
  B Yes, but it has now *levelled off*. We need to encourage more hits.

7 **A** Our profits *fell slightly* last month.
  B They're *decreasing steadily* every month. I'm worried about it.

UNIT 8 Career paths

1 **A** I *had an interview* yesterday.
  B Really? How did it go?
  A Great. They *offered me the job*!

2 **A** Hiro *got a promotion* at work.
  B I'm pleased to hear that. He's a great manager.
  A Yes, and they have *transferred him to another branch* too. In Sydney!

3 **A** Did you *see this job advertisement* online?
  B Yes, I did. I *applied for the job* this morning.

4 A I *graduated from university* in 2013.

B Me, too. And I *started my first job* the next week.

5 A Did you do a *six-month probationary period*?

B No, it was three months. I *did some training courses* at the same time too.

6 A I saw this job advertisement in the paper. It's perfect for you – you have all the right *qualifications*.

B Yes, you're right. Thanks. I'll *send in my CV* and apply for it.

7 A Is the job *full-time*?

B No, it's *part-time*. The hours of work are 8 a.m. to 11 a.m.

8 A The *salary* is €1,200 a month. Are you interested?

B Yes, I am. Does it include a *pension*?

A Yes, it does. And we provide private *health care* for all our employees.

9 A This table shows you your *reporting lines*.

B I see. So I report to Carol Thorpe.

A That's right. She will tell you about *your responsibilities* at work.

UNIT 9 Staying in and going out

1 A Are you *doing your homework*?

B Yes, but I'm *having a break* at the moment.

2 A Shall we *have dinner*?

B Yes, but let's *get a takeaway*. I don't want to cook tonight.

3 A Would you like to *go for a run*?

B I'd prefer to *go for a bike ride*, actually.

4 A We're *going out for a meal* tonight. It's our wedding anniversary.

B Lovely. I'm *going to a friend's house*. They invited us round for dinner.

5 A Do you *do a lot of exercise*?

B Not really, but I often *go for a walk* at the weekend.

6 A Mickey, we're *going to the concert* in half an hour.
B OK, I'll *get ready* now.

7 A What time do you *get up*?
B 6 a.m. – and I *go to bed* at 11. I don't get a lot of sleep.

8 A Who *does the shopping* in your house?
B My wife, but I *do the washing* and I *do the washing-up*.

9 A How often do you *go to the gym*?
B Twice a week. I really want to *get fit*.

10 A I'm playing really badly at *pool* today.
B Why don't you get a different *cue*? That might be the problem.

11 A I'm buying my daughter a tennis *racket* for her birthday.
B That's a good idea. She loves *tennis*.

12 A Do you want to play *table tennis*?
B Yes, but I don't have a *bat*. Can I borrow one?
A Of course you can!

13 A Do you play *golf*?
B Yes, but I don't have my own *clubs*. I use my dad's.

14 A Did you play *American football* at high school?
B No, I played *baseball*.

15 A Do you *do aerobics*?
B Yes, and I *do gymnastics*. I love sports like that.

16 A How often do you *go swimming*?
B About once a week. I also *go running* at lunchtimes.

1 A We *hope to send* a company news email to all our customers next year.

B Great idea. I *don't mind writing* it for you.

2 A We *aim to expand* our sales in South East Asia next year.

B Yes, we *need to increase* business across all the ASEAN countries.

3 A We're *planning to arrive* at your office at about 3 p.m.

B Excellent. We're *looking forward to meeting* you.

4 A The number of visitors to the ski resort is *likely to rise* over the next few years.

B That's good news. People really *enjoy coming* here. It's a perfect family resort.

5 A I *expect to visit* our new suppliers in Bangladesh soon.

B Really? *I'd like to go* with you. Is that possible?

6 A Fernanda has *decided to recruit* some new sales representatives.

B I know. I *want to talk* to her about it.

7 A My brother and I are *planning to cycle* across South America.

B Wow. I can't *imagine doing* anything like that.

8 A What will the weather be like in Oslo?

B It *might snow,* so wear warm clothes.

9 A I *probably won't go* on holiday this year. It's too difficult with the baby.

B Yes, sometimes it's nice to stay at home.

10 A Can I visit the factory on Saturday morning?

B Yes, it *will definitely be* open.

11 A We *probably won't get* a bonus this year.

B I agree. The sales figures aren't very good.

12 A I'll phone the office in Mexico now.

B They *might not be* at work yet. It's 6.30 a.m. in Mexico.

13 A How long does it take to get to the airport in a taxi?

B At this time of day, you*'ll probably* need about 45 minutes.

Work skills

UNIT **1** Talking about your job

1 A What do you do?
 B I'm an engineer.
 A Who do you work for?
 B I'm self-employed. I run my own company.
 A Do you travel a lot for work?
 B Yes, I travel to Ireland once or twice a month.

2 A Who do you work for?
 B I work for Delphi.
 A What kind of company is it?
 B It's a parts manufacturer.
 A What department are you in?
 B Human Resources.
 A Do you work full-time?
 B Yes, I do.
 A Can you tell me what you do in your job?
 B I'm responsible for recruitment.

3 A What do you do?
 B I'm an accountant.
 A Where do you usually work – in an office?
 B Yes, I do.
 A Who do you work with?
 B I work with another accountant and an assistant.
 A How many hours do you work a week?
 B Around 60 hours a week.

1 A Good morning. Johnson's Music.

B Could I speak to Melanie Johnson, please?

A I'm sorry, Melanie's on another line.

B Could you ask her to call me back?

A Sure. May I ask who's calling?

B It's Sawako Oshiro. She has my number.

A I'll give her your message.

B Thank you. Bye.

2 A Thur Construction. How can I help you?

B Could I speak to Daniel Thur, please?

A Could you hold the line?

B Sure.

C Daniel speaking. How can I help you?

A Daniel, it's Pedro Lopez here. I'm just returning your call.

3 A VBB Plumbers.

B Hi, is that Victoria?

A No, it's Belinda. Hold on a second.

B Sure.

4 A Thank you for phoning.

B My pleasure. It's good to speak to you again.

A I'll call you next week.

B OK. Bye.

5 A Well, I think that's everything. We're ready for the meeting on Monday.

B OK, I'll call you when I get to your offices.

A OK, bye.

6 A That's everything. Thank you for all your help.

B You too. It's good to speak to you.

A Thanks very much. I'll be in touch again soon.

B Bye.

UNIT 4 Meetings 1: Stages of a meeting

1 **A** Welcome to the meeting. Shall we make a start? Let's introduce ourselves. My name is Bernard Miles.

   B I'm Clarissa Jenkins.

   C My name is Tony Young.

2 **A** The main objective today is to talk about our new office. Alessandra, would you like to start?

   B Yes, the first item on the agenda is the new office phone number. From next month, this will be 960 0923. Could everyone check that all our customers know the new number and get back to me?

   A OK. Everyone happy? Good. Then let's move on to the next item on the agenda.

3 **A** The last item for today is the new name for our watches for teenagers. Abdul?

   B We have hundreds of possible names. So thank you very much for your ideas and suggestions.

   A OK. Has anyone got any questions?

   C No, that's all for today, I think.

   A Good. Thank you, everyone. We meet again at the same time next week.

UNIT 5 Presentations 1: Basic staging and signposting

1 **A** Good morning. Today I'm going to talk about doing business in the USA. I've divided my presentation into three areas. First, we'll look at key markets. Second, US Law. Third, we'll discuss company culture.

2 **A** Now, I'd like to move on to US Law. At this point I'd like to hand over to my colleague, Brandon Klein.

   B Thanks, Justine. First of all, thank you all for coming.

3 **A** That brings us to the final part of the presentation: company culture in the USA.

4 **A** To sum up, I'd like to make some general conclusions. Firstly, our key markets in the USA are all on the West Coast: in California and Oregon. Secondly, US law is complicated but our Law Department can solve any problems you have. Finally, company culture in the US is similar to this country, but there are some important differences. Thank you all for listening.

UNIT 6 Telephoning 2: Answering the phone

1 **A** That's my phone. Do you mind if I take it?
 B No, go ahead.
 A Hello?
 C Pam? It's Tony here.
 A Tony! Hi! Sorry, I can't speak right now. I'm in a meeting.
 C OK. Can you call me back as soon as possible?
 A Sure, no problem. I'll call you back in about twenty minutes. OK?

2 **A** Oh, sorry. Is it OK to answer this call?
 B Sure, that's fine.
 A Hello?
 C Dave. It's Caroline.
 A Caroline. It's difficult to talk right now. I'm visiting a factory. Can I phone you later?
 C Sure, no problem. I'll be here all day.

3 **A** Good afternoon. GU Insurance.
 B Good afternoon. I'd like to speak to Ms Grey, please.
 A I'm sorry. Ms Grey isn't in the office today.
 B Oh. Could you put me through to her assistant?
 A Can I ask who's calling?
 B It's Alan Bromley.
 A Please hold…. I'm sorry, his line's busy. Would you like to hold?
 B No, but can he call me back urgently, please?
 A Of course. I'll see that he gets your message, Mr Bromley.

4 **A** Sprint Leisure Centres. Nina speaking. How can I help you?

   B Could you put me through to your press officer, please?

   A Yes. Could you tell me your name, please?

   B It's Amanda Leclerc.

5 **A** Could you hold on a moment?

   B OK.

   A She's on another line at the moment. Do you want to hold?

   B No, I'm in a bit of a hurry.

   A Do you want her to return your call?

   B Yes, please. I'm calling because we want to write about the centre in our newspaper. My number is 0141 496 0911.

   A OK. I'll give her your message.

UNIT **8** Meetings 2: Turn-taking and turn-giving

1 **A** Does anyone have any suggestions?

   B May I say something?

   A Sure, Ivan. Go ahead.

2 **A** We start the project on 23rd March. Louise?

   B Sorry to interrupt but we can't start then. It's a public holiday.

3 **A** Everyone needs to send me their sales figures by Thursday and then …

   B Could I just say something here?

   A Sorry, could you let James finish?

4 **A** So we'll start on Monday 4th and finish on Friday 29th. Is that OK for everyone?

   B I'd just like to say that I'm on holiday from Wednesday 13th to Friday 15th.

   A How about you, Oliver?

   B Those dates are fine for me. I don't have any holidays this month.

5 **A** We plan to open a new factory in China in February and another one in Mongolia in April. Any comments?

   B Excuse me, but I think Chinese New Year is in February. It's probably not a good time to open the factory.

1 **A** To use the office Wi-fi, you need the password. It's 'visitor9123'. OK?

 B Sorry, was that visitor9123?

 A Correct.

2 **A** Xavier's office number is 020 7946 0955.

 B And the extension number?

 A Dial 16 for his office.

 B 16?

 A That's right.

3 **A** We can offer you bags of brown rice at $12 each and bags of basmati rice at $15.70.

 B Sorry, I didn't catch the second price. $15.17?

 A 70 not 17. $15.70.

Functions

UNIT 1 First meetings and greetings

1 A Can I introduce myself? I'm Ismail Anwar.
B Very pleased to meet you, Ismail. I'm Ursula Weiss.

2 A Harry, let me introduce you to Anja Nowak.
B Nice to meet you, Harry.
C Nice to meet you too, Anja.

3 A You must be Wayne Clarke. I'm Dave Richards.
B Oh, hi Dave. Pleased to meet you.

4 A Samantha! How are things?
B Luther! Fine, thanks. Great to see you.
A It's nice to see you again, too.

Reference: Student's Book **p. 17**

UNIT 2 Talking about schedules and arrangements

1 A Are you free for a meeting on Tuesday?
B No, I'm giving a presentation in Amsterdam.
A How about Wednesday?
B Yes, that's fine with me.

2 A Barry, I'm really sorry but I can't make the phone conference tomorrow. I'm going to be on a training course. Can we arrange another time?
B Sure. When would be good for you?
A How about Friday morning?
B Yes, that's fine with me.

Reference: Student's Book **p. 29**

UNIT **3** Asking for and giving advice

1 A We have a long flight to Australia with the kids. What should we do?
  B You should bring some games to play on the plane.
  A Yes, that's a good idea.

2 A What's the best way to get to the airport?
  B Why don't you ask your hotel to arrange a taxi?
  A Good idea. Thanks!

3 A We're travelling all around Sicily in August. Should we book our hotels before we leave?
  B If I were you, I would book all the hotels before leaving. Sicily is very busy in the summer.
  A That sounds like good advice.

Reference: Student's Book **p. 41**

UNIT **4** Asking for and giving opinions; agreeing and disagreeing

1 A What do you feel about making Petra the new Marketing Manager?
  B I think she's perfect for the job.

2 A How do you feel about changing the company name?
  B I'm not sure but our current name sounds strange in English.

3 A Don't you think we need more staff training days?
  B I see your point, but training is very expensive.

4 A Don't you think that Eric's presentations are really funny?
  B Do you think so? I don't really like them.

5 A Do you think that the office photocopier is too old?
  B No, I don't think so. It works fine.

6 A I think we need a sales office in Mexico. It's a big new market.
  B I totally agree.

7 **A** Don't you think that the new uniform is cool?

   B No, I don't. I don't like the colour.

8 **A** I think that the new receptionist needs to speak English, Spanish, and German.

   B I think you're right.

Reference: Student's Book **p. 52**

UNIT **5** Eating out; requests

1 **A** Have you got a table by the window?

   B Yes, we have. This way, please.

2 **A** Could I have the salmon, please?

   B Certainly. And for you, madam?

   C I'd like the salmon too, please.

3 **A** Excuse me. Have you got any butter?

   B Yes, sir. I'll get some for you.

4 **A** Would you like dessert?

   B Yes. Could we see the menu again, please?

   A Here you are.

   B Can I just ask? Does the fruit cake have any nuts in it?

   A Yes, it does.

   B OK, I'll have the ice cream, please.

   A And for you, madam?

   C I'd like the fruit salad, please.

5 **A** Excuse me. Could you bring the bill now?

   B Yes, of course.

   A Can I pay by credit card?

   B Yes, sir. We accept Visa and American Express.

Reference: Student's Book **p. 65**

UNIT **6** At a hotel

1 **A** Good afternoon. We'd like to check in, please.

B Do you have a reservation?

A Yes, here's our reservation number. Two rooms.

B Thank you. Could I have your passports, please?

A Yes, here they are.

2 **A** Hello. Do you have any rooms free?

B Yes, we do.

A I'd like a single room, please.

B How many nights are you staying for?

A Just tonight.

B OK. The room is €80 a night. Breakfast is included in the room charge. Service is from 7 to 10 a.m.

A That sounds fine.

B Could you fill out this form, please?

A Sure. Do you have a pen?

3 **A** Here is your key card. You're in room 319 on the third floor.

B Thank you very much.

A Is there anything else I can help you with?

B Yes, I'd like a wake-up call at 7 a.m., please.

A OK, no problem.

B Thanks very much.

A Enjoy your stay at the Clifton Hotel.

4 **A** Hello, reception.

B Oh hello. I'm in room 319. I'm calling about the air conditioning. I can't get it to work.

A I'm very sorry to hear that, madam. I'll get someone to fix it immediately.

Reference: Student's Book **p. 77**

UNIT **7** Job interviews

1 **A** Have you ever worked in an English-speaking country?
  B Yes, I have. I worked in Canada last year.
  A Where did you work?
  B I worked in the Redstone Café in Ottawa.
  A How long did you work there?
  B I worked there for six months.

2 **A** What do you do now?
  B I'm a tour guide in Stockholm.
  A What's been your best experience as a tour guide so far?
  B I was on a TV programme about tourism in Sweden. I really enjoyed that.

Reference: Student's Book **p. 89**

UNIT **8** Invitations and offers

1 **A** Would you like to visit our research centre next week?
  B Yes, I'd love to.

2 **A** Would you like me to give you a lift to the station?
  B Thanks for the offer but I've already got a lift with Paulina.

3 **A** Would you like to go sightseeing this afternoon?
  B I'd love to, but I have another meeting at 3 o'clock.

4 **A** Would you like some breakfast in the canteen?
  B I'd love some, thanks.

5 **A** Would you like me to book your flight for you?
  B Yes, please. That would be great.

6 **A** Would you like a coffee?
  B Yes, please. I'd love one.

Reference: Student's Book **p. 101**

UNIT 9 Making suggestions

1 **A** How can we encourage new customers to come to our cinema?
   B We could have half-price films for students on Mondays.
   A Yes, that's a possibility.
   C What about starting a Saturday kids club? Parents could bring their kids to a children's film.
   A That's a good idea.

2 **A** We need to reduce our costs. Does anyone have any ideas?
   B How about moving our office to the new business park?
   A Absolutely not. We have to be in the town centre. All our clients are here.

3 **A** I want to translate all our documents into Arabic, but I'm not sure how to arrange that.
   B Why don't we use an online translator?
   C I'm sorry but I don't think that will work. Automatic translators make lots of mistakes.
   A I agree. Let's use a professional translator.
   C I suggest we hire World Translate Incorporated. They're very professional.
   A OK, let's do that.

Reference: Student's Book **p. 113**

UNIT **10** Asking for information with indirect questions; farewells

1 **A** Do you know if the banks are open on Saturday?
   B No, they're closed at the weekend.

2 **A** Could you tell me where conference room 113 is?
   B Yes, it's on the fifth floor.

3 **A** Do you know when the presentation starts?
   B No, sorry, I don't know.

4 **A** I really must be going. Thank you very much for your hospitality.
   B You're very welcome. Thank you for visiting us.

5 **A** See you back in Paris.
   B Yes, have a safe flight.

6 **A** That's the end of the project. Thanks for all your hard work.
   B No problem. I enjoyed it. I hope we can work together again some time.
   A Me, too.

7 **A** It was a lovely evening. Thank you for the dinner.
   B You're very welcome. I enjoyed it, too.

8 **A** Thank you for telling me about the new position in your company. I'm very interested.
   B Great. Well, I'll be in touch.

Reference: Student's Book **p. 125**

Classroom language

Here are some phrases to use in the classroom.

Phrase	Translation
Could you say that again, please?	
How do you spell 'internet'?	
What does 'reception' mean?	
How do you say 'autobus' in English?	
What's the past participle of 'forget'?	
Sorry, I don't understand.	
What should I do?	
I don't know the answer to number 3.	
I'm not sure but I think the answer is 'False'.	
I've finished.	
Who is my partner?	
Sorry I'm late.	
I need to leave early.	

Here are some phrases to use for pair work.

Phrase	Translation
Do you understand the instructions?	
Are you ready?	
Let's start.	
Is it my turn?	
I think you're right.	
I don't agree because …	
Are you sure?	
Maybe the answer is …	
What do you think?	
It's your turn.	
What's the answer?	
Let's ask the teacher.	
That's a good idea.	
Have we done everything?	

Grammar terms

Here are some grammar terms to help you with your studying.

Word	Definition
adjective	a word that describes a person or thing **Example** This drink is *hot*.
adverb	a word that tells you how, when or where something happens **Example** Please speak *slowly*.
article	*a* or *an* are indefinite articles, and *the* is the definite article **Example** There is *a* computer on *the* table.
comparative	a form of adjective that compares two things. **Example** The Bristol Hotel is *cheaper* than the Ritz.
conditional	a sentence that we make with if. It describes the possible effect or result of an action. **Example** *If* it rains, I'll take a taxi.
gerund	a noun that we make with the –*ing* form of the verb. **Example** *Walking* is great exercise.
infinitive	the basic form of a verb. The bare infinitive is the verb: *work*. Infinitives are also *to* + verb: *to work*. **Example** I'll *work* from home tomorrow. I want *to work* with you.
noun	a word that you use for a person, place, thing or idea **Example** My *company* has an *office* in *Munich*.
past participle	a form of the verb that you use with the passive and the present perfect **Example** The meeting is *cancelled* because Tony has *missed* his flight.
plural	more than one person or thing: **Example** He has got *two jobs*.
possessive adjective	the form of a word that shows that something belongs to someone **Example** It's *your* notebook.
preposition	a word that tells you where, when, how, etc. **Example** He is travelling *from* London *to* Paris *on* 5th March.
pronoun	a word that you use in place of a noun **Example** *She* gave *it* to *you*.

singular	the form of the verb that shows there is only one person or thing **Example** There's one *man* in the meeting room
superlative	a form of adjective that shows the highest degree of something **Example** Shell is the *largest* company in the world.
tense	a form of a verb that shows time, for example the Past Simple. **Example** The Past Simple of *do* is *did*.
verb	a word that tells you what somebody does or what happens **Example** She *lives* in Windsor and *works* in London.

Irregular verbs

Verb	Past Simple	Past Participle
be	was / were	been
become	became	become
begin	began	begun
break	broke	broken
bring	brought	brought
build	built	built
buy	bought	bought
catch	caught	caught
choose	chose	chosen
come	came	come
cost	cost	cost
cut	cut	cut
do	did	done
drink	drank	drunk
drive	drove	driven
eat	ate	eaten
fall	fell	fallen
feel	felt	felt
fight	fought	fought
find	found	found
fly	flew	flown
forget	forgot	forgotten
get	got	got
give	gave	given
go	went	gone

Verb	Past Simple	Past Participle
grow	grew	grown
have	had	had
hear	heard	heard
hit	hit	hit
keep	kept	kept
know	knew	known
learn	learnt	learnt
leave	left	left
let	let	let
lose	lost	lost
make	made	made
meet	met	met
pay	paid	paid
put	put	put
read	read	read
ride	rode	ridden
run	ran	run
say	said	said
see	saw	seen
sell	sold	sold
send	sent	sent
shut	shut	shut
sing	sang	sung
sit	sat	sat
sleep	slept	slept
speak	spoke	spoken
spend	spent	spent
stand	stood	stood

Verb	Past Simple	Past Participle
steal	stole	stolen
swim	swam	swum
take	took	taken
tell	told	told
think	thought	thought
throw	threw	thrown
understand	understood	understood
wake	woke	woken
wear	wore	worn
win	won	won
write	wrote	written

OXFORD
UNIVERSITY PRESS

Great Clarendon Street, Oxford, OX2 6DP, United Kingdom

Oxford University Press is a department of the University of Oxford.
It furthers the University's objective of excellence in research, scholarship,
and education by publishing worldwide. Oxford is a registered trade
mark of Oxford University Press in the UK and in certain other countries

ISBN: 978 0 19 459789 0

Printed in China

This book is printed on paper from certified and well-managed sources